WHO ARE 'THE PEOPLE'?

Unionism, Protestantism and Loyalism in Northern Ireland

Edited by

Peter Shirlow and Mark McGovern

Pluto Press

LONDON • CHICAGO, ILLINOIS

First published 1997 by Pluto Press
345 Archway Road, London N6 5AA
and 1436 West Randolph, Chicago, Illinois 60607, USA

Copyright © Peter Shirlow and Mark McGovern 1997

The right of the individual contributors to be identified as the
authors of this work has been asserted by them in accordance
with the Copyright, Designs and Patents Act 1988.

British Library Cataloguing in Publication Data
A catalogue record for this book is available from the British
Library

ISBN 0 7453 1213 6 hbk

Library of Congress Cataloging in Publication Data

Designed and produced for Pluto Press by
Chase Production Services, Chadlington, OX7 3LN
Printed in the EC by Redwood Books

Contents

Abbreviations

AIA	Anglo-Irish Agreement
APNI	Alliance Party of Northern Ireland
CAJ	Committee on the Administration of Justice
CBI	Confederation of British Industry
CCRU	Central Community Relations Unit
CEC	Campaign for Equal Citizenship
CLMC	Combined Loyalist Military Command
CRC	Community Relations Council
CTG	Cultural Traditions Group
DED	Department of Economic Development
DL	Democratic left
DUP	Democratic Unionist Party
EOCNI	Equal Opportunities Commission for Northern Ireland
EU	European Union
GDP	Gross Domestic Product
GNP	Gross National Product
HC	House of Commons
IFI	International Fund for Ireland
INLA	Irish National Liberation Army
IPLO	Irish People's Liberation Organisation
IRA	Irish Republican Army
MEP	Member of the European Parliament
MP	Member of Parliament
MSR	Mode of social regulation
NIARLA	Northern Ireland Abortion Law Reform Association
NIF	New Ireland Forum
NIO	Northern Ireland Office
PAF	Protestant Action Force
PUP	Progressive Unionist Party
PWC	Protestant Working Class
RHC	Red Hand Commandos
RUC	Royal Ulster Constabulary

SDLP	Social Democratic and Labour Party
UDA	Ulster Defence Association
UDP	Ulster Democratic Party
UFF	Ulster Freedom Force
UUC	Ulster Unionist Council
UUP	Ulster Unionist Party
UVF	Ulster Volunteer Force
WP	Workers' Party

Notes on Contributors

Arthur Aughey is a Senior Lecturer in Politics at the University of Ulster. He is the author of the book *Under Siege: Ulster Unionism and the Anglo-Irish Agreement* (Blackstaff: 1989). He has recently co-edited Northern Ireland Politics (Longman: 1996). Arthur is also a member of the Community Relations Council and the Cadogan Group.

Alan Bairner is a Lecturer in Politics at the University of Ulster. He is the co-author of the book *Sport, Sectarianism and Society in a Divided Ireland* (Leicester University Press: 1993). He has written widely on the theme of sport and sectarian division. His other academic interests include Swedish politics and socialist thought.

Colin Coulter is a Lecturer in Sociology at St Patrick's College, Maynooth. He has written several analyses of Unionism and the Conservative Party in Northern Ireland in *Fortnight* and *Irish Political Studies*. He recently contributed to the book *Unionism in Modern Ireland* (Gill and Macmillan: 1996).

Alan Finlayson is a Lecturer in Politics at Queen's University, Belfast. He writes on social and cultural theory, he has written several articles on theories of nationalism and has recently contributed to *An Introduction to Contemporary Social and Political Thought* (Longman: forthcoming).

Brian Graham is a Professor of Human Geography in the School of Environmental Studies at the University of Ulster. He is a co-editor of the book *An Historical Geography of Ireland* (Academic Press: 1993). In relation to the themes of revisionism and cultural identity in Ireland he has also contributed articles to the journals *Ecumene*, *Transactions* and the *International Journal of Heritage Studies*. He has recently edited *In*

Search of Ireland (Routledge: 1997). Brian has also written widely on transport geography.

James McAuley is a Senior Lecturer in Sociology at the University of Huddersfield. He is the author of *The Politics of Identity: A Loyalist Community In Belfast* (Avebury: 1994). He has written extensively on the theme of Loyalism in the journals *New Society*, the *Irish Journal of Sociology* and *Études Irlandaises*. He has also contributed to the books *Culture and Politics in Northern Ireland* (Open University Press: 1991) and *Ireland's Histories* (Routledge: 1991).

Mark McGovern teaches Irish Studies at Edge Hill University College, Ormskirk. His PhD (University of Liverpool) focused on the siege myth within Protestant identity, in his home town of Derry. He has written widely on Republican and Unionist ideologies and recently contributed to the book *The Irish Peace Process* (Avebury Press: forthcoming).

Duncan Morrow is a Lecturer in Politics at the University of Ulster. He was previously employed at the Centre for the Study of Conflict. He is the author of *The Churches and Inter-community Relationships* (Centre for the Study of Conflict: 1991) and co-editor of *Northern Ireland Politics* (Longman: 1996). He is actively involved in community relations issues and is a member of the Community Relations Council and the Corrymeela community.

Rosemary Sales is a Senior Lecturer in the School of Sociology and Social Policy at Middlesex University. She has recently authored the book *Women Divided: Gender Religion and Politics in Northern Ireland* (Routledge: forthcoming). She has also written about Fortress Europe, refugees and also on social policy in Europe.

Peter Shirlow is a Lecturer in the School of Geosciences, Queen's University Belfast. He is also a founder member of the Socio-Spatial Research Unit at Queen's University which undertakes research into deprivation and labour market inactivity. He is the editor of *Development Ireland: Contemporary Issues* (Pluto Press: 1995). He has written several articles on Loyalism and Republicanism for the journals *Antipode*, *Political Geography* and *L'Éspace Geographique*.

Preface

A common piece of graffiti in Northern Ireland is the slogan 'We are the People: Prods Rule OK'. This legend was something to which many of us who grew up in a Protestant community accepted as a truism. On one particular wall in Lambeg, in the late 1970s, somebody wrote at the end of this slogan 'Ask Charlie Nash'. This additional slogan was written after the boxer Charlie Nash, a Catholic from Derry, had been beaten by Jim Watt, a Protestant from Glasgow, in a world contender fight. The boxers themselves had a significant admiration for each other and the question of religious affiliation had not been an issue to either of them. Both were united by their devotion to their sport.

To many of us who were Protestants the fight itself threw up a crucial issue over who to support. After all, Charlie Nash lived in our country, there was a lot of media interest in him, we knew more about him than Jim Watt and, most of all, he was Irish. As was the case with much of our identity this fight brought to the fore many of the contradictions that confront us in terms of who and what we are, and to whom we should owe allegiance.

In many ways it is this confusion of identity which is the main inspiration for this book. Most of the contributors to this collection come from Protestant backgrounds but not all of us are pro-Union thinkers. Some would support the reunification of Ireland, some would wish Northern Ireland to be fully integrated into the UK. Others may even admit to being ambiguous about future constitutional arrangements. However, one constant and shared concern is that present constitutional arrangements and representations of political identity do little to resolve the nature of socio-cultural antagonism. For too long the communities or traditions of Northern Ireland have been represented as bi-polar opposites. In this book we begin the task of challenging the 'myth of the homogenous communities', by establishing the diversity and variance which exists among Protestants.

This is a crucial task which is based upon the assumption that Irish society will not progress or resolve its antagonisms without a deconstruction of cultural animosity and division. Unfortunately the main argument has been that each community must respect the other and that each must support the notion of 'parity of esteem'. But how do we achieve this when the majority of politicians and the main political ideologies are based upon the perpetuation of antagonism itself? Moreover, how do we do this in a highly segregated society in which a divided people rarely come into more normal forms of social contact? The simple answer is to start a project in which each community or tradition begins its own introspection. A process in which individuals declare that they find the cultural representations, whether Protestant or Catholic, Nationalist or Unionist, which are forced upon us all, both alien and unacceptable.

Within our society we have many dissenting voices which disagree with community norms, voices which wish to raise us all above the sectarian quagmire in which we have all been encased. But this process is not about simply turning Catholics into Unionists or Protestants into Nationalists; it is about finding a new cultural framework in which we share diverse sociocultural experiences. We need to respond to our circumstances, learning to respect ourselves through challenging the instability that our cultural claims make, cultural claims we have clamoured to support and reproduce as the body bags were filled and the dole queues lengthened.

We need to look at the divisions within our own traditions, challenge the sectarian representations of who we are and resolve to produce a more secular understanding of what we want to be. In this book we challenge what for many of us is our own community's representation. This should not be read as a negative account of the Protestant community. Instead it should be seen as a representation of our concerns about our own community. We have and will continue to invest in our own community through challenging what we feel to be erroneous and unwise. We hope that one day this task will be undertaken by those who grew up in Republican and Nationalist communities alike.

Introduction: Who are 'the People'? Unionism, Protestantism and Loyalism in Northern Ireland

Peter Shirlow and Mark McGovern

Whether it is written on the walls of Belfast, spoken by the Apprentice Boys of Derry, or sung at Windsor Park, the phrase 'We are the People' is a clear and unequivocal statement of loyalty and devotion to and from the Protestant people of Ulster. Throughout and before the conflict this aphorism has been an emotive rallying call as well as a familiar part of everyday language in Northern Ireland. It is a phrase which has stood the test of time. As the traditional wall murals of King Billy and the Battle of the Boyne have slowly faded away to be replaced by more contemporary images of Loyalist paramilitaries, as the character of Unionist hegemony slowly dissolves and fragments, this phrase has been constantly used and reproduced as a reminder of the need for cultural cohesiveness and solidarity in the face of what is perceived as Irish irredentism and British state-inspired betrayal (Dunn and Morgan, 1994).

As such, this adage is a grand signifier of loyalty, devotion and identity. If anything it is a constant reminder of a self-identified community who sense that they are besieged and threatened by socio-political and cultural dissipation. In such circumstances and throughout Irish history, the inherent political instability which has plagued this island has always meant that strategies for socio-cultural survival have included fabricating notions of cultural solidarity, foeism and unified strength (McNamee and Lovett, 1992; O'Brien, 1994).

It has been one of the central myths used when diagnosing the conflict, as is the case in the Framework Documents, that the supposed two traditions (the pro-British and pro-Irish communities) contain identifiable and unitary characteristics which remain authentic. In reality the opposite may well be the case. In many ways those who have been and are embroiled in the pursuit of conflict and socio-cultural antagonism are the very people who are trying to create or maintain an illusionary form of socio-cultural homogeneity. They revel in excessively biased historical interpretations and strive to promote blinkered political objectives which are driven by devotional nationalisms. In many ways this devotion to a pure and uncontaminated notion of cultural and national homogeneity denies the relevance of a more pluralistic interpretation of identity which could effectively challenge sectarian discord.

The abstraction that such a solid form of socio-cultural conformity exists among Protestants, as well as Catholics, is not only myopic but in many ways fictitious. The authentic and more appreciated reality of 25 years of conflict, street violence, boycotting and heightened sectarian animosity is that there has been no significant movement towards much needed mutual understanding or socio-political agreement. Furthermore, and it has been the case throughout the conflict, the communities are divided not only between but within themselves. For many Protestants there has been a desire to distance themselves from events and actions, such as the Drumcree stand-off and the besiegement of Harryville Catholic church. Many people believe these actions are inappropriate and out-moded forms of political representation. Similarly, many Catholics find little or no pleasure in the boycotting of Protestant businesses or the re-mobilisation of the Provisional Irish Republican Army (IRA). Regrettably, such distancing tactics, which in many instances are attained through a process of apoliticisation, are more commonplace than a forceful condemnation of community representatives and politicians who thrive upon sectarian asperity.

The continual failure of individuals to point the finger at their own community, through questioning how and why it reacts in such conflictual ways, is undoubtedly part of the overall problem. It is evident that in many instances, due to the threat of violence and rejection by one's own community, it has been easier to accept ontological security through conformity with a given identity than it has been to advocate dissent. However, it may also be the case that socio-political fragmentation within each community is so profound that many individuals or sub-communities do not feel that violence or atavism emanates from their actions and/or political beliefs. In both instances the general problem still remains that for many the task of encouraging the regeneration of cultural identity and conviction through the promotion of an anti-sectarian discourse is simply anathema.

Therefore, it is not surprising that in most instances it is assumed that the resolution of conflict will come in some form of negotiated settlement between the pro-British and pro-Irish sections of the population. Such a position is in itself illegitimate as it relegates the importance of intra-community diversity, on the one hand, and hides the reality of identifiable inter-community solidarity, on the other (Shirlow and McGovern, 1996). Without any clear understanding of intra-communal plurality we are left with an inappropriate and generalisable model in which the bulk of the population is placed within one or other of the two (supposed) traditions. Lamentably, socio-cultural heterogeneity, within each of these conjectural traditions, is being lost or misrepresented, as monolithic depictions of identity silence and/or dilute the importance of nonconformist voices which dissent from wider community norms (McGovern and Shirlow, 1997).

Of course, for many the use of the two traditions model is wholly unproblematic as well as politically calculated. For the British and Irish states it permits the interpretation that the conflict is more about religion and history than it is about issues such as class, socio-economic competition and the impact of shifts in the character of Irish society. Furthermore, for certain community representatives, the mobilisation of a binary ideological framework of division sanctions a form of censorship over inter-community dialogue as each side purposely promotes differences over similarities. Dividing the population into two blocks also allows sectarianism to thrive upon the demonisation of the 'other'. In all societies divided by conflict it is always the case that we judge the opponent more than we judge ourselves.

As such the aim of this book is to promote an understanding of the Protestant community and its diversity. This does not mean that there are no shared values or beliefs within the Protestant community. Evidently, most Protestants consider themselves to be British as is clearly indicated through the ballot box. But what is less clear are the divisions which 'dare not speak their name'. Without any understanding of the plurality that exists within each community it will be impossible to develop a support base capable of challenging ideas, beliefs and actions which retard social progress, on the one hand, and block the utility of a new socio-cultural direction for us all, on the other.

Who are 'the People'?

To describe and account for any people as 'a people' usually leads to the employment of stereotyping, whether negative or positive, from within. For many Protestants a concept of oneness and the existence of 'the People' is wholly unproblematic, a situation which is not unique to Protestants or the Irish context (O'Connor, 1994). However, as noted by Sparke, '"The People" is one of the trickiest and most dangerous of all political phrases. That being so, no occurrence of it ought ever to be taken for granted or allowed to pass without examination' (1994, p. 32).

Not only is the use of the legend 'We are "the People"' problematic when it is used by Protestants themselves, but it is also equally harmful when it is mobilised to portray the Protestant community as a unified cabal who are both politically intransigent and culturally myopic. Condemnation of this supposedly unified Protestant community comes in many forms. Protestants have been depicted as unified agents of oppression or as dupes of an imperial past. Moreover, their articulation of a British identity is challenged as erroneous and unwise. As was noted in October 1994 in the Chicago Tribune, 'Protestants are less humorous than their Catholic counterparts. They are sombre and hard-working. They feel British and deny their Irish past and future.'

Paradoxically, the Chicago Tribune's simplistic depiction and overtly hostile discourse aids the reproduction of the 'myth of the whole Protestant community' (Brown, 1985). Such monolithic depictions, whether they are generated internally or externally, merely indicate the stamina of binary sectarian and ideological divisions. Furthermore, for many Protestants the sense that they are denigrated both at home and abroad only furthers the sense of besiegement and promotes a further drive towards illusionary homogeneity. As such, and due to the effects of conflict and denouncement, communal homogeneity becomes even more pervasive and persuasive for those who can see no further than the permanence of sectarian demarcations. As a consequence the reality of class, gender and other axes of social division are underplayed in the context of a highly politicised ethnic separation. Furthermore, the call for communal solidarity, in the face of the perceived threat of the 'other', has in turn limited the space for an exploration of intra-communal heterogeneity. This in turn means that allegiance to 'the People' prevents the abstruse question being asked, 'Who *are* "the People"?'

If this question is not asked then it is important to substantiate a claim that 'the People' possess a series of concepts which constitute a discourse of political legitimacy. Whether such an ideological project is built upon civic or ethnic foundations, and whether or not it is conceived as the basis for a right to self-determination, it is a process which lies at the heart of modern political theory and of the organisation of power and authority in modern societies (McGarry and O'Leary, 1995). Such a process is taking place when speaking of Ulster Protestants as of any other community, although their status as a distinctive 'People' is undoubtedly more inherent and disputed than most. Furthermore, the conflict itself is closely fixed to reproducing and sustaining the idea of 'the People' in the face of its detractors.

In reality, communal devotion emerges as a mode of domination, in which shared class, gender and cultural experiences, which are inter-community in character, are concealed. Moreover, contriving or accepting monoliths is, for certain sections of both communities, an apparently satisfactory pursuit even if it sows the seeds of future discord.

A Protestant or Unionist History?

The imagined heritage of historical continuity of any collective people emerges through a historiography of selection, adoption and adaptation. Many Protestants perceive their history as being centred upon a distinctive past in which specific action, norms and beliefs remain immutable. A particular element in the historiography of Protestantism has been the dilution and removal of any significant Irish dimension. What are perceived as unacceptably dissenting voices and shifts in the character of Protestant politics and identity have been purposely obscured (Gellner, 1983; Tonkin, 1992), and a history of collective allegiance to the crown, constitution and the 'Protestant People' remains. This process of historiographical incorporation and elimination has played a key role in establishing the hegemonic hold of Ulster Unionism.

The litany of a populist Protestant history draws upon 'rarefied tableaux' of key historical epochs, figures and events. Whilst the professionalisation of historians' writing has done much to curb the interpretative excesses of earlier generations, the extent to which such 'inorganic' intellectuals influence a long-established and commonly held perception of the past is somewhat limited (Stewart, 1967 and 1977). As such the 'rarefied tableaux' still have wide appeal and popular valence.

The cycle of the past, as told in popular Unionist histories, has been seen to contain distinct elements, each of which has contributed to a centripetal construction and reproduction of not only a Protestant but a Protestant–Unionist unity (Jackson, 1989 and 1996). For example, the actuality of conquest and colonisation has traditionally been conceived as a battle between 'British civility' and 'Irish barbarity'. Historically, the civility–barbarity thesis not only legitimised Protestant domicility in Ireland, but continues to suggest the need and right to defend such a position *vis-à-vis* the Catholic/Nationalist community. Furthermore, the relationship between the British state and the Protestant people has been sanctified in commemorations of sacrifices made in the past by the latter for the former. A sacrificial ethos, which has underpinned the construction of the Protestant community (and which in many instances has excluded the contribution made by Catholics), has been evoked not only in histories of Derry and the Boyne, but even more powerfully in the memory of the Somme.

This celebration of sacrifice has been evident not only in the writing of history but also (and with far greater influence) in the popular practices associated with the street culture of Loyalism and the marching season. In addition, the imagery of the 'Honest Ulsterman' (distinctive in tongue, race, religion and custom) has become a central motif utilised to justify the foundation and continued existence of the Northern Irish state. The particularity of the 'Honest Ulsterman' not only sets the community apart from Catholic Ireland but also, somewhat paradoxically, from the rest of the British polity.

These overlapping and interlinking circles of historicised identity forge not only a 'flag of collective allegiance' (the 'right to be') but also dictate a 'charter for action' ('to defend the right to be'). History tells a significant section of the community who they are and what they must do to ensure their survival as 'the People'. This important ideological use of history, in a situation where there is a real or perceived threat to the continuance of the Protestant community will invariably mean that elements or ideas within the collective past, which challenge or deviate from the narrow confines of accepted orthodoxies, are liable to be lost. As such the complex mosaic of socio-political and cultural heterogeneity within the 'Protestant community' has been reduced to an ever-repeating cycle of threat, siege and deliverance. The 'siege mentality' so evident among sections of the Ulster Protestant community owes much to this conception of the past.

Recent histories of the Protestant past have begun to challenge such orthodoxies through revealing something of the lost (and non-Unionist) history of the Protestant community (Jackson, 1996; English and Walker, 1996). Evidence to support diversity and conflict within the Protestant community has a long and at times distinctive lineage. During the period of settlement, in the seventeenth century, antagonisms within the Protestant community were signified by conflicts over land ownership. Moreover, disputes over political rights and intra-Protestant denominational differences were also prominent. Such socio-cultural differences continued into the eighteenth century and were combined with a growing antiquarian interest in Irish culture and folklore, with explicit political implications. For some, this fed into an embryonic identity of Irish patriotism. By the end of the eighteenth century the nature of a specifically 'Protestant' identity could be historicised as the very essence of radicalism, the rejection of not only 'Popish' but also British tyranny. To be a 'virtuous Protestant' could mean to be a good Irish patriot.

This constant caveat of heterogeneity was reproduced through the nineteenth century but was successfully countered by three powerful ideological forces which fomented the character of modern Protestant identity: Orangeism, all-Protestant Union and the imperial patriotism of Unionism itself. Furthermore, the space for dissent narrowed post-partition as the politics of the new state were conditioned by perceived and real threats both internally and externally from Irish Republicanism.

Social tensions did, however, produce antagonisms, evident in labourist and at times communist politics, but such hostilities did not effectively challenge the dominance of Stormont-based Unionism which was able to discharge a form of pan-class solidarity (Purdie, 1991). As with labourist politics the continued fragmentation of Unionist hegemony through the emergence of

liberal, Loyalist and fundamentalist discourses has been tied to
the overarching supremacy of a pro-union congruity and agenda.
The end result has been that particular readings of the past have
led to a definition of Protestants as a 'pro-Union People'. The
abandonment of dissident traditions from popular mythologies
has been paralleled by a celebration of Britishness in which the
symbols associated with the constitutional link have come to take
on a significance far beyond the realm of institutional govern-
mental arrangements. It may be that, as a result, we can talk of
this community as the 'pro-Union People'.

A Pro-Union People?

Even though 'loyalty' to the concept of the Union is not always
reciprocated by the British state and the wider British population, this does not detract from the salience and attractiveness of
pro-Union belief. As such, pro-Unionism has emerged as a creed
invented and re-invented through the incorporation of shared
social norms and actions which are constructed as distinctly
British. The so-called 'British way of life' is constituted as
rational, clear and intuitively natural.

Unionism as a political doctrine is centred on the principle
that the United Kingdom should be preserved as an integral unit.
For Ulster Unionists it is the principle that Northern Ireland
must remain in the Union of Great Britain and Northern Ireland.
Clearly, Unionism adopts a nationalist form; like Irish Nationalism it has distinct ethnic, language and civic dimensions. In
relation to the latter the Union is visualised as a union of invari-
ant citizenship of the United Kingdom, irrespective of cultural,
religious or racial origins. In terms of its ethnic construction,
Unionism is explicitly linked to a sense of achievement, in which
the allegory of Protestant forefathers (excluding foremothers)
importing civilisation to Ireland continues to play a pivotal role
(Clayton, 1995).

The fundamental rationale of Unionism is the desire to resist
any coercive incorporation into a reunited Ireland. Justification
for such action and belief emanates in most instances from a
predominantly Protestant community. However, pro-Unionism is
not a static or unified doctrine in itself, but instead it contains a
wide body of strategies, goals and representations. Pro-Unionism
can represent a stand against what is perceived as Irish irredentism; an endorsement of economic and other benefits; sectarian

atavism, consocialisation or a seemingly and increasingly positive thesis that the Union supports pluralism, multi-culturalism and equality of citizenship. In each case the 'People' emerge as those who are the vanguard of a more respectable civilised and responsible body of citizenry on the island of Ireland.

Certainly a new wave of Unionist rationalism, as articulated by the Cadogan Group, Robert McCartney, the *Ulster Review* and others, grounds itself upon a liberal-democratic thesis of reconceptualising the state–society relationship. Yet, even within its own terms, this project faces two fundamental problems: First, the need to decouple the association of pro-Unionism and the 'Protestant' people and second, to convince a sufficient section of the Catholic community that the preservation of the Union is desirable. The dilemma is one of squaring a supposed drive for pluralism with the potential alienation of large sections of the Protestant community for whom the Union enshrines far more than merely the nature of state institutions and the rights of the citizenry.

The seemingly insurmountable task facing 'new' Unionism is precisely how it might reconceive and reconstitute the 'pro-Union people' so that it might come to include the 'whole body of the enfranchised citizenry'. The task facing 'revised Irish nationalism' is the mirror image of this problem. It too is engaged in an attempt to renegotiate its ethnic and civic dimensions in order to recreate an inclusive vision of the 'Pro-unification People'. In overall terms the crisis facing Ireland, North and South, Catholic and Protestant, Nationalist and Unionist, is to reconceptualise who 'the People' are in order to achieve a new social and political consensus.

Unionism, Protestantism and Loyalism

The ethnic and civic elements of Unionist politics, the impact of history and culture and the diversity of experience in terms of gender and class are the main areas of concern within this book. It is designed to illuminate the character and disposition of the Protestant community as well as indicate the very nature of conflict and social tension within Northern Ireland. In promoting a pluralistic collection the book also treats the concept of 'the People' with the care it so evidently requires and deserves.

For too long, commentators on the conflict in Ireland have carelessly thrown diverse groups into general categories which are wholly inappropriate and insensitive. The end result has been to convince many on the ground that there actually is an identifiable and unified foe which must be resisted. If a more cautious commentary were produced which indicated that there is significant intra-communal heterogeneity, then it is possible that inter-community similarities would also be exposed. The significance of such alliances would be to undermine the demagogues and political manipulators who mobilise contrived homogeneity and in so doing block alternative syntheses and strategies.

The book is organised into three main areas of concern: the politics of contemporary Unionism, the relationship between history, culture and Protestant ethnicity, and the impact of divisions of class and gender on Unionism and Loyalism today.

In different ways the first two chapters explore this critical moment of contemporary Unionist political discourse, and thus also make a valuable contribution to the ongoing debate on the future direction which Unionism might take. In Chapter 1 Arthur Aughey, one of the leading exponents of 'new Unionism', argues that it is a rational and modern political ideology centred upon conceptions of citizenship and the state–society relationship and not (as it is often viewed by its critics) a form of nationalism. In essence, Aughey denies that an ethnic conception of 'the People' is either true or useful when attempting to understand the nature of Unionism. Echoing Jennifer Todd's (1987) definition of 'two traditions' within Ulster Unionism, Aughey argues that within the Unionist fold there have indeed been these two (potentially contradictory) conceptions of 'the People' of Northern Ireland. One is an essentially ethnic construction, which tends to exclude the Catholic population, the other is 'constitutional' and is rooted less in notions of identity and ethnicity, but rather upon the relationship between civic society and the institutional organisation of political power. Through an analysis of recent Ulster Unionist Party documents, and their reaction to the 'Talks Process' of 1990–92, the Downing Street Declaration and the Framework Documents published in February 1995, Aughey argues that the future lies in promoting an 'expressive constitutionalism' capable of calling upon the allegiance of all the citizens of Northern Ireland (Ulster Unionist Party, 1986). Calling for a 'new and intelligent form' of Unionist politics, Aughey sees in the rejection of an 'ethnic construction' the basis for political rights and responsibilities which negate Northern Ireland's socio-sectarian divisions. Coherent and thorough in its argument, Aughey's vision of a 'Unionist constitutionalism' is ultimately rooted in a wider tradition of conservative political philosophy.

For Brian Graham, on the other hand, it is in the cultural, rather than the constitutional sphere, that Unionism must revisit its ideological message. As a geographer Graham emphasises the importance of people's understanding and sense of attachment to spatial entities and territories. For Graham, the historical failure of the Northern Ireland state was its inability to construct a cultural affinity between its spatial limits and 'the People' contained within. Clearly, any future constitutional arrangement faces the same dilemma. As a consequence, if Unionists are to be successful in the project of promoting their political philosophy as being pluralistic and inclusive in character they must, as Graham suggests, formulate a 'positive cultural iconography'. This might, he argues, allow for a 'sense of place' to develop which can provide the social cement for a new consensus amongst all of 'the People' who live there.

In line with this form of argument and in the second part of the collection the focus falls more upon the part culture plays in defining different aspects of identity within the contemporary Protestant community. In Chapter 3 Alan Finlayson examines different ways in which the past has been recalled by Ulster Loyalists, and the manner in which these various tellings of the past construct identities in the present. For Finlayson 'identity' and 'community' are ultimately contestable concepts, not unlike the notion of 'the People' with which they are so closely bound.

According to Finlayson, 'essentialist' identities should be deconstructed by dissecting the conception of 'mythic communities'. Far from being essentialist in nature he argues that identities are constituted and reconstituted through time to give particular definition to those who 'belong' and thereby also to define the interests which are supposed to be self-evident. To assess the discursive character of Ulster Loyalism, Finlayson examines a number of instances in which 'Ulsterness', 'Britishness', 'Protestantism' and 'Democracy' are invoked to 'hail' the hearer to the ethnic fold. Rather than reworking understandings of the past, this means that 'the People', however they are imagined, must first of all go beyond essentialist conceptions of identity if any new future for Northern Ireland is to be realised.

It is impossible to understand Unionism and Loyalism without understanding the role of 'fundamentalist Protestantism' in Ulster Protestant political culture. That is the starting point for Duncan Morrow's examination of the importance of a series of symbols, myths and rhetorical motifs within the discourse of contemporary Unionist ideology which are derived from theological, and, in particular, 'fundamentalist Protestant' perspectives. Morrow is not simply arguing, *à la* Steve Bruce (1986), that fundamentalist preachers, churches or theological tenets in and of themselves are influential, but rather that they define a moral universe within which the parameters of an Ulster Protestant identity takes shape and is expressed. He argues that much of contemporary Protestant ideology is constructed via a series of structural oppositions: the 'sinned against and the sinning', the 'righteous and the damned', the 'good and the evil'.

Not only are such binary oppositions established rhetorically, but they are the essence of the ritual re-enactment of identity contained within the culture of the marching season. Indeed, they are the basis upon which an identity among sections of the Ulster Protestant community is established, ensuring that the political projects and agenda for which they are invoked are invested with a meaning beyond the realms of the transitionary and the ephemeral, but rather stand as moral absolutes in a universalised struggle of the 'elect' and the 'dark forces' ranged against them. Within the context of ongoing conflict such an ideological configuration has great sway. In the absence of that conflict its power may wane. In a sense Morrow is suggesting that the 'sacred past' enshrined in a fundamentalist world view permeates the thinking of people far beyond those who would consider themselves to be 'evangelicals'. This telling of a 'sacred past' helps to ensure that the 'elect' (conceived as the Protestant community) becomes synonymous with 'the People'.

It is in the realm of culture that any community comes to an understanding of itself and there are a myriad of cultural forms and arenas within which this process can take place. Alan Bairner examines the importance of football, and an affinity with certain football teams (the Northern Ireland side in particular) as a focus of identity for the Protestant working-class males. Sport plays an important role in the construction of identities in the modern world, and in Northern Ireland that means not only gender and class-specific identities, but also a fusion of sectarianism and the 'imagined community' of the Ulster Protestant.

Given the impact of profound socio-economic change, football in certain instances provides a means for the cultural enactment of empowerment in the absence of real power for sections of the Protestant working classes. The consequence is that football can, at times, provide an arena for a deeply masculine, defensive, violent and anti-Catholic definition of Protestant working-class identity. For some, with Stormont gone and the shipyards largely silent, there is only Windsor Park or the Oval left as visible places of belonging.

In the final section of this book the impact of gender and class divisions within the Protestant community are examined. In Chapter 5 Rosemary Sales provides a wide-ranging survey of the socio-political position of Protestant women. Ethnic division, she suggests, is deeply rooted in the fabric of Northern Irish society and as a result it has certain gender-specific consequences. According to Sales, the 'closed systems' of Unionist, Loyalist and Protestant ideologies aid the construction and legitimation of particularly virulent patriarchal relationships within the Protestant community. Similarly, the conflict in Northern Ireland directly and indirectly affected the lives of Protestant women, as 'armed patriarchy' has disempowered women in both the home and in public arenas. In terms of employment and political participation, the struggle for gender equality has been severely hampered by the dominance of ethnic antagonisms and constitutional issues. In a whole range of ways, therefore, 'monolithic' constructions of communities have resulted in a social conservatism which has insured that the cause of women's rights has been marginalised. For Sales the 'peace process' has represented a real opportunity for issues, neglected by 25 years of war, to come to the fore. Her argument would also confirm that the confrontations of the summer of 1996 provide further evidence on how difficult it is to establish a meaningful peace when the role of women continues to be relegated to the sidelines by a masculine-centred culture. She may well ask the question: Are 'the People' all male ?

Colin Coulter focuses on the politics of the Unionist middle class, arguing that this 'mainstream' of Unionism is often overlooked in academic analyses due to the 'exoticism' of Loyalism and its ideological perspectives. Coulter traces the development of a middle-class Unionist tradition given the impact of the major political and structural changes since the early 1970s. In particular, he identifies the complex and contradictory impact of long-term Direct Rule from Westminster, with its commensurate

loss of localised political power and cultural assimilation with
Britain, alongside the potential avenue of cultural (as well as
economic) *rapprochement* with the Republic of Ireland. Character-
ising the politics of the Unionist middle classes in terms of
'inertia, ambivalence and indifference', he suggests that these
factors have contributed directly to the conflict being prolonged.

The final two contributions examine the relationship
between Ulster Loyalism and class. Jim McAuley is concerned
with the changing nature of Loyalist politics in the wake of
the cease-fires and the development of the 'peace process'
through 1994 and 1995. By analysing the changing discourse of
the fringe parties linked to Loyalist paramilitaries during this
period, McAuley argues that their reaction evidences an embryonic break into new forms of politics within the Protestant
working class. The hegemonic hold of Unionism over the
working class had tended to preclude aspects of Protestant
working-class culture which might have been antithetical to the
interests of the Unionist party. At the same time the ongoing
conflict in Northern Ireland similarly tended to exacerbate
those elements within Protestant working-class culture which
accentuated communal and sectarian division. In the absence of
conflict, and in the context of shifting social and economic
conditions, a more class-based politics then becomes possible.
It is in this light that Jim McAuley examines the continual
emergence of the Progress Unionist Party (PUP) and the Ulster
Democratic Party (UDP). Divisions in Northern Ireland are
such that the development of a cross-community working-class
political movement is, in the short term, difficult to envisage.
Similarly, the precarious character of the 'peace process' means
that any political and ideological shifts will inevitably be
partial and tentative. However, McAuley suggests that the
absence of social and sectarian strife might, in the longer term,
allow common ground to be found around class-based issues
between political parties ostensibly organised and supported
within particular communities.

The last chapter combines an analysis of the ideological
nature of Loyalism with a study of the changing social and
economic character of Northern Irish society. Echoing
McAuley, Mark McGovern and Peter Shirlow regard the Loyalism espoused by Protestant paramilitaries as a distinctive
ideological force within the broader parameters of Unionist
political culture. They also suggest that this ideological tradition reflects the class-specific experiences of Protestant workers

who consequently also perceive and comprehend the impact of shifts in both the local and the international economy through a pre-existing mental framework. That ideological tradition similarly sets 'limits of possibility' for political articulation. World-views in Northern Ireland are, in a range of ways, profoundly affected by the central binary opposition of the 'collective self' and the 'collective other'. Since the inception of the Northern Irish state that divide has also conditioned the regulatory practices of the state, which in turn underwrote Unionist party hegemony. However, the 'post-industrialism' of recent years (and the specific impact it has had upon the Protestant working class) has substantially undermined those hegemonic practices, resulting in the political and ideological fragmentation of Unionism. The emergence of working-class Loyalism must be seen in that context. The dilemma for the future, however, is whether or not the absence of violence is indicative of a fundamental move away from sectarian division.

1 The Character of Ulster Unionism

Arthur Aughey

The purpose of this chapter is to examine three features of Ulster Unionism. First, I set out what I take to be the common central propositions of Unionist argument. Secondly, I go on to examine the issue from these general propositions of two different versions of what constitutes 'the People' of Northern Ireland. I intend to show that the first of these understandings is substantially constitutional and only residually ethnic in its emphasis. The second of these understandings, by contrast, tends to be substantially ethnic and only residually constitutional in its emphasis. Both these understandings together form the character of Ulster Unionism and its ambiguous idea of 'the People'. Finally, I attempt to test these understandings by exploring the way in which both have found expression in the most recent and exhaustive examination of these matters. This examination took place in the two sets of discussions about political progress in Northern Ireland which have become known as the 'Brooke Talks' and the 'Mayhew Talks'. These were conducted in the spring and early summer of 1991 (the Brooke Talks) and from spring to late autumn of 1992 (the Mayhew Talks). I conclude by assessing briefly the difficulties posed for Unionists by recent political developments, in particular the proposals contained within the *Frameworks for the Future* published on 22 February 1995.

In the growing body of literature on Unionism, it has been defined variously (to take a few recent examples) as a colonial mentality (MacDonald, 1986); the political expression of evangelical Protestantism (Bruce, 1986); an aberrant substitute for nationalism (Nairn, 1977); a covenanting tradition of conditional loyalty (Miller, 1978), and a 'Herrenvolkean democracy' (Lee, 1989). Some of these interpretations have helped to illuminate particular aspects of Unionism. Some have not. Indeed, the purpose of the latter has been, more often than not, to condemn rather than to understand. If one were to generalise from the body of established literature on Unionism there are some limitations which are worthy of note. The first has been a tendency to interpret Unionism as somehow deviating from an established norm of political argument. It has been defined by what it lacks rather than what it might positively express. This was especially evident in some of the studies written in the 1970s, for example in the arguments of Tom Nairn (1977) and David Miller (1978). The second has been a tendency to portray Unionism as a pathological condition obstructing the natural and inevitable course of Irish history. This is a tendency still to be found, of course, in Nationalist writing, which has a long lineage and has dressed itself in a number of different forms, from Third World Marxism and liberation theology to radical-chic cultural criticism (Bennet, 1994).

Even the most insightful analyses, for instance Jennifer Todd's essay, 'Two Traditions in Unionist Political Culture' (1987) was marred by the use of a practical index of measurement. Todd's useful distinction between the 'Ulster British' and the 'Ulster Loyalist' identities is flawed in the sense that understanding has become implicated in political recommendation (i.e. the Ulster British identity is to be praised because it is more likely to transform itself into a British-Irish identity appropriate for a 'new' Ireland), and the purpose of recommendation has become implicated in the engagement to understand (i.e. the attributes of both identities should be so defined as to lead to the conclusion which she feels is necessary to reach). This is unfortunate, because I think Todd's characterisation of these respective identities does provide a useful preliminary perspective on important and relevant distinctions within Unionist argument. Before I consider and try to illustrate these relevant distinctions, I want to establish as succinctly as possible what might be the common ground of Unionist political argument.

Two Propositions

At the heart of Unionist political argument has been the 'fact' of the Union, a fact which involves two distinct though practically interrelated ideas. The first holds that membership of the United Kingdom represents a clear and unequivocal definition of British political status. To live in Northern Ireland, in other

words, ought to mean that one is accorded equality of citizenship with everyone else who lives in the United Kingdom. As
the 1984 Ulster Unionist Party (UUP) policy statement *The
Way Forward* argued 'only rights can be guaranteed, not aspirations' (Ulster Unionist Party, 1984). To adapt a Burkean
phrase, the proposition is that real rights and not pretended
rights are founded in the fact of the Union. Fact is nine points
of the law in Unionist politics. In practice, this is an idea
which has issued in a determination to accept no political
initiative which could be judged to attenuate British citizenship in Northern Ireland. It is a position which has been held
with a stubborn constancy, and which has come to be taken as
definitive of the general Unionist mentality – 'not an inch',
'what we have we hold', 'no surrender'. In the nature of things
in Irish politics this is not an irrational position to hold. It is
only one part and not the whole of political immobilism. The
Unionist 'no first step because it is a step towards a united
Ireland' corresponds to the Nationalist 'no first step unless it is
a step towards a united Ireland'. Both are mutually dependent
and mutually reinforcing dogmas.

The second and related idea is that this British status,
founded on the democratic consent of the majority, should be
durable. This attitude is fixed in terms of the justice of the
constitutional arrangements guaranteeing Northern Ireland's
place within the United Kingdom. In other words, partition is
legitimate and there ought to be no change in the status of
Northern Ireland unless and until there is a change in the will
of the majority, understood now, at least in (polite) Ulster
Unionist circles, as the 'greater number'. The exercise of that
will has always had a ring of finality to it. To the former
Prime Minister of Northern Ireland Sir James Craig, for
instance, the Government of Ireland Act of 1920 had been
accepted by 'the People' of Ulster as 'a final settlement and
supreme sacrifice in the interest of peace'. It is noticeable,
indeed, how frequently that same language of finality and permanence has recurred ever since in Unionist argument. In
1992, for example, Ulster Unionist Party MP William Ross
could speak of the Brooke/Mayhew Talks involving deliberation
about a 'final conclusion', in short, an end to all such political
initiatives and a stable recognition of partition. 'When I say
final', he proclaimed, 'I mean final' and none of his audience
was in any doubt about what he meant by finality (Ross, 1992).
It means a durable guarantee for the position of Northern

Ireland, based on the will of its majority, within the United Kingdom.

Historically, these principles of status and durability have provided a clear mandate for Unionist politicians to reject any set of arrangements predicated on the idea of the natural political unity of the island of Ireland. For Ulster Unionists today, whatever may have been the case in the past, there is no natural political unity in Ireland. There are held to be two states or two nations or two peoples on the island of Ireland. This is something to which I will return when considering the Unionist position in the Brooke/Mayhew Talks and their response to the Framework Documents. Therefore, Unionist hostility towards Articles 2 and 3 of the Republic's Constitution is not a manufactured political tactic as has been claimed recently by Nationalists. It reflects a long-standing claim for the mutual recognition of these distinctive entities.

The ideas of status and durability allow us also to interpret what self-determination has traditionally meant for Unionists. That membership of the United Kingdom is a clear definition of political status and that that status should be durable and properly acknowledged represents the traditional statement of Unionist self-determination. The exercise of self-determination in that form has been negative rather than positive. It has been concerned to minimise where possible separate political development from the rest of the United Kingdom rather than to encourage it. The 'People' of Northern Ireland have been determined to remain part of the United Kingdom (Aughey, 1991).

Of course, what is meant by 'the People of Northern Ireland' is not self-evident. Not only are there differences on this matter between Unionists and Nationalists. There have been and remain differences within Unionism itself. I would argue that two influential ideas of 'the People' together constitute the character of Ulster Unionism. These ideas may be considered separately but in practice they have been entangled one with the other. Unionist argument may shift insensibly or incoherently between one idea and another, depending on circumstance, depending on the audience (a tendency which is equally noticeable in Nationalist discourse). The first of these ideas is a conservative idea, the idea of the 'constitutional People'. The second of these ideas is a radical idea, the idea of the 'sovereign People'. This is a distinction which has been employed with some sophistication, though in a very different context, by the American political theorist Harvey C. Mansfield Jr (1987). The relationship between these

two ideas of 'the People', the constitutional and the sovereign,
may go some way to explaining that apparent contradiction
which observers have often noted in Unionism between, on the
one hand, its loyalty, prostrating itself before the Union flag and
every sympathetic utterance of a member of the royal family or of
a British politician; and, on the other hand, its rebelliousness,
taking to the streets with an almost anarchic fervour whenever its
interests appear threatened. My argument is that these forms of
behaviour are really two sides of the same political coin.

The Constitutional People and the Sovereign People

In a number of essays published in the journal *The Public
Interest*, Mansfield Jr has tried to define the forms and limits of
constitutionalism and democracy. Constitutionalism, he argues,
involves restraining the confidence of democratic majorities 'in
their own sovereignty, which is responsible for the fractious-
ness' (1987, p. 56) of modern politics. Ultimately, constitutionalism 'demands a people that is independent, but not so much
as to think itself capable of governing without a constitution;
it needs a sense of responsibility that is aware of the limits of
responsibility' (1987, p. 57). If it is to be viable, constitutionalism must mean that 'the sovereign people has been replaced by
the constitutional people' (1987, p. 57). These are suggestive
insights which may be translated from the American context,
which Mansfield Jr is discussing, to Northern Ireland's case.

The idea of a constitutional people, in other words, is the
idea of a people defined mainly by the status and the durability of its institutional life. In this (Unionist) sense, the identity
of 'the People' of Northern Ireland is secured by the fixing of
Northern Ireland's formal position as a part of the United
Kingdom. In this particular form, it is not Britishness as some
peculiar spiritual substance, and certainly not as a 'cultural
tradition', which defines Unionism but the acknowledgement of
the authority of the constitutional relationship of Crown-in-
Parliament. This is the Unionist claim to 'constitutional patriotism', a stable practice which pre-dates Jurgen Habermas's
theory of the same name by about a century. And it was James
Craig who put this idea rather neatly when he pledged Northern Ireland to the British war effort in 1939: 'We are King's
men.' The identity claimed here is a political one. Over half a
century later, during the Brooke/Mayhew Talks, the constitu-

tional formality of this political idea was central to the UUP's defence of the Union (see St John Ervine, 1949).

This idea of the constitutional people embraces a traditional understanding of the history of Britain as the history of a free people, a freedom not unrelated, of course, to their Protestantism. Free, though, in a very peculiar and in a very British way. The British genius is believed to lie in the capacity to fashion institutions which reconcile order with personal liberty. This tradition of Ulster Unionism, like modern British Conservatism, involved the coming together of two nineteenth-century ideas: Whiggish constitutionalism (and its providential – 'Whig' – theory of history) and Tory traditionalism (and its 'national' appeal). As both Thomas Hennessey (1993) and James Loughlin (1990) have shown recently, this celebration of the balanced constitution as historical providence was an important aspect of the Unionist case against Home Rule. And equally, the case against Home Rule turned the notion of traditional constitutionalism into an article of political faith. This faith has tied traditional Unionism into the 'Conservative political nation', in both the ideological and party political senses of the word 'Conservative'. The Conservative nation is nothing less than a people defined by the procedures and the forms of its established constitution. This is the understanding which some Tories have called 'One Nation', that is, classes, peoples and interests which transcend their cultural differences and their distinctions in a common political allegiance. And this common allegiance, expressed through the authority of a sovereign parliament, channels and constrains the power of a modern democracy. Indeed, it was not an Ulster Unionist but the Conservative Prime Minister, John Major, who gave a notable exposition of this idea. Addressing prospective parliamentary candidates in Glasgow in February, 1992, Major stated:

> I believe that we should stand for the historic union of 'the Peoples' of the United Kingdom. A union in which our nations work together but each sustains and develops its rich and varied traditions. Let me tell you why. Because England and Scotland, Wales and Northern Ireland together are far greater than the sum of their parts. (Conservative Central Office, 1992)

Major's formulation was about as clear and positive an idea of the Union which it is possible to get. It is one to which Ulster Unionists subscribe for they are included within the constitutional people. That, if you like, is the expressive idea of 'the People', a people, however internally diverse, whose interests are expressed by and through established institutions and whose political identity is filled out by the effective and affective procedures of state. It is recognisable as an expression of Unionism – 'High Unionism', if you like. It is very much alive and most recently had its clearest elaboration in arguments put forward by the Campaign for Equal Citizenship. In sum, it proposes that we (the Northern Irish) are 'the People', 'the People' of the United Kingdom.

The idea of the sovereign people, on the other hand, is the assertive idea of 'the People'. It is the idea of 'the People' conceived apart from all institutions and conventional practice. It is 'the People' invested with a metaphysical principle, the right to self-determination. As such it is potentially very un-conservative with the capacity to challenge fundamentally the procedural conservatism of the first perspective. This assertive idea has been well described as a type of populism displaying aggressive informality, and 'overflowing informality is a source of tyranny and rebellion' (Mansfield Jr, 1983, p. 128). Populism of this sort respects constitutional form only in so far as it satisfies its need for self-assertion. Form is a means to an end and not an end in itself. In the Unionist case, it has involved the assertion of local majoritarianism, of a communal and defensive patriotism. 'Our wee Ulster' or 'the British people of Ulster' or simply 'the Protestants of Ulster' is the *fons et origo* of all political consideration. It is self-consciously ethnic in that its spiritual substance is a religious one (the specific truth of which the work of Steve Bruce (1986) has reminded us).

The idea of the sovereign people has always been a current in the history of Ulster Unionism and is at its most vital whenever the position of the constitutional people of Northern Ireland appears threatened. The strength and the persistence of the idea of the sovereign people – indeed, the necessity – in Unionist politics is founded upon the very insufficiency of the idea of the constitutional people in itself. Paul Bew's study, *Ideology and the Irish Question* (1994), has revealed the interplay of these two notions in such political crises. The expressive formality of the constitutional people depends upon conditions of political security. Of course, Unionism has rarely, if ever, had such political security. It has always felt under siege and with very good reason. The assertive informality of the sovereign people is the measure of that insecurity and that experience of siege. This local dialect of popular sovereignty is what David Miller in *Queen's Rebels* (1978), took to be the essential characteristic of Unionist politics, namely its 'conditional loyalty'.

Miller's seminal thesis of conditional loyalty is but another way of saying that the expressive ideal of Unionism, the secure and certain acknowledgement of Northern Ireland's place within the British state, has never been confirmed. Miller's argument stresses the conditionality of Unionist loyalty, suggesting a self-serving disposition. Yet looked at another way, it is the British state which may be said to be conditional in its loyalty to 'the People' of Northern Ireland. And in these circumstances it is quite rational for Unionists to reserve their judgement. To adapt another Burkean phrase, it is logical to qualify the expressive value of the civil state (constitutionalism) with the assertive value of the uncivil state (popular sovereignty). In other words, if the policy of a British government appears to undermine the rights of the constitutional people, then the uncivil state of the sovereign people may be the way to reassert those rights. This too is recognisable as a characteristic of Unionism – 'Low Unionism', if you like – and it has a tendency to merge at the edges into support for an independent Ulster. The Ulster Workers' Council strike of 1974 – 'constitutional stoppage' as it was revealingly termed – was its most effective recent political statement. In sum, 'Low Unionism' proposes that we are 'the People', the Protestant people of Ulster.

In the practical politics of Northern Ireland today it is tempting to identify the UUP as the institutional embodiment of this idea of the constitutional people, and the DUP as the institutional embodiment of this idea of the sovereign people. It is equally tempting to identify their respective leaders accordingly: David Trimble (leader of the UUP) as the quintessential and expressive constitutionalist and Ian Paisley (leader of the Democratic Unionist Party – DUP) as the assertive man of 'the People'. This approach has a superficial truth. But the whole truth is that these two ideas of 'the People' have been implicated one with the other in both parties and implicated one with another in the history and practice of Ulster Unionism (Trimble, 1988).

At a practical level, as Bew, Gibbon and Patterson (1995) have pointed out in their book *Northern Ireland: Political Forces and Social Classes*, devolved government at Stormont was reasonably, if not entirely, successful in reconciling both the constitutional conservatism and radical populism of the Unionist tradition. Once Stormont was challenged in conditions of political violence, it became impossible to keep Unionism organisationally unified. If there is such a thing as the Unionist family, it is not a very harmonious one. At a conceptual level, the reconciliation has been made in a slogan like 'self-determination within the United Kingdom', which may be taken to mean that the only legitimate action of a government which seeks to modify the conditions of the constitutional people is to submit those modifications to the test of popular consent in Northern Ireland. As Peter Robinson (MP/DUP) has argued, putting these two ideas together, the citizenship of people in Northern Ireland must be on the same basis as everywhere else in the United Kingdom. If the government chooses to change the terms of that citizenship it 'can only be done if there is consent, and the consent not only of the Government and Parliament, but of "the People" of Northern Ireland' (House of Commons, 1985). Not to do so is a calculated act of misrule and justifies Unionist non-compliance. David Trimble, for instance, also argued that

> the Treaty of Union and the Acts of Union specifically provide that in all treaties 'the People' of Northern Ireland are to be on the same footing as 'the People' of Great Britain. It would be wrong therefore for the government to enter into a treaty which treated Northern Ireland differently, for if it did it would be breaking the Treaty of Union. (1986, p. 8)

These propositions notwithstanding, the Anglo-Irish Agreement of 1985 between London and Dublin was signed and implemented over the heads of Unionists and did place 'the People' of Northern Ireland on a different footing from those in the rest of the United Kingdom. Consequently, there have been problems for Unionists in remaining faithful to the fundamental wisdom of the Union and nothing but the Union. This had obvious implications for the idea of the Unionist people. The determination of James Molyneaux (former leader of the UUP) and Ian Paisley (leader of the DUP) to find an alternative to and a replacement of the Anglo-Irish Agreement involved some very obvious political dangers.

For example, Molyneaux, when leader of the UUP, asserted that talks about an alternative to the Agreement would not involve any constitutional adjustment because 'Northern Ireland already has a constitution enshrined in statute, precedent and practice' (Molyneaux, 1992). That, he argued, should be the solid foundation upon which all else is to be built. Unfortunately for Molyneaux, of course, the Anglo-Irish Agreement had already become part of the precedent and practice (though not the statute) upon which the government of Northern Ireland is based and thereby the potential, even the likely, benchmark for any future development.

Unionist opposition to the Anglo-Irish Agreement also provoked a response of popular sovereignty, one embraced enthusiastically by the unashamedly populist DUP: the assertion of an absolute right to self-determination. There were obvious, if ironic, echoes of this attitude recently in Scotland. As Canon Kenyon Wright asked in a provocative address to the Scottish Convention, referring to Margaret Thatcher: 'What if that other single voice we all know so well responds by saying, "We say no, and we are the state"? Well, we say yes – and we are "the People"' (cited in Marr, 1992, p. 113). This was voiced in a Convention which was in principle and intention avowedly non-separatist (as are Unionists). In the Ulster case, the reverse was true. Unionists said 'No' and Margaret Thatcher said 'Yes'. In both instances, of course, they were ignored.

From the spring of 1991 to November 1992, the parties of Northern Ireland were engaged in the intermittent, though intensive, Brooke/Mayhew Talks about arrangements of government to replace the existing Agreement. As a part of these talks the parties were required to set out as concisely as possible their views on identity and what they understood the nature of the problem in Northern Ireland to be. The papers submitted by the Unionist parties provide us with a useful insight into their views on these matters. Of course, the propositions in the Unionist papers were engaging with claims made by the Social Democratic and Labour Party (SDLP) which were, in turn, consistently backed up by the Irish Government. It is appropriate, therefore, to consider briefly the position of the SDLP before examining the arguments of the Unionist parties.

People, Traditions and States

The SDLP's concept of 'parity of esteem' based on the 'legitimacy of both traditions' was the logical spine running through the SDLP submissions at all levels of the Brooke/Mayhew Talks

(SDLP, 1992a, 1992b, 1992c, 1992d). Their argument was as follows:

(1) There are two traditions on the island of Ireland. While the Unionists assert that their tradition is wider than the six counties of Northern Ireland (i.e. British), Nationalists know that their tradition transcends the boundary of Northern Ireland (i.e. exclusively Irish).

(2) The political reality of the Troubles is that the two traditions must aim to reach agreement on how best to share the island of Ireland.

(3) The conflict of two traditions and identities is expressed in a conflict about political structures. Because these traditions transcend existing political structures it is then pointless attempting to deal with the present crisis by taking those political structures for granted. Existing political arrangements in Ireland are artificial constraints upon one tradition, the Nationalist, and cannot accommodate its fullest expression.

(4) Each tradition has an absolute right of self-definition. The SDLP claimed to be content for Unionists to define their own relationships but reserved to itself the right to define its own relationships. This right of self-definition demands not only parity of esteem for fellow citizens but also thoroughgoing constitutional change to accommodate a political demand.

(5) The SDLP defined its identity in terms of allegiance to the Irish state. They believed that that identification conferred the right on the Irish Government to involvement in the affairs of Northern Ireland.

In the opening submission to the Brooke Talks in June 1991, Ian Paisley advanced a number of propositions about the identity of the Ulster people. He stated first that he 'would never repudiate the fact that I am an Irishman but that is a geographical term'; secondly, that 'Ulstermen are not Englishmen living in Northern Ireland'; and thirdly, that 'we in Northern Ireland are a race apart' (Paisley, 1991). The DUP returned to these themes a year later in the Mayhew Talks. Its paper, having criticised Nationalists for all their misconceptions about Unionists and their patronising attitude towards their culture, then proceeded to repeat familiar clichés, for example that Ulster Protestants love the Royal Family, have a strong 'work ethic', are sincere, humorous, caring and hold their convictions deeply (DUP, 1992b). Such particular values notwithstanding, the DUP's argument was that the distinctiveness of Northern Ireland meant that only those within Northern Ireland could properly sort out its problems. There would, for example, be no truck with the SDLP's formula about traditions. The status of the sovereign people of Northern Ireland was the principled underpinning of the DUP's case.

The UUP argued that, contrary to nationalist assumption, Unionists did not feel confused about their identity. They felt British, which was defined as acknowledging the authority of a political order which embraced diversity and plurality. There was resentment expressed at the purely 'negative' definition of the Unionist identity in the New Ireland Forum (see, for example, p. 5 of the Forum Report, paras 8 and 9). The theme of diversity was also at the heart of the UUP's defence of the Union. In the UUP document, *Nature of the Northern Ireland Community*, it was stated:

> We identify with a culture and ethos which is not exclusive to this part of Ireland, but which has traditionally had a broad international outlook. Unionists do not have a single view of their Britishness – there is considerable diversity within our community – and why not? (1992a, p. 6)

What Unionists had traditionally found within the United Kingdom, Irish Nationalists were only now beginning to find within the European Community. As noted in *Nature of the Northern Ireland Community*:

> The reality of the Irish Republic's membership of the Community has seen it turn its back upon the narrow parochial nationalism which saw its birth, and espouse a recognition of the strength of divergence and of its role within the wider world. (1992a, p. 9)

For the UUP, then, their basic political heritage is their Britishness. This Britishness, it was argued, is at the heart of Unionist philosophy: '... the feeling of belonging; the feeling of sharing with our fellow-citizens in Great Britain in great national events; of being part of something larger than simply six counties in the north-east corner of our island' (1992b, p. 11).

To support the Union represented a clear preference for continued membership of a modern, pluralist and liberal democratic state 'of 4 nations, 3 linguistic groupings, many ethnic minorities and a multitude of religious denominations' (UUP, 1992b). This UUP position was thus a classic restatement of the idea of the constitutional people. The political logic of such cultural self-definitions became clear as the Unionist parties elaborated their positions. For the Unionists, the Brooke/Mayhew Talks were not about reconciling traditions but about adjusting the relations between two states in Ireland. A paper presented by the DUP went to the heart of what was common to the Unionist position. Three propositions were made about the SDLP's language of identity, its idea of self-determination and its notion of statehood. First, on the language of the Talks, the DUP pointed:

> to the disservice done to clear thought by the use of metaphysical language, loose characterisation of groups as reflecting traditions, simplistic stereotyping of groups as monolithic communities, and the identification of political groupings as communities with traditions. (1992b, p. 7)

Secondly, on self-determination, the DUP denied that it is meaningful to speak of 'the Nationalist community in Northern Ireland having self-determination'. As the DUP paper put it 'Only "Peoples" have the right to self-determination, and since 1920 there has been a "People of Northern Ireland"' (1992b, p. 9).

Thirdly, on statehood, it was proposed that the 'reality is that the island is not divided between two traditions. It is divided into two states each with a right of self-determination' (1992b, p. 9).

This was the logic which informed common Unionist arguments in Strands 1, 2 and 3 of the Mayhew Talks. Each of these Strands can be dealt with separately. In Strand 1, since the Unionist parties did not acknowledge the legitimacy of the 'two traditions' analysis proposed by the SDLP, i.e. two traditions on the island of Ireland demanding full parity of esteem at all levels of government and administration), they were concerned to create arrangements for the governance of Northern Ireland as a region of the British State. As an integral region of the British state there may be some need for special arrangements to deal with peculiar problems. But these special arrangements should be limited and should certainly not attenuate the status of Northern Ireland as a part of the United Kingdom.

There were clear divisions between the two Unionist parties over what was possible in Strand 2. The 'Robinson letter' to Sir Ninian Stephen of 23 October 1992 (which was leaked to the press) denounced a suggestion by the UUP that there was any possibility of agreement on measures of North–South institutional co-operation which would involve executive powers (The *Newsletter*, 23 October 1993). The division between the two parties, however, was mostly rhetorical rather than practical. The UUP had anticipated Robinson's letter by stating a fundamental principle: '... the principle the UUP applies to this proposed relationship with the Irish Republic is that it must be constitutionally correct' (UUP, 1992b).

What this meant was that there should be no fudging of the distinction between tradition and statehood and therefore no qualification of the right of 'the People' of Northern Ireland to self-determination. Any relationship between North and South must be based on the constitutional, political and institutional integrity of the two separate jurisdictions on the island of Ireland. Hence the arrangement which the UUP considered appropriate was only a competence to set up joint bodies such as the already existing Foyle Fisheries Commission.

Both Unionist parties saw Strand 3 as an opportunity for the British Government to confront the Irish Government over Articles 2 and 3 of the Republic's Constitution. One thing which the UUP was careful to avoid, in Strand 2 as well as Strand 3, was getting involved in international negotiations. That, it claimed, was the responsibility of the British Government. The necessity of maintaining the principle of negotiations between states and not negotiations between traditions was central to this concern. The purpose of Strand 3 – for both the UUP and the DUP – was to establish 'an unequivocal recognition and acceptance of Northern Ireland's position as an integral part of the United Kingdom (UUP, 1992c).

The Brooke/Mayhew Talks have come and gone. Since their closure in November 1992, the British and Irish Governments have together come up with the Framework Document of 22 February 1995. The Framework Documents are supposed to provide a balanced view by the two Governments of the way forward from the talks impasse between State and identity. What has been the Unionist response?

The Framework Documents

If there is a single political formula informing the Framework Documents it is the formula of Irish unity by consent. The immediate lineage of that formula may be traced back to articles of the Anglo-Irish Agreement and to the language of the Downing Street Declaration. Unity by consent is a simple, though not a new, formula. Its meaning, however, is not self-evident. First, if one were to accept that the principle of consent governs the principle of unity then, to all intents and purposes, the Union would be 'safe'. Unionists would have to live, of course, with the possibility of eventual Irish unity. But then Unionists have always had to live with that possibility. They would not like the formula but they could learn to accept its implications. It would also mean, of course, that such unity might never come about. Nationalists might be persuaded to accept an arrangement which was substantially British and only residually Irish. That outcome would depend ultimately upon a new and intelligent form of Unionist politics.

If, on the other hand, the principle of unity were to govern the principle of consent then a very different set of expectations emerges. In this case, the balance would be towards those structures designed to facilitate Northern Ireland's transition from its present UK status towards some form of all-Ireland arrangement. It would suggest that it is not the active consent of the 'greater number' in Northern Ireland to unity which is being sought but merely acquiescence in political arrangements which promote that end. The outcome would then be (ultimately) substantially Irish and only residually British. Persuasion of Unionists by Nationalists would be not by argument but by circumstance.

In their response, Unionists have read the Framework Documents to mean that the principle of unity does indeed govern the principle of consent. This is judged to be an assault on their identity as British citizens (the constitutional people) and the right of the majority within Northern Ireland to self-determination (the sovereign people). The two ideas of 'the People' are now combined in an assault on the logic of the Framework Documents. As John Taylor of the UUP combined them succinctly in a speech to the Irish Association in Dublin in May 1990:

The documents represent a conditional surrender to Sinn Fein/IRA in that self-determination is increasingly centred on the island as a whole. Until consent for a united Ireland can be manufactured efforts will be made to harmonise all aspects of policy between Northern Ireland and the Republic – inevitably causing disharmonisation between Northern Ireland and the rest of the United Kingdom until we can be extracted from the UK with ease.

A similar view is to be found expressed by the DUP. The Prime Minister, it argues:

> will not impede the road to a united Ireland – but he will not help anybody who wants to keep Northern Ireland within the Union, so the balance is tipped in advance towards the achievement of a united Ireland and the destruction of the United Kingdom ... 'the People' are not going to be able to say yes or no. (DUP, 1995)

In both cases it is being proposed, first, that any meaningful content to the status of Northern Ireland as a part of the United Kingdom would be removed under the new dispensation (Unionists, according to the Downing Street Declaration, for instance, are part of 'the People' of Ireland and not part of 'the People' of Britain). Secondly, it is argued that the will of the majority will not be allowed to determine the 'process' of change in Northern Ireland. In other words, neither conservative constitutionalism nor radical populism will have an effective purchase on policy. The option proposed in the Framework Documents, it is claimed, is an option which every Unionist rejects, namely the option of (progressively) terminating the Union. Such a dismal consensus would seem to offer little reassurance to Unionists for the future.

Conclusion

One might conclude, therefore, by asking the question: where is Unionism going? There is no clear answer anyone can give to such a question. In the words of Humphrey Lyttleton, when asked a similar question about modern jazz: 'If I knew it I would be there already.' Some think they know where Unionism is. If it is not yet beaten it is on the way to being beaten. In the words of the 'independent Republican' Anthony McIntyre, 'While the British government have for now refrained from acting as persuaders for a united Ireland they are unmistakably acting as dissuaders of the Unionists from staying within the UK (1995, p. 60).

That is a step, he argues, towards the IRA/SF position which 'once taken, will close the gap between what the British government is doing now and that of being persuaders for Irish unity (1995, p. 60). Unionist fear of the apocalypse and Nationalist hope of salvation are once again to be seen in intimate embrace. Both are possibly deluded.

Events since 1985 have indeed shown the extent to which British policy makers have adopted the language of Irish nationalism in the presentation of their proposals. This has threatened Unionism in both its modes of expressive constitutionalism (as Molyneaux discovered twice – first in November 1985 and then in February 1995) and in its mode of assertive populism (as Paisley experienced in his 'freezing out' after December 1993). Nevertheless, there can be no settlement without Unionist support for that settlement. That is one simple democratic fact of life which is often overlooked by Nationalists in their moments of triumphalism and by Unionists in their moments of self-pity. What sort of settlement may emerge is not the concern of this chapter. However, it is interesting to note how one of the architects of the Anglo-Irish Agreement, Sir David Goodall, has now come to understand what is essential to the Unionist sense of identity.

What is lacking in present circumstances, argues Goodall, is recognition by Nationalists 'of Northern Ireland's continued status as part of the United Kingdom so long as the majority of its population so wishes' (1995, p. 37). Nationalists, North and South, appear not to understand that it is insufficient to provide reassurances about the Unionist 'tradition' if Unionists 'are being invited to live out that identity in a society which is being edged away from the United Kingdom into a progressively closer, *de facto* union with the Irish Republic' (1995, p. 37). In principle, then, Goodall shares the same perspective as Taylor. He concludes:

Terms like 'identity' and 'tradition' blur the hard edges of the real division between Nationalist and Unionist in Northern Ireland and conveniently obscure the fact that an essential element in their 'identity' is precisely the Unionists' sense of living on territory which is part and parcel of the United Kingdom and not of the Republic. (1995, p. 37)

Of course, this is the unresolved question. Whether Nationalists can ever accept that Northern Ireland is legitimately and constitutionally part of the United Kingdom by the will of its 'people' remains doubtful.

2 Ulster: A Representation of Place yet to be Imagined

Brian Graham

The purpose of this chapter is to examine the crisis that attends issues of Protestant identity in Ireland. In particular, the discussion addresses the proposition that Protestants in general and Unionists in particular lack an agreed representation – or imagery – of place to legitimate and validate their domicile in the island of Ireland. It is further argued that the negotiation of a future, sustainable political structure requires a prior resolution to these more fundamental underlying cultural dilemmas. At the outset, it must be observed that although the shaping of power in Northern Ireland is broadly disputed between Nationalist and Unionist discourses, it is also a contested concept within both these broad perspectives. Furthermore, these terms are not necessarily synonymous with Catholic and Protestant. A considerable proportion (perhaps almost 50 per cent) of Catholics are unionists, while some Protestants are republicans (with deliberate usage of lower-case 'u' and 'r' respectively). Thus, the issue of contested images of Protestant place overlaps with, but is not equivalent to, the disputed iconography of Unionist place.

The proposition that forms the title of this chapter originates in an essay by the literary critic, John Wilson Foster. Embracing a theme that has often been addressed by liberal Ulster Protestant writers who cannot fall back on religion to define their own Irishness, Foster 'turns to the landscape that seems on occasions to join the sects' (1991, p. 159). He argues that regionality – by which is meant a continuity of identity vested in place – might provide Catholics and Protestants in Northern Ireland with a common individuality. Drawing upon the vision of the poet John Hewitt, Foster seeks a primarily indigenous synthesis, one that locates Ulster's Protestant and Catholic inhabitants culturally within a representation of place that encompasses, to quote Hewitt, 'geographical and economic coherence, ... some sort of traditional and historical identity and which ... in some measure demonstrates cultural and linguistic individuality' (cited in Clyde, 1987, p. 294).

Implicit in such a synthesis is the poet's belief that Ulster culture should be more than an echo of the thought and imagination of another people or land. Foster contends that Ulster people have for long suffered the 'twin psychological colonialisms of Irish nationalism and British nationality that have falsified their consciousness and diverted them from the true task of self-realisation' (1987, p. 294).

It is argued here that this condition accurately describes the relationship between Ulster Unionism and the territory which it seeks to control. In turn, this is reflected in what the Opsahl Report describes as a 'conflict, even a confusion of identity' (Pollack, 1993, p. 95). The reason for this is apparent in Miller's (1978) cogent argument that Unionists have never developed a nationalist ideology, the most powerful form of metanarrative linking social groups and territory. Rather, they have operated continuously within a pre-nationalist contractarian discourse, defined by allegiance to a British crown that is the symbolic expression of the constitutional reality of the United Kingdom state which protects their interests, particularly in terms of religion (Brown, 1991). Further, despite the New Right onslaught on the structure of the welfare state, radical working-class Unionism (as expressed for example in the ideas of the Progressive Unionist Party (PUP)) has sought to retain those institutions of social communality created by the post-war Keynesian consensus (Progressive Unionist Party, 1996). Thus, the link with Britain is sufficient to define Unionist 'allegiance'. But, as it is a contractarian relationship, one is released from that covenant if it is broken. However, this underlines the dilemma of Unionist identity. That cannot be defined by political criteria alone if those are debatable and, under certain circumstances, even ultimately expendable.

Thus, the insistence upon the negotiable nature of the relationship with Britain forces the acknowledgement that Unionists' identity must embrace their domicile in the island of Ireland and the legitimation conferred to power relationships by a social solidarity fixed in that place. The failure to come to terms with this paradox lies at the root of the downfall of the Unionist polity. The link with Britain may indeed be sufficient to demarcate allegiance but remains in itself insufficient to

define Unionist identity as anything less transient than that
often misunderstood and ill-informed echo of another land.

Thus, the Protestant dilemma embraces both cultural and
political dimensions. The primacy given to the latter by the
1995 Joint Framework Documents reflects a characteristic and
customary arrogance that derives in part from the centrality of
party political processes within a UK state that lacks any written constitution to protect the principles of citizenship. As
Hutton (1995) persuasively argues, this results in the aspirations of that state being defined as those of the party with a
majority of seats in the House of Commons. Arguably, however, the key crisis facing Northern Ireland, indeed Ireland as
a whole, is not the negotiation of a framework for accountable
government. Rather, that is predicated upon a resolution to the
contested and confused sense of identity which characterises
the Ulster population as a whole but its Protestant majority in
particular.

Territory and Identity

The underlying assumption of the present argument is that identity, upon which the legitimacy of political processes depends, is
a function of a symbolic relationship with place. On one hand,
socio-political institutions must refer to the territory within
which they exist and over which they claim dominion. The exercise of political power cannot be conceived without a geographical basis. Conversely, the articulation of political power involves
a conscious moulding of space in order to generate the degree of
legitimacy that derives from the synonymity of territory and
authority. In all states, whether nation-states or otherwise, an
historically derived and validated iconography of place and ritual
is used to encapsulate a people's image of itself and validate its
exclusive right to that particular territory. In turn, history in its
manifestation as a heritage is used to legitimate particular power
structures and related political frameworks. At a simple level,
this explains why Unionists have sequestered the old provincial
name – Ulster – as a synonym for Northern Ireland, even though
the latter comprises only two-thirds of the province's nine
counties.

The imagery employed in such representations of the past
is not fixed because history is a set of relative values, subject
to continual re-evaluation and modification in response to con-

temporary demands. None the less, the ensuing depiction of place will seek to embody elemental continuities, their perceived longevity part and parcel of the processes of legitimation. Therefore, places are social contexts for human behaviour, settings in which social and political activity is caused and takes on meaning and purpose. Furthermore, they constitute the location for the reproduction and transformation of social relationships (Pred, 1984). Contemporary cultural geographers regard landscape not only as ways in which human groups see their worlds, but also as the intellectual and material transformations of nature through which those groups represent and contest their worlds within and between themselves (Cosgrove, 1993). Landscape is thus a means of human signification, not simply a text but also a context – a way of thinking and doing and asserting dominant power relations.

Consequently, landscape unavoidably possesses an ideological context. Baker (1992) identifies three particular characteristics of association. In the first instance, an ideology offers an ordered, simplified vision of the world, represented in landscape. Secondly, ideologies exert authority and find expression, not only in language, but in a landscape that is rich in signs of identity and social codes and which acts as a system of signification, expressive of that authority. Finally, ideologies employ individual, sacred landscape symbols to signify their own holistic character. The nation-state is perhaps the most obvious manifestation of these symbiotic relationships between landscape, ideology and identity. But state-building in general, whatever the constitutional arrangements, depends on a perpetuation of the hegemony of particular cultural forms, a dominance that must be perceived as legitimate by at least a majority among the population. The state can survive and prosper only so long as it can hold together that territorial coalition of places which gives it geographical form (Agnew, 1987). Consequently, all states sponsor intensely territorial state-ideas in support of their sovereignty, a factor also critical in the evolution of regional identity within states.

Northern Ireland and Territorial Identity

Foster, like Hewitt before him, believes in a primarily indigenous synthesis of identity vested in Ulster place, which separates it from the residue of Ireland but also from the

remainder of the UK. However, it is my argument that the
quest for such an identity induces irreconcilable tensions,
themselves part and parcel of the specific failure of Unionism
to come to terms with its cultural location in the island of
Ireland. In constructing a popular ·consciousness, Unionists
have always faced the quandary that any form of self-realisation that locates them in Ireland requires an acknowledgement of an Irish element to their identity, unless, that is, a
particularly Ulster cultural nationalism can be simultaneously
created which establishes that region's authentic separation
from the remainder of Ireland while accommodating it under
the protection of British allegiance. Almost by definition,
therefore, Unionists have displayed an ideological unwillingness to come to terms with Ireland.

They hold that there are two distinct peoples in the island,
the core of the political problem being the refusal of Northern
Nationalists to recognise this and accord Unionists the same
rights of self-determination they claim for themselves. However, this is to ignore the point that both Nationalism and
Unionism are contested concepts, the former riven by the success of a British political agenda of embourgeoisment which
has undermined Catholic middle-class support for sectarian
politics, the latter fractured by the class, and also gender, politics that have re-emerged in the face of the bankrupt political
philosophy of traditional Official Unionism. Internal schism is
the characteristic that unifies the hypothetical 'two nations' of
Ulster politics.

Nevertheless, the constitutional institutionalisation of de
Valera's ideal of an agrarian, homely Catholic society ensured
that Protestant, industrialised north-east Ireland could not be
accommodated in the post-independence Irish Free State. The
Catholic Church in Ireland pursued an extremely successful
power strategy in which the nineteenth-century Gaelic version of
history, created in response to the demand for independence, was
co-opted to underpin its own agenda for Irish identity. Thus, the
decisive ethos within nationalist Ireland after 1922 was Catholic
rather than Gaelic (Ó Tuathaigh, 1991). Faced with this ideological victory, representing the sequestration of everything Irish as
Republican and Catholic, Protestants, even those opposed to
Unionism, increasingly lost, abandoned, or were excluded from
any sense of being Irish (Brown, 1991). Crucially, however,
Unionism failed to develop an alternative indigenous cultural
synthesis, instead relying on the political dimensions of the

British link to delimit Northern identity. But undermined by the ambiguities of that relationship, the traditional poverty of Unionist historical awareness and a political unwillingness to develop a representation of Northern Ireland that transcended the sectarian dichotomy, the result has been cultural incoherence and political impotence (Brown, 1991).

Prior to the collapse of the Stormont regime in 1972, successive Unionist governments displayed only the most selective concern in manipulating Ulster's cultural past as an ideological artefact, failing not only to acknowledge the importance of landscape and place as systems that might signify and legitimate their authority, but also to appreciate that these settings were crucial to the reproduction of the social relationships that would have perpetuated their hold on power. The failure of the Unionist polity was a reflection of the absence of legitimacy conferred by an agreed representation of place. The only leading Unionist who apparently recognised this dilemma was Terence O'Neill who, together with Estyn Evans, was instrumental in establishing the Ulster Folk Museum at Cultra Manor, Co. Down, an institution created specifically in order to depict a cross-sectarian representation of Ulster's rural material culture. Irrespective of whether that Ulster is within, or apart from, Ireland, the (perhaps unagreed) intention of its founders was to articulate the integrative ideal of regionalism (Graham, 1994b). But in general, the official Unionist view of history eschewed such attempts to link representations of territory with a non-sectarian version of authority.

Apart from the inherent contradiction with an allegiance defined by the political link with Britain, Brown (1992) also believes that one singular reason for the Unionist failure to exploit the concept of national identity lies in a Calvinism which to some extent renders history insignificant. Working-class (increasingly non-working) Protestant identity can be defined along two schizophrenic axes. An element of class politics does exist, reflected in a radical Unionist consciousness which traditionally depended on, as it continues to do, the alienation of the Protestant underclass from its leaders. In general, however, that class consciousness has been at best diluted, at worst subsumed, by a sectarianism derived from the sacred sense of Protestantism. Emphasising Catholic treachery and duplicity, contemporary politicians (most notably Ian Paisley) depend upon this sense of religion to substantiate their legitimacy (Bruce, 1986). The Opsahl Report concluded that, for many Protestants, religion is a

far more important element in defining identity than is either
Unionism or Britishness, the negativity of their attitudes to the
Republic of Ireland being largely explicable in these terms. Paradoxically, therefore, even if individuals do not personally believe,
their identity tends to depend on religious symbols, leading –
ironically – to the position that, while commitment to religion is
weaker among Protestants compared to Catholics, the ideological
position of the former 'is ultimately much less readily secular-
ised' (Wallis *et al.*, 1986, p. 7).

Thus, for Unionists, single events, often of sectarian hue,
substitute for the powerful cultural synthesis that Nationalists
derive from the meshing of place and past. Set outside place, and
indeed time, these events lack any continuity of theme, a narrative that might connect them together Above all, they singularly
fail to provide a coherent text of place. Whether it is the 1641
rebellion when Protestant settlers were massacred by Catholic
rebels, the Battle of the Boyne in 1690, or the first day of the
Battle of the Somme in July 1916, Unionist history is absurdly
reductionist, its imagery, displayed on orange banner and wall
mural alike, depicting these and similar iconographic events in
terms of blood sacrifice and/or Catholic duplicity.

The poverty of this historiographical representation means
that traditional Unionism lacks any classical historical synthesis,
vested in the landscape, which might illuminate the illustrious
past of the Ulster Protestant community. Irish history and its
cultural landscapes have instead been suborned to the iconography of Republican nationalism. Unionism occupies not so much
'a place apart' as 'no place', a failure of legitimation which
ensures that it is an ideology that commands little, if any, significant external support. The liberal ethic firmly advocates the
Republican cause, particularly because of the oppressive sectarian
legacy of the pre-1972 Unionist state. Although Unionists may
indeed articulate a case, it is in a language that no one else
understands because of that failure to legitimate their authority
over the territory which they seek to control.

The largely negative territorial definition of traditional
Unionism is in part a reaction to the opposing ideology within
Ireland. The hegemonic, one-nation imagery of traditional Irish
nationalism offers a remarkably successful contrast to the indi-
gence and uncertainties of its Unionist counterpart. This metanarrative, espousing Gaelic and rural values in an imagery in
which the western Atlantic fringes of the island (those further-
most removed from Anglo-influences) were depicted as the

authentic cultural heartland and was a conscious creation of the
nineteenth-century evolution of Republican nationalism as an
alternative to Home Rule (Johnson, 1993). Meshing with other
elements, again notably blood sacrifice, this version of Irish
nationalism was, as observed above, subsumed within the Catholic Church's pursuit of power. The eventual outcome was the
incorporation of what Lee (1989) describes as a 'supreme imagi-
native achievement' into the 1937 Constitution as the definitive,
moral core of the Irish State. This representation depended on a
sense of place which denied heterogeneity in the interests of a
communal solidarity, defined by the seamless interweaving of
Catholic dogma and state ideology. Within this discourse, there
was literally no place for Protestants. Fatally, however, for a
Unionist cause, faced with a reactionary sectarian dogma, it was
adjudged sufficient to say 'no', rather than contemplate the tensions induced by the continued British political allegiance of a
part of Ireland that lacked any coherent, internalised cultural
synthesis.

Unionists have persisted in saying 'no', the perpetuation of
their antipathy to cultural representations vested within Ireland
or embracing elements of Irishness depending upon a belief in
the assumed continuity of the relevance of Gaelic-Catholic
ideology. In this, they share a curious cognitive symmetry with
the IRA and Sinn Fein. As John Dunlop, former Moderator of
the Presbyterian Church (the largest Protestant denomination in
Ireland) argues, IRA violence was based on a fundamentally
flawed analysis of the Irish problem (Presbyterian Church in
Ireland, 1986). The IRA decided to fight the British, but
Republican ideology does not allow them to acknowledge that the
problem is their dissenting neighbour. However, the persistent
Unionist recourse to a siege mentality, demonstrated so clearly in
the reactions to the 1985 Anglo-Irish Agreement and the 1995
Joint Framework Documents, articulates an equally defective
vision. Unionists and their militant Republican opponents are
locked into dramatically opposed representations which nevertheless share a common nineteenth-century provenance.

In contrast, Northern Ireland is surrounded, geographically,
by forces of positive intellectual and political re-evaluation.
These reflect the general point argued by Michael Mann (1986)
that societies are constituted of multiple, overlapping and intersecting socio-spatial networks of power. As the boundaries of
these rarely overlap, and social control is never sufficiently complete, the interstitial emergence of new or extended networks of

power cannot be prevented. Within Northern Ireland, the intransigent Unionist reliance on a nineteenth-century sectarian discourse opposed to, and partially defined by, an equally partisan Republican ideology, leaves Unionism in an extremely vulnerable position in responding to the continuing evolution of external power networks. If Unionist identity is largely vested in the negativity of defining oneself by whom one is not, that is, Catholic Irish, then the failure to articulate a response that addresses the political and cultural complexity of Northern Ireland's location is effectively condemning the Unionist cause to ultimate destruction. Three principal sets of processes, promoting change in power networks, can be identified.

In the first instance there is little evidence of a Unionist recognition of the need to respond to the sustained attempt during the past several decades to amend traditional representations of Ireland's past. The fractured process of 'revisionism', which seeks to replace the monolithic cultural matrix of Catholic, Gaelic and rural values that combined to produce the iconography of 'Irish-Ireland' with a culturally more diverse or pluralist articulation of Irish identity, has instituted a continuing and vitriolic debate on the nature of Irishness and the relationships between North and South (Brady, 1994). Ranged against those who advocate a diverse and comprehensive vision of Irishness, are 're-revisionists' or neo-traditionalists who see any attempt to reinterpret 'the beneficent legacy of expression' as patronising of the suffering in Ireland's past and apologetic of the role of the Anglo-oppressor. This is, of course, the viewpoint that continues to isolate Unionists as fellow-travellers of English coercion and indifference and confirms their intellectual isolation in the face of the pro-Republican, pro-Catholic alignment discernible in international opinion towards Ireland. By refusing to address the ideological implications of revisionism, the evidence of increasing secularisation in the Irish State, changing attitudes to the role of women in society and the clear evidence that the British Government lacks any ideological commitment to their cause, Unionists have been bypassed in an argument that, although as yet inconclusive, will continue. This suggests that Unionists no longer understand the terms of that to which they are so implacably opposed.

A second dimension of change that demands, but has not produced, a coherent intellectual response from Unionists is the continuing debate on the nature of the UK State. Adopting Benedict Anderson's (1983) definition of the nation as 'an imagined political community', Linda Colley argues that Great Britain can plausibly be regarded as an invented nation – forged above all by war – and 'superimposed, if only for a while, onto much older alignments and loyalties' (1992, pp. 5–6). It is defined, not by any domestic political or cultural consensus, but in reaction 'to the Other beyond their shores'. The dismantling of the apparatus of local government by a New Right administration has transformed the UK into the most centralised state in the European Union (EU). Despite this centralisation, the cultural tensions of this invented nation, fuelled by political discontent with the geographical concentration of the Conservative hegemony in south-east England and alienation from a Government that defined the national interest as its own survival, are readily apparent in demands for devolution and regional assemblies in Wales and Scotland. The debate within Scotland between those who seek to express their cultural nationalism within a UK political structure, and others who see cultural nationalism as the basis for political independence, is one further indication of the illusory unity of the British State. In a sense, this evidence of fragmentation and the questioning of the continued validity of regional alignments and loyalties, offers positive encouragement to Unionists who could depict Northern Ireland in a similar vein. As we shall see, there is indeed evidence that some Unionists do belatedly recognise the need to articulate a cultural underpinning to their political ideology. In general, however, the orthodox Unionist leadership continues to define its relationship with a changing and contested British State through traditional political criteria alone. Again, there appears to be little recognition of the need to formulate more flexible responses in a context of shifting alignments of identity and power.

Finally, membership of the EU has fundamentally altered notions of territorial sovereignty in both the UK and Ireland. While European legislation is applicable to both parts of Ireland, the most potent cultural representation is that of membership of a complex fusion of state, nation and regional identities. The argument that a 'Europe of the regions' is set to replace a 'Europe of the nations' echoes John Hewitt's earlier commitment to regionality as a solution to the dilemma of cultural identity in Northern Ireland (Ascherson, 1991). As Foster (1991) observes, the cultural entity of the region is reinforced by EU economic policy which directs financial aid at the regional level. The entire island of Ireland currently qualifies for inclusion among EU Objective 1 Regions, those which are lagging behind the remainder of the Community. Within these, per capita incomes and gross domestic product (GDP) per capita are respectively less than 75 per cent of, and between 25 and 46 per cent lower, than EU averages (Williams, 1994). Such regions are the principal recipients of EU structural funds which aim to promote the convergence of poorer areas towards Community norms.

Inevitably, these interventionist policies constitute an homogenising political and economic resource within the EU. Although Ascherson, for example, may have been precipitate in visualising the decline of national identity in favour of regional consciousness, EU policy constitutes yet another overlapping and intersecting socio-political network of power to which Unionists have yet to provide any sustained and lucid response. Thus, the poverty of Unionist historical awareness is primarily responsible for that ideology's inability to come to terms with change in the palimpsest of manifestations of power to which Northern Ireland, like any territorial entity, is subject. Others could be added – the international system of capitalism, the interventionist agencies and programmes funded by US government – but the point remains. Traditional Unionism, locked into the negativity of its own incoherent and vapid cultural consciousness, largely continues to say no, irrespective of whichever proposal is being formulated.

Territoriality and Political Frameworks in Northern Ireland

The remainder of this discussion is concerned with the characteristics of the contested Protestant representations of place which seek to transcend sectarian division, no matter how inadequately, in the interests of binding together a sustainable Northern Ireland polity. Although the discussion is pitched at the aggregate level, this is not to ignore that Protestant perspectives are contested along locality, gender, class and cultural axes that strongly influence the relative acceptability of the various representations (Graham, 1994c). For example, as a generalisation, working-class Protestants are more likely to be opposed to any *rapprochement* with the Republic of Ireland, compared to a middle class whose material interests would not be unduly compromised by the political unification of the island. None the less, beyond what might well be an intense local affiliation within the intimate geography of place demarcated by the finely-differentiated and complex intermeshing of religious distributions (incidentally a factor that strongly militates against repartition of Ireland as a feasible political solution), a Protestant will occupy a position inside a contested set of political representations, each matched by a synonymic

Table 2.1 Contested political explications of Northern Ireland and their synonymic cultural representations

Political perspective	Variants	Cultural representation
Integration of Northern Ireland into UK state	–	Denial of Irishness; denial of nationalism; citizenship as principle of unity of multi-national, multi-ethnic UK state.
Devolution	Repartition	Ulsterness is defined by location in separate region, culturally and historically distinct from remainder of Ireland.
Independence	–	As above but with emphasis on internal cohesion rather than dependence on UK allegiance. Ulster is portrayed as a conflict of nationalities.
Unified Ireland	Federal state Unitary state	Ulster is depicted as one distinct region within culturally and geographically heterogeneous Ireland.

cultural representation (Table 2.1). This prolixity of perspectives reflects the absence of agreement on identity and the acceptability of proposed political structures for the future of Ireland. In essence, four broad contrasting political structures can be identified: the integration of Northern Ireland into the United Kingdom; devolution; an independent Ulster; a unified Ireland of some kind.

Integration

As the 1995 Joint Framework Documents demonstrate, the political integration of Northern Ireland within the UK State is not seen as a feasible political solution by either the UK or Irish Governments. Nevertheless, it provides a useful basis of discussion here because of the outlook which it provides upon issues of cultural identity. Furthermore, the election of Robert McCartney in the June 1995 North Down by-election on a pluralist, cross-sectarian, integrationist platform suggests a measure of middle-class support for this perspective and a disenchantment with the devolutionist impulse of Official Unionism. None the less, the integrationist cause is one that is riddled with contradiction. In a vigorous advocacy of its virtues, Aughey (1989) argues that the character of Unionism cannot be explained in terms of 'nationality assumptions'. It has very little to do with the idea of the nation and everything to do with the concept of a multi-national, multi-ethnic state in which a citizenship derived from the structure of that state provides the essential principle of unity. The link with Britain is necessary for Northern Ireland because of the guarantees which it offers of a more pluralist and progressive way of life. Thus, Aughey disputes the commonplace notion that Unionists are a people in limbo who have failed to come to terms with Ireland because of that traditional sectarian and aggressively Gaelic version of Irish identity. Indeed he argues that any attempt at formulating a distinctive Northern Irish identity constitutes no more than an acceptance of the postulates of the Nationalist argument. Thus, the very concept of a cultural representation that in any way locates Northern Ireland in Ireland is a form of embryonic separation and an ideological danger to the integrationist discourse.

In pursuit of this argument, Aughey is driven to the conclusion that the modern state does not depend on any form of substantive territorial identity. But the effective legitimacy of any state, even a 'union state' like the UK, is vested in the sovereignty of territory. The defence of that territory and the imperialist superimposition of its will upon the 'Other' constitute powerful forces of integration, particularly when reinforced, as in the case of Britain, by a broadly Protestant culture. But as Colley (1992) argues, nationalistic impulses of Welshness, Scottishness, and Englishness, combined with forces of regionalism and localism, remained powerful divides in the eighteenth-century invention of the British nation, and continue to do so. Common codes of citizenship, inevitably applied unequally in both spatial and social terms, do not in themselves constitute a sufficient principle of unity, particularly if those values are rejected by a substantial percentage of the population – as is the case in Northern Ireland.

Devolution and Independence

Majority Unionist opinion and the UK and Irish Governments all favour a devolutionist solution to the constitutional future of Northern Ireland. While there is widespread disagreement concerning the extent of that devolution and the concomitant issues of consociation and even joint authority, all the various permutations that comprise this fractured and diverse discourse share increasingly apparent reservations concerning the authenticity of defining Northern Ireland's cultural location solely through the Union. As observed earlier, the logic of the negotiable, contractarian nature of that link demands that it be defined by more than political criteria alone.

Adherents of the devolutionist perspective agree that the island of Ireland is not a natural socio-geographic entity, the belief that there are separate and distinct peoples inhabiting the island being fundamental to Unionist philosophy. Hence, partition is legitimate and 'there is no historical imperative that Ireland should ever be united', Northern Ireland being 'an agreed entity, rather than a non-legitimate one' (Pollak, 1993, p. 17). Thus, unity with a state perceived to be defined by Catholic principles is neither a feasible political or cultural goal. Traditionally, the Stormont regime addressed this issue of the two peoples by minimising the separation of Northern Ireland from the remainder of the UK, this being the principal reason for that selective, episodic and sectarian history which Unionism chose for itself. However, contemporary Unionists are increasingly aware that Northern Ireland cannot survive culturally or politically by a dependence on an allegiance to a Britain that is at best ambivalent and, at worst, overtly hostile. The Joint Framework Initiative may enshrine a political acknowledgement that the Protestant majority in Northern Ireland has the right to determine its own future, but the ethos and language of the documents underscores the lack of long-term British ideological commitment to the Unionist cause. As the Downing Street Declaration also made clear, Britain has no remaining strategic interests in Ireland. Faced with this dilemma, combined with the Catholic cultural (if not necessarily political) rejection of Britishness, and the need to define some project of legitimation that might transcend sectarianism, Unionists increasingly seek an indigenous, synthetic representation to authenticate and legitimate their domicile within the island of Ireland.

As we have seen, the recognition that landscape iconography is one overt signifier of a common ground between Protestant and Catholic, has a lengthy provenance among the Protestant middle classes and Unionist intellectuals. It is true to say, however, that the latter have largely failed to exploit such ideas to influence external opinion on Ireland. In addition to poets like Hewitt, historians including A.T.Q. Stewart (1977) have created representations in which Planter and Gael are so intertwined in their complex matrix of localities that the essence of a solution to the Northern Ireland problem lies in coming to terms with 'the two dramatically opposed political wills that must coexist on the same narrow ground' (Stewart, 1977, p. 130). To Hewitt, Ulster was a landscape of singular geographical and cultural coherence, one which conveyed a traditional and historical singularity to all its people. Thus, he saw the province in contrasting terms to the sectarian landscapes depicted in the poetry of Seamus Heaney and Tom Paulin (albeit expressed in 'Heaney's courteous, compassionate, and unaggressive way' to cite Watson, 1991, p. 4). For Hewitt, landscape was the medium that depicted the regional loyalties which might subsume sectarianism, that region being: 'an area of a size and significance that we could hold in "our hearts", a local expression of universal impulses' (Ormsby, 1991, p. 32).

Such ideas are clearly relevant both to the contemporary revisionist impulse in Irish historiography and to the contested nature of Unionism itself as it struggles to formulate a response to the Joint Framework Documents. However, a further ideological tension occurs because of the nature of Unionist allegiance. If that is indeed contractarian, and if the

British Government is seeking to change the terms of the Union, the premises of devolution can logically be extrapolated into an argument for the dissolution of the link with Britain altogether in favour of an independent Ulster. The ways in which the devolutionist discourse can shade into independence are apparent in recent attempts to delineate an indigenous cultural synthesis for Northern Ireland. These aim to create an origin myth that establishes a representation of place legitimating the claim of Ulster's Protestants to their territory within the island of Ireland. Central to such projects, whatever their attitudes to the Union, is the construction of an image of place that underscores Northern Ireland's (Ulster's) cultural distinctiveness from the remainder of the island. Such propositions are not in themselves sectarian if Catholics are prepared to share in the imagery of place so defined. Apparently sound historical evidence supports the concept of the province as the distinct and separate region within Ireland. For example, the drumlin belt that stretches across South Ulster from the Down coast to Donegal Bay is one of the island's most enduring frontier regions. To its north, Planter and Gael shared in a striking commonality of material culture until urbanisation and industrialisation swept away traditional rural lifestyles of the sort depicted in the Ulster Folk Museum.

Among others, Adamson (1978, 1982 and 1991a) has speculated on an origin-theory for an indigenous Ulster subculture. His ideas locate this in the communality of a cultural province, extending across the Dalriadan Sea, to link north-east Ireland, Argyll and Galloway. In turn, this echoes Heslinga's contention (1971) that the real frontier in Ireland is that between Ulster and the remainder of the island, a religious divide that extends westward the equally significant cultural boundary between England and Scotland. Somewhat ironically, Adamson's origin-myth adopts precisely the same foreshortening of time which MacDonagh (1983) identifies as a primary characteristic of traditional Irish nationalism, the distant past being used in both representations to validate and legitimate contemporary social order.

Adamson contends that the primordial evidence of contemporary Ulster's glorious past is to be found within the seventh- and eighth-century tales and sagas, the Táin Bó Cúailgne, that constitute the earliest written record of the province's Iron Age heritage. The original inhabitants of what is now Ulster, the

Cruthin, controlled an Ulster-Scots cultural province prior to the
Iron Age incursions of the Celts (synonymous with Gaelic in
traditional iconography). The provincial name 'Ulster' derives
from the Ulaid, one of the Iron Age tribes, perhaps the pre-
eminent one, occupying the region by the second century AD.
During the succeeding centuries, these people were driven east
into the area that now constitutes Counties Down and Antrim by
the rise of Airgailla power in South-central Ulster and that of the
Uí Néill in the west (Mallory and McNeill, 1991).

Down and Antrim thus had close political religious and trad-
ing links with Scotland, symbolised most presciently by the
island monastery of Iona. Consequently, the Scottish migrants
who crossed to Ulster in the seventeenth-century Plantations
were returning to 'the lands of their ancestors' rather than acting
as the oppressive colonisers of Gaelic myth. Even the Ulster
Gaels who had displaced them originally had more in common
with their ethnic kindred in Scotland than those in the remainder of the island. To paraphrase Pred's terms (1984), Adamson is
seeking to appropriate Ulster time and space in the creation of an
indigenous regional metanarrative, arrived from symbolic place
icons and intermeshed with pseudo-history. Irrespective of the
academic validity of this representation' (Mallory and McNeill
(1991) dismiss the Cruthin as archaeologically invisible),
Adamson's is a conscious attempt to erect a signifying system
which communicates and reproduces a separate but ethnically-
integrated representation of the North, its contemporary stature
legitimated by the longevity of its independent and once glorious
past and its Ulster-Scots heritage.

Ideologically, such depictions of the past provide at least a
framework, a rearrangement of the pieces in more surprising
patterns, for an authentic expression of Ulster culture that is
no longer a pale reflection of those 'psychological colonialisms
of Irish nationality and British nationalism' (Foster, 1989). But,
and herein lies one of the dilemmas that underlay traditional
Unionist ambivalence to Ulster cultural regionality, attempts
such as Adamson's to create an indigenous Ulster cultural synthesis can be exploited by advocates of devolution and independence. The somewhat tortuous interpretation necessary to
distance Ulster from the remainder of Ireland reduces the
thrust of the British cultural connection to the link with Scotland. However, rather as Scottish cultural nationalism can be
mobilised in support of political independence, the logic of an
indigenous representation of Ulster points in this direction as

well, particularly given the absence of reciprocal political support within Scotland for any Ulster-Scots identity.

A Unified Ireland

Although the concept of an Ulster-Scots cultural province does underscore the failure of the Union to provide anything more substantial than an increasingly compromised political allegiance, and also demonstrates that devolution and independence are separated by degree rather than kind, it does appear to address Unionism's other cultural dilemma, the necessity of locating Northern Ireland apart from the remainder of the island. Clearly, this representation depends on the assumption that, historically, Ulster differs from the remainder of an Ireland that is culturally and historically homogenous. Such a conjecture, however, is ideologically constructed, one significant and enduring repercussion of the monolithic, Catholic 'symbolic universe that constituted the dominant public myth of post-Famine Ireland' (Lee, 1989, p. 648). However, the Gaelic-Catholic metanarrative is but one possibility, now heavily, perhaps terminally, compromised by the revisionist historiographical ethos that identifies a geographically heterogeneous Ireland, the personality of which is largely defined by its multiplicity of regional differences among which Ulster's particularity is but one. Such a discourse constitutes a specific threat to the fragile edifice of an Ulster-Scots epic that seeks its legitimacy through distancing Ulster from Ireland.

In the traditional Gaelic-Catholic metanarrative, the wider cultural geographical contexts of Ireland's complex history were generally either ignored or manipulated into an iconography of oppression. Conversely, a number of geographers, most notably Estyn Evans (1981) and W.J. Smyth (1993), have argued that Ireland is no different from the majority of European nations and states which have evolved through a fusion of regional loyalties. Evans, for example, placed Ulster within an essential unity of Ireland, one distinctive element in the island's diverse habitat, heritage and history (Graham, 1994a and 1994c). Smyth contends that we need to set aside simplified stereotypes and explore instead those diversities and pluralities of Irish identity which were subsumed within what he terms the period of 'necessary closure' of the country during the late nineteenth and first half of the twentieth centuries, as the struggle for political and cultural independence was intensified, consolidated and achieved. However, the Gaelic-Catholic discourse still survives. Lee (1989) for example, offers succour to

Unionist negativity, describing the representation of the island as a cultural patchwork as mere heroic self-deception. All that is important is Celt and English, any redefinition of Irishness being no more than what he believes to be a relentless pursuit of Anglicisation. Lee's depressing, ultimately sectarian analysis demonstrates the critical and enduring paradox within traditional Irish nationalism. Theoretically comprehensive, inclusive and non-sectarian, its emotional appeal has always derived, however, from the exclusive myth of a culturally homogenous Irish nation struggling to free itself from Anglo-oppression (Boyce, 1991). As the Nationalist MP Stephen Gwynn once privately admonished, the inevitable consequence is 'if Ireland as a nation means what de Valera means by it, then Ulster is not part of the nation' (quoted in Bowman, 1982, p. 338).

Conversely, if Ulster is to be but one specific variant within a regionally diverse society, the cultural depiction of Irish-Ireland as a hegemonic landscape of Gaelic omnipotence is no longer an acceptable representation. Instead, new definitions of Irishness build upon a discourse which stresses the myriad regional particularities of Ireland's hybrid society. In a wider context, the arguments of cultural omnipotence advanced by intellectuals such as Lee can be seen as little more than delusory. It says little for the maturation of the Irish State to argue that the removal of illusions of homogeneity would bring the whole edifice tumbling back within the English hegemony. Rather, the exclusive imagery of traditional nationalism reflects less upon the evidence of the island's historical landscape, as the ideological success of the Gaelic-Catholic metanarrative, Northern rejection of and exclusion from its imagery, and the symbolic importance of partition to Unionists and Nationalists alike (Graham and Proudfoot, 1993).

Conclusions

The absence of a political consensus within Northern Ireland is a reflection of the contested nature of the Protestant, and indeed Irish, identities discussed here. If any future political structure is to be accepted as legitimate by both Unionists and Nationalists in Northern Ireland, a cultural environment must first be created in which ideology creates an integrative place consciousness which, in turn, will signify the holistic and inclusive nature of that philosophy. Without this cultural cement, no political framework can succeed. Tuan (1991) observes that regions may have no existence outside the consciousness of geographers who, by their eloquence, are able to create place. No matter how impaired that rhetoric might be, the challenge in Ireland is to create landscapes in which pluralist myths might be embedded.

It has been argued here that the integrationist case contains too many contradictions to constitute a feasible proposition. By extrapolation, the ambiguous, negotiable, contractarian link with Britain is also an insufficient basis from which an overarching sense of identity for Northern Protestants might be created. The signifying system of largely disconnected events and dates, through which successive Unionist governments attempted to communicate and reproduce their vision of Northern Ireland, was inadequate. The political economy of Unionist Stormont failed to create a cultural landscape, a representative imagery, through which Protestants might come to terms with, and legitimate, their domicile in Ireland. Thus, the contested political representations of Ulster have not been informed by positive delineations of cultural imagery but by a Protestant exclusion from and negative reaction to the immensely successful Gaelic-Catholic iconography, vested in place, which has been so potent an influence on the shaping of space – and thus power – in the Republic of Ireland. Just as Unionists defined the Union largely through political criteria, they attempted to represent Northern Ireland as a political entity alone, a distant echo of another land. Stormont's distancing of Ulster from Ireland reflected the dilemma that any internal cultural synthesis would have to embrace, or at least acknowledge, elements of Irishness.

The development of a culturally separate Ulster narrative, integrated into the Ulster-Scots epic, has been the principal response to this impasse. However, not only does it embrace connotations of alienation from the Union by its imperceptible shading into an argument for independence, but it further depends on the assumption that Ulster is the distinctly different region in an otherwise geographically homogeneous island. As observed here, the contemporary revisionist ethos argues against this, depicting a heterogeneous Ireland in which Ulster is one particular region among a number. Thus, the Unionist predicament remains that, while the development of an indigenous synthetic cross-sectarian cultural representation of Ulster is necessary to legitimate power, inevitably that construct will

also support the efficacy of a pluralist depiction of a unified
Ireland of some form. However, as overlapping and intersecting
socio-political networks of power change Europe, the cultural
problem for Ulster Unionists remains a vexed one. They cannot continue to say 'no' but must instead formulate the positive cultural iconography necessary to imagine their place and
thus legitimate their cause. Inevitably, such a construct must
take them closer to Ireland, but only to a revised and pluralist
representation of that society, one in which regional and
cultural heterogeneity is the defining ethos.

3 Suffering for Righteousness' Sake? Fundamentalist Protestantism and Ulster Politics

Duncan Morrow

It was [my family's] proud boast that no Paisley ever married a Roman Catholic. Long may it continue! And they were known for their espousal of the principles of civil and religious liberty.

Ian Paisley (1973)

In a post-cease-fire radio interview in 1994, the security spokesman for the UUP, Ken Maginnis, widely considered too liberal to become leader of his party, expressed the view that the Protestant community regarded itself as 'more sinned against than sinning'. In choosing his words, Maginnis did at least two important things. He was undoubtedly expressing a widely-held view among Protestants and Unionists in Northern Ireland. His words are consistent with the self-image of all Orange and Unionist institutions throughout modern history. Quoting Edmund Burke, the Revd M.W. Dewar justified the need for the Orange Order on the basis that 'when bad men combine, the good must associate, else they will fall, one by one, an unpitied sacrifice in a contemptible struggle' (1958, p. 22).

Secondly, and importantly, he invoked traditional Christian imagery to explain a modern struggle played out on the secular stage. The image of the persecuted innocent is at the heart of the Christian gospel. Without further reference, or even deliberate intent, Maginnis re-established the basis for a coherent ideological identification of the Protestant and Unionist communities with the crucified Christ. It is an image with profound resonances in a society with a high percentage of churchgoers and recent ex-churchgoers. If Protestants are the sinned against, we can be in little doubt about who constitute

the sinners. Furthermore, in spite of this persecution, the innocent still hold on. Instead, persecution rallies all to the cause.
This too has deeply religious resonances. Speaking about his
late father, Ian Paisley explicitly conveyed the response to such
sentiment in theological terms: 'My father ... was uncompromising in his character. He did not care. The more he was
opposed, the more he was persecuted, the more he excelled in
his evangelism' (1973, p. 10).

Persecution and suffering for the sake of righteousness have
long been central leitmotivs in Northern Irish politics. By in-
voking such imagery once more, political leaders make obvious
what has always been implicit. Conflict in Northern Ireland is
not only a struggle for simple political power but is a moral
and spiritual battle. The importance of Protestantism as the
assurance of fundamental moral superiority of the cause cannot
be denied. There can be no serious moral equality between the
actions of the persecutors and those of the persecuted. Pushed
to its conclusion, there is an absolute moral difference between
the groups. As a result, the parties of Ulster, the good and the
evil, the sheep and the goats, the saved and the damned, the
sinners and the sinned against have parallel scriptural anteced-
ents. Read through this prism, Christian scripture is the ideological quarry from which sustenance can and should be drawn
in the last battle for secular as well as sacred supremacy. The
unquestionable premise is and must remain that 'we are the
sinned against and they the sinners'.

Numerous explanations have been advanced to explain why
Christianity has remained relatively impervious to secularisation in Northern Ireland; these range from the sociological
such as the relatively rural nature of the society, to the historical and traditionally deep attachments to religion, and the
theological. One further factor is that the ideological relevance
and explanatory power of the good/bad dichotomy has
remained obvious. The explanatory power of fundamentalist
religion resonates with the experience of persecution and violence. In the face of violence and chaos, people are driven back
to the comfort of a knowledge of righteousness and order.
Aggressive certainty replaces chaotic self-doubt. Neither theological liberalism nor secular modernity offers such solace in
this context, while traditional religion offers both immediate
comfort and the hope of triumph. The power of fundamentalism is its capacity to interpret this reality even to those who
doubt the core doctrines on which it is based.

Given ongoing violence, there is no need to change the interpretation of history because its fundamental structure appears unchanged. There is, or it appears that there is, nothing to revise. Experience, lived within a nearly uniformly Protestant mental framework, can only understand the Northern Ireland conflict as another onslaught of evil Republican violence on a God-fearing and law-abiding people. This prism, proclaimed as true Protestantism, thus becomes to Unionist tactics what Marxism was to East European communists (Moxon-Brown, 1983). The image of the persecuted innocent contains within it the central Christian hope of ultimate victory in the Resurrection. Persecution will not triumph but represents the call to ever greater efforts in the bid to overcome, whether by evangelism or political struggle. For evangelism we might benevolently read 'persuasion' in the secular realm, although there are many who would claim that the boundary between persuasion and coercion depends more on political conditions than on semantic definition.

Ultimately two identifiable yet apparently contradictory trends have to be reconciled: within Unionism, there is clearly an enormous blurring of the doctrinal and the ideological and thus of the border between the religious and the political. Nevertheless, fundamentalist religion does not act as a universal transcendence for Northern Irish Protestants. Of course, it is necessary only that the slipperiness between the secular and the Church can be plausibly and regularly demonstrated in social reality for it to be of political and social importance. Such assertions of connection are patently not true. Yet, while Church and politics cannot be separated it is also true to say that they cannot be elided.

It may be, however, that Maginnis unwittingly provides the bridge between these two phenomena, revealing in the process not so much the secular unity of Church and politics as the religious basis inherent in Irish Nationalism and Unionism as crusades against evil. Being 'more sinned against than sinning' represents the fundamental *sine qua non* of all moral division. This is not, as such, a statement of doctrine, but it is a description of the moral universe to which both doctrine and reason speak. The influence of fundamentalist Protestant doctrine is not that it leads people to this conclusion but that it provides a firmness of conviction once this premise is conceded. It is this quality of independently grounded certainty which gives doctrine its relevance not only for those who explicitly share fundamentalist beliefs but to all those who share the premise that this is a battle against evil people. The primary importance of fundamentalist Protestant religion is not its doctrinal Protestantism but its absolutist religiosity, its ferocious attachment to the division into sinned against and sinning.

Protestantism and Political Myth in Ulster

Protestantism, whether in an actual present-day form or in an archaic post-belief echo, clearly shapes Northern Irish Unionism in all of its significant moments. When Unionist Prime Ministers declare their system to be a 'Protestant parliament for a Protestant people', the die is well and truly cast. Unionism in Ireland over the last two hundred years is, without any exaggeration, absolutely incomprehensible without an understanding of Protestantism and its theological uses. Theological Protestantism and anti-Catholicism can lay claim to a longer unbroken historical pedigree in Ulster than any other still-existent ideological rival. There is a degree to which all modern representations of the anti-Nationalist ideological case are recent additions or alterations to Protestant anti-Catholic sentiment. This, perhaps more than anything else, is the underlying argument of Steve Bruce in his assessment of Paisleyism (1986). He then develops this argument to suggest that the antithetical nature of Protestantism to Catholicism is what makes the emergence of a liberal centre in Northern Ireland impossible.

Given the relative newness of modern political ideologies and current political institutions in both Britain and Ireland, Protestantism certainly provides our most direct link to a primordial narrative and myth of origin in non-Catholic Ireland. It is to this crucial connection between Protestantism and myth that we should look if we are to understand Protestantism's ongoing ideological function. In his essay, *Science and Ideology*, the French philosopher Paul Ricoeur defines the relationship between myth and ideology as follows:

> Ideology expresses a social group's need for a communal set of images whereby it can represent itself to itself and to others. Most societies invoke a tradition of mythic idealisations whereby they may be aligned with a stable, predictable and repeatable order of meanings. This process of ideological self-representation frequently

assumes the form of a mythic reiteration of the founding-act of the community. (quoted in Kearney, 1988, p. 14)

Protestantism in Ulster is clearly no stranger to ritual re-enactment of the self-justifying story of its own past. Any society may be expected to cherish such a past. Nevertheless, there are three elements which distinguish the case of Protestants in the North of Ireland.

Firstly, the representation of myth through ritual and symbolic displays may indeed unite the Protestant community at times. At the same time, however, the reality of an ongoing and hostile Catholic presence, both socially and politically, means that the ritual does not unite the political nation but divides it into two: those who belong and those who are seen as enemies. Ritual re-enactment of Protestant myths, in particular Orange parades and symbolic uses of the Union Jack at important all-British occasions are therefore both central communal festivals for those involved, and reminders of the fundamental division that structures political life. Ritual re-enactment of purely secular myth within the North of Ireland does not produce closure and social harmony but instead may indeed come perilously close to restimulating the original conflict.

René Girard (1987), the French social critic, suggests that all myth is structured around the memory of expulsion of a scapegoat-victim from the group. From this expulsion stems both the identity and unity of the group as it simultaneously creates human and moral differentiation. Myths act not only to tell the story of the expulsion but to reinforce the unity of the group. Thus myth functions to create unity at the expense of a victim. Of course, given that the victim is driven out, he or she is represented only in the telling of the victimisers. The fact that the victim is indeed a victim is usually invisible to those doing the re-enactment. Ritual re-enactment of the expulsionary event therefore takes place without the presence of the victim and thus functions to bind the group together without unveiling the truth of the violent origins of the group. Girard calls the structures, myths and rituals which stem from expulsionary events 'Religion': transcendent unifying bearers of whole cultures (Girard, 1987).

The predicament of Protestants in Ulster is that the opponent, against whom the whole community has its identity, remains in the midst. The victim is not expelled, and the consciousness that one could be the victim remains. Furthermore, ultimately the rituals in Northern Ireland do not hide violence but tend to raise its profile to the point of making it largely impossible to deny the victimising consequences of one's own actions. The potential that re-enacting the ritual will inflame rather than abolish passions means that there is an ever-present danger of becoming yourself the victim. Orange bravado, for example, never creates final security, especially in times of tension. As such, many myths and rituals of Ulster remain permanently ambiguous.

The second dimension of Protestantism is related to this very partial success of other myths in providing sustenance in Ulster. Fundamentalist Protestantism enables people to 'read back' the events of the North of Ireland into a mythical reading of the Bible. Thus Protestantism invests Protestants with a universal significance by identifying with Jesus on the cross, the persecuted innocent. Hence it provides the assurance that, at root, the Protestants of Ulster are part of the struggle of universal good in the battle against evil. In this version, Ulster Protestants, although currently the persecuted victims, will ultimately be justified by divine retribution. This combination is summed up in the last sentence of Steve Bruce's book when he quotes Ian Paisley asserting in relation to Protestant Ulster: 'God who made her mighty will make her mightier yet' (1986, p. 270).

In this reading, the Book of Revelation in particular functions not as a vision but as a mythical interpretation of current political events in which there is the final certainty so absent in other myths. As noted by Deane:

> On an awesome scale, the Book of Revelation works like a great folk story. It is a symbolic story, in code, of what is happening now. It tells of the great battles of repression, anxiety and fear, the collision between heaven and hell ... But it is essentially a vision, not a myth. Used as a myth, it ratifies a version of history in which the forces of good overcome those of evil. (1988, p. 27–8).

To this degree, Protestantism rescues myth when more secular versions appear less reliable. We can understand the appeal of radical evangelicalism even to the unchurched once we understand the power which such Protestant myths have in ideological terms. Many may be agnostic on the contents of the Book of Revelation but they are moved by the security and ideological consequences arising from the believers. The rather overused parallels between Afrikaaner and Ulster Protestantism have a clear relevance here. The assurance that, despite persecution, the cause is good, provides a deep well of sustenance which, in the context of political fear which characterises so many Ulster Protestants, is deeply attractive. One of the dimensions which distinguishes Protestantism from Catholicism in Ireland is the relative absence of any necessity on the part of twentieth-century Catholic Ireland to resort to any such reading of the Bible to prove the fundamental goodness of the cause. Indeed, the fact that Nationalism has founded its case on the same grounds as liberation movements with 'recognised' causes has been one of its strongest international political cards. The two most clear-cut exceptions to this are the icons of Irish Republicanism, Patrick Pearse and Bobby Sands.

There may also be a third dimension to all of this, however. Protestantism may indeed also demystify the mythical dimension of the Ulster predicament even as it adds to its mystification. The example of South Africa may illustrate this point more largely. The defeat of Afrikaaner apartheid ideology was as much a theological as a political defeat. The connivance of Protestantism with an ideology of ontological superiority was found to be unsustainable in the light not only of secular political pressure but also in the light of the New Testament. Of course this is not the whole story, but changes in the Dutch Reformed Church were crucial to the articulation of a 'New South Africa' and the political possibilities which emerged after 1990.

According to Girard (1987), the most radical insight of the Judaeo-Christian scriptures is of the connivance of all human beings in violence. The crucifixion and resurrection of Christ unmask such violence and suggest that the only way beyond violence is for each to take responsibility for one's own violence before pointing at that of others. In other words, it reverses in practice the concept of 'more sinned against than sinning' by proclaiming relative indifference to the sin of others.

Within the Protestant churches, there are many who have not shared the absolute abhorrence of Catholicism that characterises the stereotypical fundamentalist. Indeed, there are numerous examples of self-consciously inter-church or ecumenical groups and activities. Such ecumenism is, however, a serious breach of Protestant solidarity, not so much because it sups with the devil, which is ultimately 'merely' the symptom of its depravity, but because it does not and cannot accept the myth of the Protestant fundamentalist reading of the bible and still proclaim itself Protestant. Potentially then, it undermines the certainty of the myth from within, rather than from without. It reduces the relationship to Catholicism to 'a problem' open to solution, not 'a conflict' founded in absolute irreconcilability. Because of its more explicitly democratic structure Presbyterianism in particular has demonstrated this tendency to strong theological division for many years. It is no coincidence that Ian Paisley's public career began by attacking the ecumenical tendencies of the Presbyterian General Assembly. As such, Protestantism in Ireland may indeed be part of the glue of Ulster Unionist ideology but simultaneously it may be the source of the most profound critiques.

The Protestant Myth and Politics

The importance of fundamentalist Protestantism as ideology in Ulster politics lies in its relative durability and reliability as myth sustaining the fundamental division between good and bad. If and when the British State or the conservative Unionist elite is perceived as unreliable, the ideology arising from fundamentalist Protestantism thus becomes more visible.

This does not mean that all its supporters can articulate the theological basis of their position. They can, however, articulate the fundamental religious divide into good and bad which the fundamentalist myth restates. Thus many participate in the most important rituals and are carried along by the real consequences of the myth. This is likely to happen as long as the fears of the 'Protestant' community that they will be made the victims of any political or military development remain high. The fears may be of death or injury by violence, of economic loss, of loss of identity after political or military defeat or even, in the most extreme case, of genocide. Grounds for all of these fears can be found in the campaigns of Republicans in history both distant and recent. When there are few such fears, in times of tranquillity, Protestant fundamentalist ideology can be rejected as extremist lunacy. When such fears are seen to be justified, as has been the case since 1969, the same Protestant fundamentalism appears to provide the last coherent articulation of rejection.

Paisleyism, of course, represents the most publicly important assertion of radical Protestantism in the modern era.

The physical reality of Republican hostility (leaving aside all matters of causality) and the political mobilisation of Catholics during Civil Rights tended to confirm Paisley's apocalyptic vision to many frightened Protestant minds. Furthermore, the machinations of successive British Governments again underlined to Protestants that Albion was perfidious. Paisley's understanding of Protestant doctrine is his explicit source of inspiration for all of his political activity. As one Free Presbyterian minister put it: 'We have a God-given responsibility. We are ambassadors for Christ. That is why we take such a strong stand against modernism, liberalism, ecumenism and Romanism' (quoted in Morrow, 1991, p. 91).

Paisley's religious defence of secular borders has secular appeal to threatened and insecure people. Doubts about Paisleyite doctrine are submerged in agreement about Paisley's enemies. Hence the DUP has become the authentic voice of an often unchurched working-class constituency, notably in East Belfast (see Bruce, 1986). Despite secularism, which is undoubtedly rising particularly in working-class urban areas of Northern Ireland, and the undoubted distaste of many for Paisley's religious utterances, nothing has stopped the DUP establishing itself within the Belfast conurbation.

By building a religious political edifice in which there are no clear boundaries between one and the other, Paisley had political appeal along the entire length of the slope connecting secular politics and religious doctrine. However, fundamentalist Protestant myth provides the core of resistance. Catholicism is defined as fundamentally evil, and loyal Catholics are, at best, misguided, and, almost certainly, damned. This approach to Catholicism necessarily relativises all possible relations to individual Catholics. They are not suitable marriage partners, they are not trustworthy with civil liberty and, most importantly, they are always tied to the hostile 'other'. Furthermore, contact with Catholics is self-limiting, eventually reducible to Catholics as 'mission field'. In condemning any other form of recognition of Catholicism, the myth of fundamentalist Protestantism therefore acts against existential or experiential change.

Such Protestantism has serious potential political implications. At the very least, in ontologising Catholicism as evil, it makes coexistence in demographic situations such as Northern Ireland extremely difficult. Protestants can never accept minority status in a Catholic society and Catholics must accept the ritual degradation of their own core religious sensitivities within a state

founded on 'Protestant liberty'. Furthermore, at the level of
wider political life, it appears to legitimise a mythology of heroic
struggle which can easily be abused by those who come within
the orbit of the myth. Witch-doctors who call on ancient spirits
cannot always control what those spirits do. The boundary between clear legitimation of virulent anti-Catholic rhetoric and
actions designed to physically attack Catholics is paper-thin in a
heightened and fearful crowd, especially for those for whom Protestant ideology is not mitigated by church-going. This is reflected in the ambivalence of many to paramilitary murder. As in
the case of revolutionaries, the 'boundlessness of their sentiment'
can quickly blind the radical counter-revolutionaries to the reality of persons. Historians can dispute at what point the French,
Russian or Chinese revolutions became murderous, but the connection between boundless ideology and actual events remains
unchallenged. The question must still be asked as to whether the
repeated calling on the fundamentalist Protestant myth creates
the basis on which violence and murder in supposed defence of
the threatened community is legitimised.

Fundamentalism and Diversity
in Religious Protestantism

Fundamentalist Protestantism myth is central to the structure of
Northern Irish politics with an influence far beyond the true
believers. At the same time, and problematically, to say that it is
part of the core is not to say that it is the only core of Ulster
Unionism. Indeed, structurally-speaking, the edifice built on
Protestantism and Unionism is far from coherent.

Within active churchgoing Protestantism, there is no final
acceptance of the fundamentalist reading of the Bible. Certainly,
Ian Paisley has built a considerable theological influence from a
base in Free Presbyterianism. The most direct route for this
expansion has been through the Presbyterian Church itself
through appeals to its fundamental anti-Catholic wing. The General Assembly of the Presbyterian Church, hostile to political
moves which were seen as anti-Unionist, notably the Anglo-Irish
Agreement, withdrew from the World Council of Churches on
the basis that it funded terrorism and from the newly-formed
Council of Churches for Britain and Ireland when it became clear
that the new body would include representatives of the Catholic
Church as full members.

At the same time, Presbyterianism has always emphasised the right of personal conscience in the light of Scripture and the Church has long been subject to disputes leading regularly to actual schism. Pluralism within the Church and an uncompromising face of the majority view to the outside world have therefore both been characteristics of Ulster Presbyterian behaviour.

Terence Brown (1985) has argued that lively and stimulating theological debate contrasts sharply with a debased political immobilism. Whether the conduct of the Presbyterian debate on doctrine and politics has been intellectually lively over the last 25 years is a moot point. However, this recognition of the fundamental theological diversity of Ulster Protestantism means that there is every reason to believe that the unity of Pan-Unionist fronts is only possible in relation to the perception of a shared external enemy and the fears which this arouses. The apparent immobilism of Unionism is the result of a coalition founded on the basis of a unity only founded against something else. There have always been divisions whenever positive political programmes have to be shaped, where individual groups have ploughed apparently conflicting furrows. Unionism as synonymous with 'No' to Republicanism has proved the only lasting glue. That the Churches have been able to show their internal differences more publicly than the Unionist parties probably results from the absence of any representative function of the Churches and the consequent absence of the three-line whip.

Of course, if internal disagreement on theology and Christian practice is the hallmark of Presbyterianism, it is clearly true for any coalition of different Protestant Churches who have not always enjoyed cordial relations. Indeed, the Church coalition only really exists in relation to commonly held fears in the secular realm. In Church terms, Paisley's Free Presbyterians remain marginal. Furthermore, the main Churches themselves are all cross-border institutions, which can never fully identify with only one state. In this sense, the Churches comprise one of those institutions which ritually and structurally keep alive an idea of common Irish identity among Protestants.

There has never been any other common theological or political platform. Famously, A.T.Q Stewart (1977) shows that in Ireland in the 1790s, anti-establishment United Irish sentiment flourished among Presbyterians where memories of massacre at the hands of Catholics such as 1641 were non-existent or dim, whereas in Armagh, which was characterised by rising inter-communal violence between Protestants and Catholics,

Orangeism transcended Protestant hostilities. The very nature of Protestantism in Ireland always mitigated against any complete Protestant theocracy in the North. The triumph of the Orange interpretation of the circumstances facing Protestants therefore represents the successful spread of existential fear among the Protestant community at large. Born into an atmosphere of existential fear and insecurity, the Northern Ireland state nearly always existed in its shadow. It is not surprising that events since 1969 have tended to reaffirm the Protestant/ Unionist front in relation to the encroaching demands of Irish Nationalism and the Catholic community who support it.

The divisions of the Protestant churches, internally, with one another and across borders, have never allowed, and probably can never allow, them to be a really solid institutional basis for Protestant integration in Northern Ireland. Indeed this is one of the most obvious contrasts with the position of the Catholic hierarchy. Until recently, the Protestant Churches never needed to unite to mediate between the State and an alienated people. The question remains whether it would ever be possible for them so to do.

The Bible against the Crown?

The immediate solution of this dilemma of common political fears and chronically divided institutions has been the emergence of new institutions. These are theoretically and actually separate from the Churches but are made up of individual church-members including the clergy while *de facto* restricting membership to Protestants. The two most obvious frameworks for this integration since 1969 have been the historically crucial Orange Order, and the young Turks represented by the DUP. Neither, however, can claim to unite all. As one looks into supposedly monolithic Protestantism, the difficulties of maintaining a coalition become more apparent.

The Orange Order, of course, represents the most historically important attempt to produce a Pan-Unionist front. The unity of the Order was always founded on the importance of the unity of Crown and Bible. As argued by Long: 'The Qualifications of an Orangeman demands a Protestant Church membership and conduct based on the Christian ethic ... There is strong Orange antipathy to Roman Catholicism, religiously and politically' (1978, p. 10–11).

Furthermore as stated previously by Dewar:

> The true Orangeman of today, deeply loyal to the British crown and a faithful Protestant is bound to support our Constitutional system which maintains the Protestant religion and preserves the Union between Great Britain and Northern Ireland. The Border is as secure a bulwark to his religious freedom, under the ample folds of the Union Jack, as were the grey Walls of Derry beneath her Crimson Banner nearly three centuries ago. (1958, p. 22)

Fifty years of Orange statehood and the public profile of such sentiments inevitably links Protestantism and Unionism in a way that profoundly influenced the identity of the state.

However, more than any other institution, the Orange Order represents the absolutely necessary connection of religion and politics in any analysis of historical Unionism. The apparent unity of Protestantism and Unionism in the Orange Order comes under stress if the two pull in opposite directions. The political crisis since 1969 has tended to weaken the institutional element of the Orange project and heighten the importance of religious fundamentalism in politics. We have also seen that this creates difficult dilemmas; the rise of fundamentalism tends to weaken the Union at the British end, while the indifference of Britain to the Union tends to encourage fundamentalism.

It is a commonplace to point out that the political monopoly enjoyed by the Orange Order under the Stormont regime has been shattered by the collapse of Stormont in 1972 (Wichert, 1991). The decline of the Order remains a relative rather than an absolute matter. Nevertheless, the decline of the Order represents the pressure under which the conservative combination of Crown and Bible has now been placed and parallels the decline of the Unionist Party itself. Partly through the vehicle of Orangeism, the Unionist Party mixed British loyalty, which is anti-Irish Nationalist but not necessarily anti-Catholic with fundamentalist Protestantism which is anti-Catholic yet willing to challenge any British Government. During the 1960s, the Unionist Party began to attempt overtures towards Catholics. Since 1969, Protestant fundamentalism has stood out as the ideological linchpin of opposition to any attempt to coerce a united Ireland.

The reliance on fundamentalist Protestant myth has meant that Unionism as a whole has a reduced capacity to reach beyond those immediately faced with the fear of the deluge.

Hence the yawning distance of Northern Ireland from the heartland of British politics. The rather plaintive insistence of Ulster Protestants on their Britishness has little impact on the average English voter for as long as they describe reality in terms of the Book of Revelation in which the forces of hell are mustered first and foremost in the Vatican via the Irish Republic. Protestantism thus unites internally and drives a wedge between Unionism and the Union.

It is at least possible to argue that the opposite is also the case. If fundamentalist Protestantism makes others regard Ulster Unionists as un-British, the failure of the British State to offer protection to its citizens has also heightened the ideological centrality of Protestantism. In the absence of any secure sense of Britishness, local communities clung to their only semi-coherent institutional and organisational bases. In historical terms, the Churches have been the only consistent structures of vertical integration within Protestant society organised within Ireland. The need to rely on an ideological and institutional framework not rooted in an entire United Kingdom framework even while struggling to remain within the State has maintained the role of Protestantism at the political frontier. In this view, the primary importance of Protestantism in Ulster is precisely that it is internally generated. In addition, it is no surprise that it has been generated among the dissenting tradition who have long doubted the commitment of a humanistic/Anglican/agnostic parliament even as they cling to 'the Crown, being Protestant'. This suggests that the more the Britishness of Ulster Unionists is denied, whether by mainland British or Irish Nationalists, the more fundamentalist Protestantism becomes the remaining ideological core of resistance (Wright, 1987).

What is important here is that Protestantism and Britishness, while interchangeable to a degree, are not necessarily the same. Orangeism is a monolith based on a presentation of this unity between the two which may no longer hold in an age of rampant secularism and British 'duplicity'. Unionists may eventually have to choose between the strands of their belonging. While the myths of fundamentalist Protestantism resonate widely in Northern Ireland and provide a mythical backbone for one part of Ulster Unionism of particular importance during times of stress in relations with British political parties, it is not clear that it forms a coherent myth even for the whole church-going Protestant, let alone Ulster Unionist, community.

Fundamentalism is not even the basis of any common theological reading of the bible within and between the Churches. There are clearly points at which fundamentalist Protestantism now actually undermines a common British identity. Unionist parties are increasingly confronted with the need either to extend their reach beyond Protestantism, and so prove their Britishness, or to retreat behind the defensive certainties of fundamentalist Protestantism and so weaken the Union.

Conclusion

Fundamentalist Protestantism thus provides a central focus for Unionist politics only under certain conditions of stress. Nevertheless, such coherence as is possible depends entirely on the existence of Republican violence. There are a number of implications of all of this. First, were Ulster to be abandoned by Britain, there is little indication that fundamentalist Protestantism would suffice as the mythological foundation for an entire ethnic nation. On the other hand, it would remain a major obstacle to the easy integration of Protestants into a new Irish State. Secondly, the importance of Protestant fundamentalism rises as Protestants feel that their Britishness is under threat. If fundamentalism is to lose its grip, Irish Nationalists and leaders in Great Britain must make clear that the Britishness of those who wish to remain so in Ireland is not under threat. This entails leaving behind the fundamentalism of nationalism that there can be no peace for as long as the British remain in Ireland, and embracing political structures which accord Britishness a serious and unchallenged long-term place far beyond the 25 years so glibly talked about by Sinn Fein. This in its turn is unlikely to happen unless a reciprocal and equal gesture is made by Unionists in relation to Irishness and Irish identity. Thirdly, fundamentalist Protestantism only unifies the community in the face of an enemy. In the absence of an enemy, or in times of confusion, fundamentalist Protestantism is not transcendent on its own. Ultimately, the choice is more likely to be between fundamentalism and Britishness.

The relationship of Protestantism to Unionist politics is therefore undeniable. However, it is not Steve Bruce's simple relationship where the religious component can be separated as immovably 'causal' and the rest as 'effect'. The conflict does not exist because Protestants are Protestants but Protestants are thrown back to fundamentalist myth because the conflict exists.

In Northern Ireland, politics and religion are a complicated series of interrelationships whose completeness can only be understood together with an understanding of the Protestant experience of violence or potential violence. The importance of the Protestant myth of the innocent crucified to be resurrected is only conceivable under the shadow of existential catastrophe. It is the common experience of the possibility of losing, of being finally blamed for this conflict, of being made the scapegoat, which gives fundamentalist Protestantism and the moral quality it assures, its key function. In the context of a secularising, confused and divided community, it is the singular achievement of violent Irish Nationalism to have achieved an apparent unity among Protestants.

Of course, as Marianne Elliot (1985) demonstrates neatly, political and theological fears not only provided the primary glue between feuding sects but these fears themselves, and the laws which were invoked to protect Protestants from them generated the very Catholic nation which was so loathed. As she argues, 'That Ireland became such an intensely Catholic nation was due to Protestant fears' (1985, p. 16).

The myth of justification by faith, and its simpler offspring innocence, which fundamentalist Protestantism celebrates, gives it an ideological hold once Protestants are convinced that they must drive out the evil which threatens them. At the same time, the very same story of the passion of Jesus means that it is always done with a bad conscience. The slaughter of innocents of those outside the community of the myth simply cannot be ignored. To acknowledge it would be to undermine the very essence of the fundamental premise about where ultimate blame lies.

On Tuesday, 10 January 1995, John Waters, the *Irish Times* columnist, not one to bow before the neo-orthodoxy of Dublin 4 revisionism, declared that it was time for England to ask forgiveness of the Irish for all the sufferings perpetrated over the centuries. Although it was not expressed in specifically religious terms, the sentiments, like much in Ireland were exactly parallel, if opposite in content, to those of Ken Maginnis. To demand to be asked for forgiveness already presumes a conception of the other as guilty, ultimately signalling that forgiveness is not, in fact, on offer. It remains very unclear whether if it were asked for, it would ever be granted. Grovelling, rather than forgiveness is required. Nationalism, too, is obsessed with its relative sinlessness. The myth that Irish Nationalism and Catholicism are unlinked was exploded by the hunger strikes of 1981. The parallel of Bobby Sands and the suffering but ultimately victorious Christ were shown to sustain not only Protestants in Ireland. Crucially, of course, for as long as we all are innocent, we can continue to murder with a (relatively) good conscience.

4 Discourse and Contemporary Loyalist Identity

Alan Finlayson

There is no such thing as a Protestant or Loyalist identity. It is crucial to recognise this before any sober analysis of that which is referred to as a 'Protestant identity' can be made. Assertions of identity are commonplace in contemporary political discourse. British politics, for example, is marked by an insistence on the part of some to an identity of Scottishness or Welshness, as well as the claims of ethnic minorities, gay political groups and, of course, the claim often made by Conservative politicians to some sort of over-arching British identity. Moreover, debates regarding European integration have occasioned much political rhetoric on the meaning of various national identities from Norway and Denmark to Greece and Turkey. Furthermore, the United States' political landscape is similarly marked by divisions and factions defining themselves by means of identity as diverse as American patriot, Jew, Hispanic, gay and Christian.

Such identity claims are a key part of political discourse but it is important not to accept them at face value. The implication of such claims is that there is a group of people who can, in some way, be regarded as constituting a coherent, maybe even homogenous, constituency on the grounds of sharing some sort of common feature which is usually portrayed as intrinsic to them and from which there flows, naturally, a variety of political interests and assertions. When it comes to ethnic or national identities these claims usually also assert some sort of historical and cultural homogeneity and continuity. They are, it is claimed, a homogenous group because they always have been so and they always have been so because they are. This solipsism is not mere mockery but a solipsism at the heart of all such claims of identity. Such claims rest on an essentialist conception of groups of persons and imply that whatever changes occur within or to a people there is something that is always and eternally the same; some sort of essence that is common to all of them. Such essentialism is essentially ahistorical as it ignores the facts of socio-cultural alteration and change.

Treating peoples as emerging from some sort of essential nature depoliticises the groups themselves. This removes from political contestation and debate the question of who and what we are and raises the question 'what shall we do to stay like this?' This depoliticisation has profound political significance since it generates a stagnation of political argumentation reducing political questions to technical ones, such as 'how do we do this?', rather than ethically reflective questions about why we are like we are, who we are and how we could or should be.

What this sort of identity claim does is to open up a particular category of belonging and assert its importance above all other identities. Crucially, such a claim inserts into that category a set of interests to be advanced by, and for, the category of people concerned. These categories have no intrinsic meaning to them. They only have meaning in as much as they are deployed in specific circumstances as mobilising ideological terms. It is only in asserting a particular claim of Protestant identity within the concrete circumstances of a political formation that Protestant identity means anything at all, or for that matter really exists. Outside of that moment the 'Protestant' community is a variegated collection of persons marked by political identities such as gender or class to mention but two possibilities. The identity exists as a meaningful category in as much as it is used in political discourse as a signifier around which a political group can be constructed and to which persons may respond. What is especially interesting about 'Protestant' and 'Loyalist' identity is the varying ways in which it has been mobilised and the ways in which its discursive deployment has altered over time, particularly since the cease-fires of August 1994.

The intention here is to examine instances of the political articulation of a Loyalist identity and to indicate how these articulations rest on a claim to an essential identity as in some instances Protestant, in others British and in others as Ulster. Such analysis reveals also the instability of such categories, showing that they rest on their continued articulation and reinforcement through various forms of community-based ritual

as well as being assisted by the social institutions that perpetuate a sectarian identity because they are themselves predicated
on a essentialist sectarian assumption. Before exploring some
instances of the discursive deployment of 'Protestant' or 'Loyalist' identity it is worth looking at two key concepts that can
assist in analysis, discourse and interpellation.

Theories of Discourse

In his selection of essays *Languages of Class*, Gareth Stedman
Jones (1983) suggests that when we interpret conflicting social
groups and classes, rather than assuming that they have opposing interests which simply find a rational linguistic expression
in the political arena, such that there is a direct reflection in
language of their essential interests, we should start the other
way round:

> Language disrupts any simple notion of the determination of con-
> sciousness by social being because it is itself part of social being. We
> cannot therefore decode political language to reach a primal and
> material expression of interest since it is the discursive structure of
> political language which conceives and defines interest itself. (1983,
> pp. 21–2)

Political actors do not merely come across a particular political
situation and then, unproblematically, articulate coherent
responses to it which people can choose to support or reject.
Politics involves interpreting the situation and providing it
with a meaning; the interpretation will dictate the sorts of
solutions that will be advocated. So, for example, orthodox
Marxists will interpret political instability as part of the inherent crises of capitalism and formulate strategies to undermine
capitalism. They will define society in class terms and appeal
to potential supporters on the basis of class. As such, political
actors are involved in constructing the arena in which the
particular ideology and political responses they advocate can
make sense.

In Northern Ireland there are two markedly different interpretations of the political situation and each defines the political
crisis and the ways in which that crisis can be resolved in its own
way. It is the constitution of these two different discursive structures that makes for the political problem. It is not a reflection of

its cause but is the cause itself. Political movements construct the interests which they represent. Recognising this, in Northern Ireland, results in a shift of our attention away from the socio-historical roots of sectarian division, away from analyses that attempt to explain a group's identity by reference to essential class, historical or ideal interests and instead, to focus on how politics itself generates the perception of interests centred around a rigid sense of community belonging.

Political discourse in Northern Ireland attempts to confirm people in mythic communities and lay before them the stark choice of either/or. Northern Irish political discourse is obsessed with establishing relations of equivalence; with drawing the world into line with sectarian preoccupations and expelling that which will not fit to the opposite, antagonistic pole. Chains of equivalence are constructed that lock subjects into a sectarian, particularistic universe. Within these chains of equivalence the discourses are entirely self-referential and self-supporting.

Republican discourse attempts to constitute itself as embodying the very identity of the movement of the mass itself, of the community whose interests it represents. Everything outside that, everything against the movement is constituted as the reverse, as absolutely opposed to the interests of 'the community', in shorthand, as part of the British State. Nothing is permitted to interfere with this classification such that Republican discourse is incapable of locating validity elsewhere. There is its side, the Irish people, and the other side, the British. It is not surprising that Republicans have such a strained attitude towards Protestants since they occupy a position both British and Irish, a position which is conceptually unrecognisable to Republicans. The identities and attitudes of the Protestant population have to be defined away within the terms of Republican discourse as false consciousness or as the ideology of the invading British coloniser. Thus they are expelled to the opposite, antagonistic pole. Republican political analysis rarely considers the attitudes of Protestants as being the attitudes of a third, separate, group. All effort is made to reduce any Protestant activity to simply a part of British activity. The actions of Loyalist paramilitaries have been interpreted as merely an extension of the British State while the British State's actions against Loyalist paramilitaries are either ignored or dismissed as insignificant. To accept them as a third player would call into question the structuring of the Republican discourse.

The crucial point to be grasped here is the constitutive nature of such discursive processes. The work of Foucault (1973) has been greatly influential in developing the links between discursivity and the construction of the social world. It was Foucault's insight to recognise discourse as constitutive. It constitutes social subjects and organises social relationships into conceptual frameworks. For Foucault, discourse analysis is concerned with investigating the variable 'discursive formations' which make it possible for certain statements to be made and attitudes to be held while others are excluded. A discursive formation is 'a set of rules', that is to say the rules by which objects, subject positions and strategies are formed. Foucault is not here concerned with just written text or spoken words but with discourse in its widest sense and with the articulatory social practice of discourse; with exploring discursive formations as the relationship between 'institutions, economic and social processes, behavioural patterns, systems of norms, techniques, types of classification, modes of characterisation' (1973, p. 45). Discourse constitutes the objects and subjects of the social world in constrained and constraining ways.

The so-called two communities in Northern Ireland are products of different imaginings of community, and these imaginings are the products of discursively constructed categories of belonging. That is to say they are the *effect* of political processes rather than, as is more commonly held, the *cause* of political processes in Northern Ireland. Recognition of the discursive and constructed nature of identity allows the reinsertion of the political into our analysis affording it a much-needed centrality. Discursive interventions are political interventions aiming to construct subject positions and effect identifications. Discourse involves an ideological interpellation.

Ideology as Interpellation

The understanding of ideology as interpellation derives from Louis Althusser's (1971) famous essay 'Ideology and Ideological State Apparatuses'. The concept has been helpful in moving theories of ideology away from an overtly simplistic base/superstructure model and towards an understanding of ideology as a process by which subjects are constructed. It is useful for an understanding of cultural identity since it enables us to avoid an essentialist conception and to take account of the political practices which, while appearing to simply emanate from a fixed ethnic identity, may actually constitute that identity. According to Althusser:

> the category of the subject ... is the constitutive category of all ideology [and] the category of the subject is only constitutive of all ideology insofar as all ideology has the function (which defines it) of 'constituting' concrete individuals as subjects. (1973, p. 32)

In short, and as is well known, Althusser understands ideology as defining notions of who and what we are such that this becomes obvious. Ideology 'hails or interpellates concrete individuals as concrete subjects'. That is to say it calls to us, tells us who we are, and in the moment of that calling we recognise ourselves. As he argues, ideology acts or functions in such a way that it recruits subjects among the individual, or transforms the individuals into subjects by that very precise operation which I have called interpellation or hailing, and which can be imagined along the lines of the most commonplace everyday police (or other) hailing: 'Hey, you there!' Ideology signals to individuals providing an identification. In recognising themselves in that calling individuals become subjects.

National or ethnic identities may be understood in these terms. The ideology of nationalism hails individuals along the lines of 'Hey, you there! Englishman' and when we respond/identify with the category 'Englishman', we are thus constituted as Englishmen. As an ideological operation nationalism, obviously, focuses on the national as the primary category with which to identify, making the nation central to our political identity and activity. Nationalism recruits individuals to this identification rather than to an identification based around class, gender and religion. In this sense nationalism may be said to produce national identity rather than simply reflect it. Indeed, any nationalist interpellation will contain more than simply a call to recognise ourselves as of a particular nation. It will also ascribe characteristics to that national identity. We may be called upon as English people such that we recognise ourselves as also proud and ready to go to war for our country, or perhaps as thrifty people who want to see our budgets balanced. It may be that in recognising ourselves as of a nation we come to see that we have a long history and heritage that we want to defend at all costs. The nationalist interpellation functions as part of a

wider political discourse, which is why we must recognise
that it is often at work in movements that are not purely
nationalist.

Ernesto Laclau (1979) has broadened the theory of ideology as
interpellation and employed it to explain the workings and success of Fascism. Laclau argues that in an analysis of Fascism it is
necessary to understand the unification of contradictions and
complexities. Without doing this 'we remain trapped in a taxo-
nomical labyrinth without knowing exactly in what consists the
peculiar fusion of contradictions from which Fascism emerges'
(1979, p. 100). He suggests that we can answer this question by
recognising that 'what constitutes the unifying principle of an
ideological discourse is the "subject" interpellated and thus constituted through this discourse' (1979, p. 101).

Moreover, an ideology constitutes subjects in a particular
way, forming their perceived identity in the very act of inter-
pellating them as one kind of subject rather than another. An
ideology achieves temporary coherence, unification, when the
elements that make up the ideological discourse, the chain of
signification, are so connected that each evokes the other. Thus
the hailing of the subject as a member of a particular ethnic
group, for example, also evokes political, religious and other
orientations. Furthermore, each evokes the other such that the
religious also evokes the political and the ethnic. We can understand nationalism as operating in this manner; as an ideological process constituting subjects in a particular way, always
intimately bound up with other ideological subject positions. A
nationalist interpellation also includes particular political, and
other, interpellations. In this way the national can become the
unifying point within an ideological discourse, the category
within which other categories are given and naturalised. The
national becomes a popular-democratic interpellation around
which the ideology of the movement is fixed.

Ulster Loyalism is just such a discourse. 'Ulsterness' and its
specificity is articulated through Loyalist discourse and is symbolic of a range of other discourses. It constitutes identification
with a closed community and sets off other identifications with
religious, political, cultural practices. As Steve Bruce (1986)
suggests, we cannot explain sectarian division simply by reference to economic factors or some such structural explanation.
As he argues, 'What guides people's actions is not the situation
in which they find themselves but their perception of their
circumstances' (1986, p. 255).

This sort of phenomenological approach is a welcome move away from structural determinism but raises the question of how such perceptions arise. Surely understandings of one's position are precisely what ideology, and politics, are all about. Loyalism offers one such understanding. It signals to individuals, offering a perception of the social world, that is coherent, within its own terms, and which is built around a communal identity. This can be explored by looking at the actual discourse used within Loyalism in order to view how it structures itself. Jennifer Todd (1987), for example, has suggested that we recognise two strands in the political culture of Ulster unionism – 'Ulster Loyalist' and 'Ulster British'. The Ulster Loyalists, she argues, primarily identify themselves with Ulster, holding a secondary loyalty to Britain. The Ulster British hold the reverse. The present argument, while differing from Todd's analysis, is concerned with the 'Ulster Loyalist' rather than the 'Ulster British' ideology.

Constructions of Loyalist Identity

A first task is to demonstrate the existence of an interpellation of Ulster specificity within Loyalist discourse; that is to define the Loyalist community as a separate in terms of its characteristics and values. The January 1993 issue of *The New Ulster Defender*, a newsheet linked to the Ulster Defence Association (UDA) carried on its cover a painting, by a Loyalist prisoner, of the four national symbols of the four nations of the United Kingdom, entwined with the phrase 'The British Family of Nations'. Included in the issue was a special pull-out centre section compiled by the Ulster Heritage Agency containing what the magazine described as

> a few of the historical points that give the Ulsterman his separateness and the facts that make Ulster a separate cultural and political entity. The Ulster Nation within the British Family of Nations. Contained within are details on Cuchulain, the ancient leader of the Ulster people, and his 'single-handed' defence of Ulster against the Irish 2000 years ago. (*The New Ulster Defender*, January 1993, p. 4)

In addition to this simple claim to identity and heritage a sense of specificity is produced by reference to the negation of that identity; to the Other of Irish Nationalism and Catholicism. In

stressing difference from this Other, Loyalist discourse sets
boundaries to itself and seals the limits of the community it is
defining – a kind of inverse interpellation. Thus, in *The New
Ulster Defender* of December 1993 a statement from the UDA
inner council denounces the 'Pan Nationalist Front' for trying to

> railroad the Ulster people into an unstoppable process which will
> destroy their state and their way of life and deliver them into an
> alien Irish Republic completely against their will. That this is being
> done in the name of peace merely confirms to us the depths to which
> Irish imperialists will go to cover their evil conspiracy. (*The New
> Ulster Defender*, December 1993, p. 6)

Here again the emphasis on the Ulster people is made. A
people with not only a state but also a way of life. We are
reminded that they are not only different from the Republic
but that the Republic is positively alien. The religiosity of the
discourse is apparent with the phrase 'deliver us into' and the
feeling of an unstoppable process contributes to a sense of
apocalypse. The notion of evil conspiracy has a resonance with
the references to pan-nationalism and plugs into a discourse of
anti-Papism. A circularity is set up wherein each element trig-
gers off the other. As such, religion separates the Loyalist
community from the Catholic community thus introducing
specificity and limiting the community. The whole demands a
political orientation which is, of course, rejection of union with
the Republic of Ireland.

A similar operation is often performed by Ian Paisley as
evidenced in his denunciation of the Joint Framework Document, in the January 1994 issue of *The New Protestant Telegraph*. Taking the clause in which the British Government
accepts that it is for 'the People' of the island of Ireland by
agreement between the two parts of Ireland alone to decide
their future, he complains

> Here we have the separate identity of 'the People' of Northern Ire-
> land submerged into 'the People' of Ireland and to that body is given
> the self-determining entity in any referenda. So there can be no
> single referendum ever again on the future of Northern Ireland with-
> out being held in tandem with the Irish Republic. So a foreign
> country which claims jurisdiction over us is to be elevated to a place
> of partnership in any self-determining referenda held to decide the
> future of Northern Ireland. (1994, p. 10)

Paisley goes on to compare the implications of the Joint Framework Declaration to Britain giving sovereignty over the Falklands to Argentina or Gibraltar to Spain. He emphasises the specific identity of the Northern Irish people and the foreignness of the Irish. It is from this separateness that there derives the right of belonging to the Union in the same way as in the cases of the Falklands or Gibraltar. Such notions repeatedly appear. The January 1994 issue of the Ulster Volunteer Force (UVF) publication *Combat* responded to the Joint Framework Declaration with an attack on British prime ministers contending that 'there are those in the British government who, had it not been for the resilience of the Ulster people would have had our identity engulfed by Eire long before now' (1994, p. 1).

Evidently, characteristics are ascribed to the Ulster people (their resilience) and it is these, situated temporally by the phrase 'long before now', that have caused the political responses of the Ulster people, that is, the defence of 'our identity'. Clearly, the identity in question is that of the Ulster people and is clearly posed against Britain. This distinct identity is again presented when the article continues with the suggestion that 'Thatcher foisted on us the Anglo-Irish Agreement and would have despite many promises destroyed our way of life and heritage' (1994, p. 1). Once more that which is defended is a specific identity and heritage. An examination of change in Loyalist discourse can illustrate both the process of discursive constitution and the political contingency of such processes.

James McAuley (1994) quotes several Loyalist popular songs. Songs are performative in nature; their purpose is to be sung publicly and most probably as part of a group, perhaps a marching band. They are ritualistic affirmations of group belonging. They are material practices that reinforce the identifications of the performers but they also act, in the Althusserian sense, to hail the listeners and recruit them to the group which the song depicts. In one such song, as a man dies from wounds caused by an IRA gunman, he says:

God bless my wife in the dear old Shankill,
God bless my home and family too
God bless the flag that I fight under
The Union Jack Red, White and Blue
(cited in McAuley 1994, p. 96)

At least that is what he used to say. The song has recently
changed and the dying man now sings:

> Will you bury me under the Red Hand,
> Will you bury me in Ulster's clay,
> Will you bury me under the Red Hand
> when my fighting for Ulster is done.
> (cited in McAuley 1994, p. 96)

From an ode to the Union the song has shifted to a Nationalist eulogy of the symbols of mythical Ulster. The protagonist
no longer fights under the Union Flag but fights for Ulster.
No longer is the sentiment one of the locality of family situated in the 'dear old Shankill' contained within the wider unit
represented by the 'Red, White and Blue'. The song is now
concerned with the lone hero defending his native Ulster until
the very end. It is tempting to see this as indicative of a shift
in Loyalist consciousness, that, as it has become increasingly
clear that Great Britain really does not care about them, Loyalists have had to search for other arenas around which an
identity can be constructed.

In the first verse all the symbols of Ulster are expressed in
possessive terms. There is 'my emblem' and 'my song'. In
singing such a song individuals can ritualistically express their
attachment to Ulster's symbols. The possessive expression of
the words creates a sense of personal loyalty and belonging
which leads up to the collective expression of defiance to the
Republic and loyalty to the 'red hand so true'. This is in
contrast to the references to the Union in the second verse.
The Union Flag is not expressed in terms of possession at all,
rather it is just a part of the cause. It is externalised as symbolic of things given from outside, 'freedom, religion and laws'.
The song reaffirms the group's commitment to itself and, by
extension, to defend freedom, religion and laws. Plainly the
defence is primarily of the Ulster land from which they will
not be driven. In an overall context the externality of the
Union Flag is contrasted to the Irish Republic and implicitly
every good Loyalist will know that the Republic has no decent
freedom, religion or law. The song does not express an attachment to Britain as a nation but rather to the Union. Indeed,
Britain is only mentioned symbolically. The primary emblems
and songs, the cultural markers, are those of Ulster. The Union
Flag is symbolic not of heritage and cultural attachment but of

a certain set of constitutional guarantees; of certain rights and privileges. The whole is sealed within the frame of a defiant positioning within Ulster. We can now look at how the inter- pellation of a specific 'Ulsterness' relates to other political interpellations in the generation of a wider and more unified ideology and at how the notion of specificity serves to justify and legitimise specific political claims such as Unionism.

Speaking at the DUP annual conference on 27 November 1993 the deputy leader, Peter Robinson, clearly demonstrated the links between different levels of the Loyalist discourse by joining the sense of a national identity defending itself against alien people with the religious discourse. At the same time he demonstrated the significance of another key point in Loyalist discourse, when stating the following:

> The battle between Unionism and Nationalism is now fully joined. It is no pallid argument between two slightly differing philosophies. This conflict strikes directly at our identity, our culture, our way of life, our citizenship, our liberties, the faith of our fathers and the lives of our sons.

The whole passage is apocalyptic in tone. The sense of a battle fully joined will inspire in the audience recognition of the battles between light and dark in the Book of Revelations. The battle being described is not just that between Loyalism and Republicanism but that between good and evil. But 'Citizen- ship' and 'Liberty' are included in the list of things threatened by Irish unification and a chain of equivalence is forged whereby religious duty, national identity and democracy are all linked; there is light, liberty and faith emerging from the past – 'the faith of our fathers', in an unbroken Burkean inheritance extending into the future – 'the lives of our sons'. The repeated use of 'our' encodes the sense of a community and of the links between the speaker, his party and 'the People' which they do not only represent but are intended to be an actual expression of. The party and 'the People' are one and the party is charged with the maintenance of the community, a sense deepened by the implication that family ties are threatened. The family is the microcosm of the greater family of the nation of Ulster.

Although the whole is encased within religious allusions, to privilege this nodal point, as Steve Bruce (1986) has done, is to underestimate the complexity of the discourse. This is not to say that religion is an insignificant part of Loyalist discourse. Bruce suggests that:

> evangelicalism provides the core beliefs, values and symbols of what it means to be a Protestant. Unionism is about avoiding becoming a subordinate minority in a Catholic state. Avoiding becoming a Catholic means remaining a Protestant. (1986, p. 264)

In a sense Bruce is entirely correct. However, the question is whether religion is important in itself, as religion, or in the way in which it functions within a wider politicised discourse. In Loyalist discourse the nationalist and the religious combine with the politics of democratic principle such that each adds weight to the other. Combined, they develop a strength far greater than they would individually.

The importance of national identity is enhanced by its association with religious inevitability and the yearning for liberty is made crucial since it is this which protects religious freedom from the perceived restrictions of Catholicism. Simultaneously, the religious aspect is enhanced by its association with nationality and democracy. The importance of religion is increased because it is able to stand as a significant marker of the ethnic group and its aspirations, and not just as a set of purely religious principles. It is religion that has differentiated the two communities throughout 400 years of history in Ireland. It has been suggested, nationalist movements do not spring from nowhere but build themselves around historically existing groups (A. Smith, 1986). In Northern Ireland, religion defines the historically-based ethnic core around which the community identity has crystallised. Political and ideological activity has transformed the meaning of these religious affiliations and it is in this sense that religion is important and why religious denomination is used as the label for ethnic groupings. Evangelicalism does not provide the core beliefs of Protestantism in Ulster; it provides the sense of specificity around which core beliefs are discursively organised. Most specifically, and here Bruce's statement is instructive, it is in the opposition to Catholicism that Protestantism has greatest importance. That Other is the negative pole against which a social and political identity is constructed. The opposition, marked by religious difference, provides a space wherein there can be generated social and political meanings beyond the simply theological; meanings of ethnicity, history and democracy. Protestantism was always about more than theology.

Historically the dissenting tradition was about the rejection of one form of authoritarian politics. These elements still combine such that, to refer back to Laclau, each element evokes another and 'operates as a symbol of the other' (1979, p. 104).

Religion evokes a national identity, a sense of Ulster specificity and, at the same time, evokes a political claim to democracy. This is why religion has continued to have such importance in spite of declining church attendance. An Ulster Protestant does not have to be practising to recognise that an attack on the religion or any weakening of it is also an attack on national identity and claims to democracy and freedom. Thus a discursive structure is made, self-supporting and with nodal points that continually reinforce each other without the need for external reference other than the negative one of the Irish Republic and Catholicism.

The importance of the democratic in the discourse of Loyalism is often underestimated, despite its ubiquity. DUP literature consistently argues a case for democracy. In their confidential document submitted to the government entitled, *Breaking the Logjam*, democracy is central to the argument. The document states that the cause of the problem in Northern Ireland is the failure of government to listen to 'the People':

> Government policy in the province has ignored the voice of the electorate. It, undoubtedly has heard them speak at election time, at the border poll and through their elected representatives but the government has not listened. It has trampled on the will of 'the People'. (DUP, 1993, p. 2)

The document describes the grievance of 'the People' as being not the intervention of Westminster as such 'but rather the way of intervention', complaining that rather than listen to elected representatives 'the government ignored their advice and instead took soundings from world opinion and Dublin government opinion'. The whole document is littered with these sorts of phrases, complaints about 'the People' being ignored, most often in favour of Dublin. If not Dublin then it's 'the northern Irish nationalist party', the SDLP.

We are told that the Ulster Defence Regiment was disbanded 'without proper parliamentary debate', that 'the electorate has been excluded from a real say in their own governance', that 'as elected representatives ... we have no power to effect changes', that 'Government accountability in Northern Ireland has become invisible. The quality of the Union is vanishing' and that the Union has been 'undermined by government policy and its rejection of the democratic process in Northern Ireland'.

The argument of the whole document is that the failure of the British Government to be fully democratic in its handling of Northern Ireland has led to the drift and uncertainty that has fostered continued violence. Rather than abide by its historic democratic duty and listen to 'the People', the Government has listened to external authorities. This is in contrast to Loyalists who have consistently fulfilled their duty. They have fought and died in wars and never shirked responsibility for the nation's defence, unlike the Irish who are always described as having seceded, and the Northern Nationalists whose irredentism shows they are unwilling to fulfil their constitutional obligations. The document concludes by calling on the government to 'express a deep consciousness of the cultural, social, democratic and historical importance of the union ...'

For the DUP, the last 25 years have been a 'series of tramplings' on the will of 'the People' in favour of Dublin and now the SDLP. The failed talks process is described, in a devious phrase, as having been 'a Dublin sponsored abortion'. The document manages to align democracy with the Protestant Unionist people, while expelling the undemocratic to the whole of the other side which is treated as if they were one thing. For example:

> Calls to restart the talks process have now become a concession to pressure from Dublin, the Roman Catholic Church leaders, and the SDLP ... These calls for talks are in a perverse way a concession to the IRA as they cloud the need for effective counter terrorist measures by turning the spotlight of blame onto politicians for not talking. (DUP, 1993, p. 12)

In this paragraph the Dublin government, the SDLP, the Church and the IRA are again linked together and made to appear is if they are acting as one. Whatever the individual differences between these groups their interests are really the same and their actions reinforce each other. Thus the Church and the politicians combine together and press for actions that are also of benefit to the IRA. This kind of argument reinforces the sense of two great, hostile camps and in stressing the unanimity of the Nationalists also stresses the unanimity of the implacable Protestant community.

The demand for democracy is common to all shades of opinion on the Loyalist/Unionist side. The Combined Loyalist Military Command (CLMC) responded to the declaration in an editorial in *Combat* by issuing a series of demands. These included that, 'there must be no dilution of the democratic procedure through which the rights of self-determination of "the People" of Northern Ireland are guaranteed'. The CLMC declared:

> We defend the right of anyone or group to seek constitutional change by democratic, legitimate and peaceful means [and that it is their] earnest desire to have an honourable and equitable peace founded in democratic accountable structures within which all of our people can play a constructive and meaningful role without let or hindrance. (January 1993, p. 2)

These democratic aspirations within Loyalist discourse are striking for their ubiquity and for the way in which they are always linked to claims of national identity. The construction of 'the People' as a people, as an ethnic category, is important for it is from the existence of this community that arguments about the rights of membership may derive. A solipsism is in effect. Certain natural and inalienable rights are held to derive from the fact of membership to a particular community and the rights are required because they allow the particular community to exist. The Ulster people have defended themselves from the Irish for 2000 years because they are the Ulster people defending their ancient rights and heritage and they will continue to do it because they have been doing it for 2000 years. Thus, although others may argue that Ulster Loyalism is not 'objectively' democratic in its practices and aspirations, 'subjectively', within its discourse, Loyalism is democratic. Within the discourse, because of the Nationalist interpellation, it is possible to regard Loyalism as democratic, seeking to defend the rights of an ancient people.

Beyond the Cease-fires: Changing Conceptions of Loyalist Identity

The IRA cease-fire of August 1994 and the subsequent cease-fire of Loyalist paramilitaries has had a marked effect on the discourse of Loyalist identity. The ending of violence, be it

permanent or not, has created a space in which the lines of
discourse are being redrawn and in which the possibilities of
new forms of identification can be glimpsed. The increased
presence of the so-called 'fringe' Loyalist parties, the Progressive Unionist Party (PUP) and the Ulster Democratic Party
(UDP), has introduced some new terms in the debate while the
DUP and the UUP have moved to try and occupy even more
distinct ground.

To take the case of the DUP first: in its strident opposition to the Declaration, mistrust of Sinn Fein and then
immediate and forthright opposition to the Framework Document, the DUP can be seen to be clearly separating itself
from the other Unionist/Loyalist parties. In doing this they
have continued, and increased, the tendency to present these
other parties as part of a long chain of equivalence tying
them in with the Republic of Ireland, the Catholic Church,
Sinn Fein, SDLP etc. The *New Protestant Telegraph* has
carried a number of short news items clearly intending to
make this apparent. For example in the July/August 1994
issue there is the following headline: REYNOLDS WELCOMES
VOTES FOR OFFICIAL UNIONISTS – the intention here being to
show that the then premier of the 'hostile foreign state' saw
it in his interest that the UUP win votes in the European
election. The implication being that voting for the UUP is
like voting for Reynolds in contrast to the DUP; as the
article continues, 'Like the British government Reynolds was
bitterly disappointed at the huge vote for the DUP leader
Ian Paisley. They see Ian Paisley and the DUP as the only
threat to the fulfilment of their joint plans for Northern
Ireland's future.' And here the British Government is made
the same as the Irish Government. All that is left standing,
all that is truly Ulster, is that represented by the DUP.

Various other little headlines go on to reinforce this image
such as this from October 1994: MAGINNIS [UUP/MP] JOINS
ADAMS [President Sinn Fein] ON TELEVISION, and in reference
to a leading member of the PUP: BILLY HUTCHINSON PARTICI-
PATES IN SINN FEIN ORGANISED CONFERENCE. These simple
headlines are left to speak volumes. The article following the
headline regarding Hutchinson tells us that he even made a
joke and laughed with the Provos. In a lengthy piece the *New
Protestant Telegraph* warns us to 'Beware of Cheap Imitations'
and in detailing the perceived errors of PUP spokesman David
Ervine asks Ulster (that interpellation again) who it wants to

speak for it. Of course the conclusion is that the only real Ulster party is the DUP.

The structuring of the discourse of fringe parties such as the PUP is strikingly different. Indeed what is most striking about the interpellation of Protestant identity in PUP discourse is its relative absence. In fact there is a peculiar reversal going on in PUP discourse. Where traditional Loyalist discourse, as examined above, uses the notion of a specific Ulster people and an interpellation of those people as a fixing point in an ideological discourse of democracy, it seems that the reverse is occurring in PUP discourse. It is an interpellation of a free-thinking democratic citizen that is used to justify the identity of the Ulster Loyalist.

In his speech to the PUP conference in February 1995, the PUP party leader Gusty Spence claims that the PUP is about 're-defining a Unionism which can involve the best of our people in pursuit of what is an honourable and politically legitimate tradition'. It is at this point unclear who Spence is referring to with the term 'our people'. The 'tradition' in question would appear to be that of Unionism. However he continues:

> We want to involve the young and the intelligent and those who demand change, we need the dedicated and those with vision but, equally, we require the sincerity of the ordinary person in the street who care and love the land in which we all were born.

The key word here is 'equally'. This passage is effectively expanding on who 'our people' is. Intriguingly 'our people' means those with a love of the land of our birth, a standard variation on the interpellation of Ulsterness, but only in as much as these people are counted in equally with the young, intelligent and dedicated. In other words, the appeal here seems to be to more than just the sons of Ulster.

In much of the speech it is clear that Gusty Spence is concerned to address a 'Unionist' people. On the one hand this does refer to a group defined by its specific politics but equally there is an element of exclusivity about it. As he argued:

> We are pragmatists and must take cognisance of the wishes of 'the People' whom we now represent. The Unionist people were not particularly happy with the Downing Street Declaration. They are decidedly unhappy with the prevarication since. (1995, Speech to the PUP Annual Conference)

It would seem from this that 'the People' represented by the PUP are Unionists. Now on one level that is of course obvious and unsurprising since the PUP is a Unionist party in name and in deed. What is curious here is that he talks of the Unionist people in the third person. It is they who are unhappy and not 'we', the PUP. When Spence uses the term 'we' to refer to anything other than the party it is thus: 'We, too, the working class Protestants have felt the slow burning agony of powerlessness and ineffectuality.' The 'we' now includes a class dimension as well as an ethnic one. The speech builds up to its final demands for prosperity, a Bill of Rights, and so forth, and it does so on behalf of 'the People' but by this stage it is not at all clear who 'the People' are.

It would seem that the PUP is in the process of articulating some sort of new political discourse. What that will ultimately be is not clear. For the moment it seems that what the PUP represent ideologically is incoherent. It does not form what Laclau (1979) described as a unified ideological discourse. Quite simply there is a confusion here over the relationship between identities of class, nation and ethnicity. This is a welcome sign. It suggests that while the DUP maintains its attempt to define persons primarily in terms of an ethno-religious-political identity the PUP is concerned to articulate a democratic political vision first and foremost and is at some level equivocating on the basis for the vision.

In my view a democratic political vision needs no basis. It can support itself in its own terms without recourse to some allegedly external category such as nation, ethnicity or class. There is a discursive space opened up in Northern Ireland and it is a space that need not be occupied by those emerging from a Unionist/Loyalist tradition. In this space it is possible to be both one thing and another and it is not necessary to capitulate to the dualistic demands that have ruled Northern Ireland for so long. This is opening up lines of division within the 'Protestant' community and allowing the expression of political ideas and aspirations not reducible to questions of the border. As Billy Hutchinson, a member of the PUP, observed, at the conference from which this book derives, working-class Protestants now feel increasingly able to criticise their Unionist representatives and the British Government without worrying about the charge of disloyalty. If this is true and if the PUP represents this dissenting voice then it may have a crucial role to play in the future of and beyond Unionism.

The difference between this new discourse and traditional Unionism is neatly illustrated by the following exchange recorded from a conference on Protestantism, entitled 'Beyond the Fife and Drum':

Speaker from the floor: 'Now I am a Unionist, but I am also an Irishman. This whole conversation seems to deny that there is such a thing as a Protestant Irishman. I object to Gerry Adams and Sinn Fein claiming everything Irish when it is part of me.'

David Ervine (PUP): 'We have put them out of each other's reach. We have tagged all the baggage, all the things that are alien to each other.'

John Taylor (UUP): 'I'm an Ulsterman not an Irishman – I don't jig at crossroads or play Gaelic Football. We've got two races on this Island; of course a Protestant can be an Irishman, but most Protestants are Ulstermen.' (Hall, 1995)

One might ask, are there any Protestants who are Ulster-women?

Conclusion

The political discourse of Loyalism/Unionism has clearly attempted to reinforce the sense that the Ulster people are a special people different from the Irish, and different from the other people of the UK, but with a historic sensibility and right to be part of that Union. This discourse is also structured along lines of religion and a line demanding and defending democracy. In the drawing of boundaries these elements – benign religion and democratic principles – are brought positively within the realms of Unionist discourse and negatively without the boundaries of the Other, of the Irish. The Irish have a repressive and medieval religion and they do not understand democracy. It bewilders many an Ulster Loyalist that the British do not understand this. They find it hard to credit how the British can allow part of the UK to slide away into this alien state. What they do not realise is that British politics inhabits a different language game in which the Irish State can be perceived as just another democratic state. In the language game of British politics the objections of the Loyalists simply do not make sense.

By conceiving of identity as the result of ideological interpellation it is possible to undertake an analysis that is sensitive to
the actual processes of ideological construction. Identity can be
placed firmly within the social plane itself rather than in some
hypothesised outside, be it a mythical 'History', intrinsic essence
or an atavistic primal urge. Such a position is flexible enough to
comprehend a variety of political formations and does not set up
an *a priori* category into which phenomena either do or do not fit.
Above all such an analysis is able to place the political at the
centre of our understanding. It is political arguments and claims
that offer up Protestant or Loyalist as the category with which
we must make our primary identification and which define the
content of that category. I do not mean to devalue sociological
analysis. To be sure there are general sociological factors that
make particular identificatory categories possible in the first
place but we have to look at the contingent ways in which a
discourse produces an identity and aims to mobilise it; at how
politics is itself constitutive of the sorts of identities that people
fight for rather than a simple reflection of something pre-given.

In Northern Ireland the religious/ethnic divide provides a
core of meaning around which political discourses form. Thus
discourses develop, and are still developing, based around the
communal identity of Ulster Protestants. These offer explanations of the social and political situation, and ways out of it. In
this sense Ulster Loyalism as a political movement relies on an
interpellation of people as Ulster Loyalists rather than as members of the working class or some other identificatory basis.
What is also crucial to analyse is the content of this interpellation. Undertaking such an analysis shows the complicated
weave of Loyalist ideology and discourse and the importance
within that of an interpellation that constructs the community
and makes it possible for the kind of politics that seeks to
defend the autonomy of that alleged community. The community is constructed by reference to its history and the reiteration of key points in that history. Defending it from any attack
becomes crucial to the ideological claims of Loyalists and
within that a centrality is afforded to a notion of democracy.
As a concept democracy has always been about freedom and
equality for a particular people. In Ulster Loyalist discourse,
democracy, freedom and liberty come to mean the defence of
the community from Irish Catholicism and any weakening of
their, the Loyalists', autonomy. Thus, defence of democracy fits
with the identity and religious affiliation to make a relatively

unified ideological discourse that constructs 'the People' as Loyalist and therefore with an interest in staying within the Union and out of the Republic of Ireland.

Recognising these processes means that we can perceive in Northern Ireland two nationalisms, both engaged in articulating popular democratic interpellations and both setting the bounds of the community by reference to the negativity of the other. But, as well as paying attention to the actual ways in which a political discourse functions, we also have to look at where it does not function. In overall terms not all interpellations are successful. Success depends, in part, on what Althusser would call the state apparatuses. How do the schools and the legal system serve to reproduce community identification for example? Demographic division, coupled with security force strategy, has also served to reproduce a Protestant/Catholic identification and, not least, IRA violence perpetrated on Protestants, as Protestants, undoubtedly reinforced the community identification of Protestants just as Loyalist violence against Catholics, as Catholics, reinforced the identification of that community. These factors assist the political discourse in successfully reaching its target since they reproduce sectarian separation in the everyday experience of individuals so that the discourse resonates effectively with the everyday world. There are social conditions that make such a discourse possible and potentially successful. It is here that sociological analysis is most important and can be allied with a theory of the politics of discourse and the discourse of politics.

In Northern Ireland there is no inevitability about the primacy of 'national' identification. People's everyday experience also reaffirms a gender and class identity. A theory of interpellation helps us to understand the ways in which ideological practice is effective and to see communal identities as such discourses that must be analysed with reference to their specific articulations and their content. In the case of Northern Ireland this position makes it possible to reconceptualise the conflict itself and to pay due attention to the 'ideological forms in which men become conscious of this conflict and fight it out'.

In the light of the cease-fires and the subsequent political developments it becomes interesting to ponder the ways in which these discourses might, or might be made to, change. It is not usually a good idea for social scientists, and especially political theorists, to make predictions. Nevertheless there are definite patterns developing which entail the possibility of a much more open and reflective construction of political identities. As we have seen, the 'fringe' Loyalist parties are beginning to be involved in a different sort of discourse from the traditional Loyalist organisations. This discourse shows an equivocation on the roots of political identity and veers between a basis on Protestant identity and a basis on a more class-oriented identity.

Set against a background of an increasingly globalised culture where a citizen of Northern Ireland is as likely to be watching satellite television from across the globe as to be waving flags in the Orange march, it seems that the possibility of maintaining rigid definitions of political identity is waning. As people got used to a situation of non-violence they were apt to go about expressing themselves in a number of ways and through a variety of cultural and political practices that cannot be reduced to a binary opposition of Catholic/Protestant, Nationalist/Unionist.

What remains to be seen is whether or not these developments will be sustained and, perhaps most importantly, what sort of changes will occur within the discourses of Catholic and Irish Nationalist politics. If there is a growing flexibility within working-class 'Protestant' politics and if this is matched by a flexibility in working-class 'Catholic' politics then major change is ahead.

Political discourse is sadly devalued in these times as politicians become increasingly concerned to present themselves as efficient technocratic operatives able to successfully manage the business of government. But political discourse is also capable of changing the way we see the world and encouraging us to change that world into something else. The challenge to do that is one at the doors of politicians. They have thus far shown little interest in changing, but the pressures and possibilities are obviously there.

5 'Up To Their Knees'? Football, Sectarianism, Masculinity and Protestant Working-Class Identity

Alan Bairner

The general relationship between sport and politics in Northern Ireland has been discussed at some length (Sugden and Bairner, 1993). Rather less attention has been paid, however, to the precise ways in which playing and, in particular, watching specific sports may have a direct bearing on the values and attitudes which have sustained a culture of political violence for over 25 years (Harvie and Sugden, 1994). Yet, as the eminent American sports historian Allen Guttmann observes, ' ... it is important to ask about the political functions of spectatorship, about their gender and social class, about the relationship between the "active" participation of the athlete and the "passive" participation of the fan' (1986, p. 2).

This chapter examines the role of association football, and specifically of attendance at senior Irish League matches, in encouraging, within sections of the Protestant working class, sectarian attitudes which, to a certain extent, have been supportive of Loyalist paramilitary violence directed at Catholics. In developing this argument, the discussion will test ideas taken from the sociology and social history of sport and also from gender theory, against the reality of the culture which surrounds Irish League football and Northern Ireland international matches. The significance of sport for the development of collective identities is undeniable. According to John Hoberman, 'Sport is a latently political issue in any society, since the cultural themes which inhere in a sport culture are potentially ideological in a political sense' (1984, p. 20).

Indeed, in the contemporary world, sport is commonly one of the most important vehicles for expressing political identity.

As John Bale suggests, 'Sport in its modern form, and arche-typically football in its modern form, provides what is arguably the major focus for collective identification in modern Britain and in much of the rest of the world' (1993, p. 55).

Often when we watch sport, we are gathering together to support the efforts of the athletic standard bearers of our community, however that is defined. As Guttmann observes:

> There is ... an apparently irresistible impulse to allegorise the sports contest and to feel that collective identity is somehow represented by five or eleven or fifteen men or women doing something with a ball or a single powerful man doing something with his fists. (1986, p. 182)

The sportsmen and sportswomen become the appointed repre-sentatives of our school, our town, our nation, our religion, our ethnic grouping or our political ideology. They become, in Hoberman's phrase, 'proxy warriors' (Hoberman, 1984, p. 6). The most frequently discussed collective identities in Northern Ireland are Unionism and Irish Nationalism, usually to the neglect of other important sources of identity, most notably gender and social class. As regards sport, therefore, most inter-est has been in the rival sporting traditions of the Unionist and Nationalist communities as well as in the relationship between members of the two communities who happen to share the same sporting space (Sugden and Bairner, 1993). However, it would be foolish to ignore cleavages within these communi-ties which may also have important political implications. To focus primarily on the two distinctive sporting traditions might appear to imply the existence of monolithic Unionist and Irish Nationalist cultures not only at the level of sport but perhaps in terms of political attitudes as well. Gender, however, has a major impact on one's social experience.

Furthermore, sport is arguably one of the most important spheres of activity in western societies in terms of the construc-tion and reproduction of gender identities. Indeed, according to some feminist analysis sport has been vital to the institutionalisa-tion of male power over women (Hargreaves, 1994, p. 26). Certainly, as David Whitson suggests, sport is 'one of the central sites in the social production of masculinity in societies charac-terised by longer schooling and by a decline in the social currency attached to other ways of demonstrating physical prow-ess (e.g. physical labour or combat)' (Whitson, 1990, p. 19). In Northern Ireland, as elsewhere, men dominate the world of sport in general and working-class sporting activities in particular. Yet gender has tended to be ignored in analyses of sport in the province just as it has been in many studies of other aspects of Northern Irish politics and society. Social class has been equally neglected.

As regards social class, the idea of a monolithic Unionist community fits well into a traditional Marxist or Irish Nationalist analysis of the Protestant working class, described by James Connolly as 'the least rebellious slaves in the industrial world' (quoted in Berresford, 1973, p. 263). According to this perspective, the Protestant working class has been manipulated consistently by the Unionist bourgeoisie. If this is correct, then presumably the ramifications of this manipulation would be apparent in the world of sport as well as that of politics and of economics. Moreover, this type of analysis would complement the orthodox Marxist view of sport as one of the most important ideological weapons with which ruling elites in capitalist societies control the working classes.

This particular analysis of sport, however, has been contested convincingly by numerous scholars who caution against regarding working-class people as totally weak and defenceless. For them, sport has never been simply an instrument of class manipulation or domination. According to Stephen Jones, 'Even in periods where there are profound economic and political inequalities, there is still scope to resist ruling interests and needs' (Jones, 1988, p. 11). Indeed, Gary Whannel argues 'The organisation of labour in sport is often primitive and inadequate but from time to time has attempted to challenge the power of the authorities' (1983, p. 61).

Certainly there is no denying the importance of sport in working-class communities. As Robert Wheeler suggests 'It is almost as inconceivable to envisage sport without the working class, as it is to conceive of a working class without organised sport' (1978, p. 207).

Thus, we can assume that working-class people or, more accurately, working-class men, enjoy some measure of control over their sporting life. This would not hold true, however, of the Protestant working class in Northern Ireland if some traditional views of its relationship to the Unionist bourgeoisie are correct. In fact, if unchallenged manipulation of the Protestant working class ever existed, its significance has long since been weakened, not least by the gradual disappearance of an important indigenous business elite. Factors such as the emergence of the DUP,

the decline in membership of the Orange Order and the growth
of Loyalist paramilitary organisations have further ensured that
Protestant working-class communities possess a very different
culture from that of middle-class Unionists together with a
substantial degree of political autonomy. As Desmond Bell argues
'Class tensions and generational differences are increasingly
manifesting themselves within the Unionist body politics' (1990,
p. 21).

Arguably, however, class differences were always more significant than Nationalist analyses of Unionism would have us
believe. Certainly in the realm of sport, the Protestant working
class has traditionally enjoyed a measure of autonomy which
has led to the construction of almost exclusively working-class
settings with their own peculiar ambience. Furthermore, the
persistence of class-based sporting activities has been guaranteed in Northern Ireland by a highly selective education
system, which separates children at secondary school level on
the basis not only of perceived academic ability but, in many
cases, on the basis of gender as well.

Although most analyses of education in Northern Ireland,
like most studies of sport, have concentrated on sectarian division, as regards the development of a sports culture and arguably of much else besides, the process of academic selection
has had as great an impact. Within the Protestant community,
for example, selection has meant that the majority of boys
from middle-class families attend schools in which rugby,
hockey and cricket are the main team sports, whereas football
is dominant in secondary schools attended largely by working-
class children. It is no surprise, therefore, that a game like
rugby retains a solidly middle-class character whilst football
can be said to belong to the working class. This does not mean
that working-class people have total control over the game of
football in Northern Ireland any more than elsewhere. As John
Clarke observes 'The formal control of football has never been
in the hands of its working class supporters' (1978: 42).

However, Jones argues correctly that 'Bourgeois control
within governing bodies did not necessarily mean that sport
was a vehicle of assimilation, whereby canons of decorum,
order and sportsmanship were simply refracted downwards into
the working class' (1988, p. 25).

Indeed, according to Jim Riordan the specific form 'sport'
takes in any culture is peculiar to that 'particular culture or
social group at a specific time'. Jones admits that 'precisely

how the working class adopted sports is still relatively obscure' (1988, p. 24). He suggests, however, that 'arguably, the working class was able to take out of games those elements, rituals and values which fitted into their own culture' (1988, p. 25). Regardless of their lack of formal control over the game, therefore, working-class people (specifically working-class men) have attained symbolic control over association football. Clarke states 'Formally and officially it has never been theirs – their relation to it is and always has been an essentially informal one, established by going through the turnstiles and supporting "their" team', thus: 'It was in the way that they watched football and supported "their" team that the working class colonised this form of entertainment and made it their own' (1978, p. 42).

These observations describe as accurately the situation in Northern Ireland as in other parts of the United Kingdom. Although local businessmen have exercised considerable power over football since it became established in Northern Ireland, the character of most of the players and supporters has ensured that the working class has 'colonised' the game in the way that Clarke describes. In addition, this 'colonisation' has been carried out by working-class representatives of both communities. Unlike the major middle-class sports which have helped to keep Unionists and Nationalists apart, football has brought them together on the field of play and on the terraces. More often than not, however, this has created tension and, furthermore, any integrative potential which the game might possess has been undermined by the overwhelmingly Protestant ethos with which it is surrounded at the highest levels.

Although the majority of sports played in Northern Ireland are organised on an all-Ireland basis, football is unusual in mirroring the division established by partition. The result of this is the presence of two national teams and separate league and cup competitions. All of the Northern Ireland League clubs as well as the national team include Catholic players and most clubs attract some measure of Catholic support, but only Cliftonville Football Club can claim to have an almost exclusively Catholic following. The majority of senior Irish League clubs are located in the predominantly Protestant eastern domain of the province and the most successful teams in recent years – Coleraine, Glenavon, Glentoran, Linfield and Portadown – all have substantial Protestant support.

At the international level, there has been a marked decline in Catholic support for the Northern Ireland team, regardless of its composition, with most Catholic football fans having transferred their affection to the players of the Irish Republic. There are many reasons for this particular development, not least the fact that the Republic's team has been relatively successful in recent years. It is fair to say, however, that Catholic disaffection is also a response to the Protestant hegemony over senior football in Northern Ireland. Whilst this has always been a feature of football in the province, given the game's British origins and the resultant opposition of Catholics involved in the Gaelic sports movement, the situation has been accentuated by the withdrawal from Irish League football of Belfast Celtic (in 1949) and Derry City (in 1971), two clubs with large Catholic followings. Loyalist songs and chants are heard at most Irish League clubs' grounds, particularly when Cliftonville provide the opposition but also when rival fans seek to establish their credentials in the eyes of their co-religionists who support other clubs. Even when emotions are not running high, the widespread interest in the fortunes of Glasgow Rangers Football Club in the Scottish League is a clear indicator of the identity of most of those who attend Irish League games.

Arguably, the stridency of the Protestant message, particularly at Northern Ireland games, has been more marked in recent years as the Protestant working class has been confronted by a series of threats to its traditional way of life. As Bell (1990) points out, a specifically Protestant sense of community is under attack from three sources – economic (in particular, deindustrialisation resulting in widespread unemployment), spatial (particularly urban redevelopment which has led to the uprooting of long-established working-class communities) and political (above all, the demise of the Stormont administration with whatever real or symbolic benefits it bestowed on working-class Unionists). These developments have had particularly serious repercussions for Protestant working-class youth, particularly young men. As one group of researchers observe: 'One of the most dramatic changes in Protestant political culture over the past fifteen years has been that the old political certitudes provided by traditional unionism have disappeared, for the young at least' (Gillespie *et al.*, 1992, p. 163).

The resultant insecurity can lead to anti-social activities, such as solvent abuse or joy-riding, which are far removed from the cultural milieu of these young people's parents and grandparents and actually represent an area of experience which is shared by young working-class Catholics. However, as the researchers point out: 'The dominant elements of the youth culture are often the same elements that dominate working class culture in general (the "parent" culture) albeit in varying degrees of manifestation' (Gillespie *et al.*, 1992, p. 5). Indeed, according to Bell:

> What has been distinctive about the youth cultural activities of working class adolescents in Northern Ireland has been their apparent continuity rather than discontinuity with parental sectarian traditions and political sensibilities ... young people in Northern Ireland, both Protestant and Catholic, have increasingly become the guardians of 'tradition'. (1990, p. 9)

According to Bell, this is exemplified by the commitment of some young working-class Protestants to Loyalist bands. Although closely linked to the parental culture of Orangeism, the 'kick the Pope' bands offer greater excitement to young people than does the Orange Order itself. As Bell (1990) describes it:

> The bands and their parades seem to provide for the dispossessed Loyalist youth of Ulster a sectarian habitus within which their generational concerns with communal identity and with winning public space become fused with the focal concerns of a parental Loyalist culture with territoriality and ethnic solidarity. (Bell, 1990, p. 100)

Bell recognises that there is some overlap between the bands and football support, in terms of their appeal to young working-class men. In fact, he argues that the combative performance of the marching bands 'is not primarily musical in character and has perhaps closer similarities with the gestural activities of football supporters – and indeed these bands undoubtedly derive elements of their style from this source' (1990, p. 100).

One could argue that proclaiming one's identity by attending football matches may have even greater value because of the regularity of football fixtures covering a longer part of the year than the Orange marching season. As Bale observes:

> Football is an example of a civic ritual which is made more attractive than other civic rituals because it possesses a serialised character; that is, it has a strong element of succession about it with its seasons and its regular and predictable fixtures. (1993, p. 56)

It should be said at this point, however, that the importance attached to following a football team has not led to serious hooliganism, as commonly interpreted. Whether this can be taken as evidence that football has contributed to a civilising process in Northern Ireland is a different matter.

Sport: The Civilising Agent?

The idea that sport has contributed to a civilising process in the western world has been advanced in particular by sociologists Norbert Elias and Eric Dunning. According to Dunning:

> The central observation on which the theory of civilising processes is based is the fact that, in Western European societies since the Middle Ages, a more or less continuous elaboration and refinement of manners and social standards can be shown to have taken place, together with an increase in the social pressure on people to exercise stricter and more even self-control over their feelings in more and more fields of social relations. (1993, p. 45–6)

The main factors held to be responsible for this process are economic growth, the division of labour, democratisation and state formation leading to stable monopolies of force and taxation, both increasingly under public control. 'At the same time,' according to Dunning and his co-researchers

> growing numbers of working-class males became more integrated into the nuclear family and the home, and, in a context where the power of women was being slowly augmented, were thus more exposed to the domesticating, 'civilising' influences of their wives. (Dunning et al., 1988, p. 231)

Sport too is regarded as having contributed to the process, particularly as women became more involved both as participants and as spectators. As Elias and Dunning indicate 'In advanced industrial societies, leisure activities form an enclave for the socially approved arousal of moderate excitement behaviour in public' (1986, p. 65).

Indeed, sport can even be regarded as having played a vanguard role in the civilising process. Certainly the behaviour of most football players in Northern Ireland supports the theory of a civilising process. There may be occasional examples at the level of junior football of the tensions created by sectarian rivalry trespassing on the field of play. But this has never been a feature of Irish League games. As for the crowd behaviour, the violence, including gun attacks, which accompanied Irish League games earlier in the century has no modern parallel (Brodie, 1980; Kennedy, 1989). There are a number of reasons for this. First, crowds are considerably smaller than in earlier decades. Second, important and potentially troublesome fixtures are watched over by large numbers of armed policemen and sometimes soldiers, concerned not with football hooliganism *per se* but with the possibility that incidents at a game might lead to more serious civil unrest. Third, setting the Troubles to one side, Northern Ireland is not a particularly violent place and there are lower rates of 'ordinary' criminal violence than in other parts of the United Kingdom (*Observer*, 28 August 1994). Finally, although football crowds consist primarily of working-class men, some further distinction needs to be made. As early as the 1970s, Richard Jenkins noted a marked difference between 'rough' and 'respectable' children on a working-class Protestant housing estate in Belfast (Jenkins, 1982 and 1983).

A significant element in this, and one which helps to explain low rates of ordinary crime in Northern Ireland, is the role of churches and church organisations in Protestant working-class life (Jenkins, 1982). According to Elias and Dunning, in most western societies, 'it is no longer a framework of religious activities and beliefs which provides scope for a balancing relaxation of restraints' (1986, p. 65). In Northern Ireland, however, religion still plays an important part in moderating people's behaviour, including that of many of the young men who attend football matches. According to Allen Guttmann 'there are signs of an increase of sports-related violence in societies where violence of all sorts is on the increase' (1986, p. 164). The evidence of Northern Ireland both supports and undermines Guttmann's claims. If we accept that Northern Ireland is not a particularly violent society, the relative absence of football hooliganism is perfectly understandable. If we take into account the violence associated with the Troubles, however, we might be surprised by the fact that hooliganism is not a major problem. In fact, this is problematic only if one regards overt hooliganism as the sole form of unacceptable behaviour witnessed at football matches.

Before addressing the actual behaviour of fans in Northern Ireland, it is worth recognising the positive contribution made by football to working-class life in the province. For example, it provides a forum for letting off steam without significant recourse to violence. Sport, according to Elias, 'offers people the liberating excitement of a struggle involving physical exertion and skill while limiting to a minimum the chance that anyone will get seriously hurt in its course' (1986, p. 165). This applies most forcefully to those who play football in Northern Ireland but it is equally true of most of those who simply watch. In addition, particularly for players but even for many fervent supporters, the game has provided an important sanctuary away from the political violence of Northern Irish society. More than that, following a football team contributes to the development of working-class communal solidarity and camaraderie which, when they occur in Nationalist areas, are usually interpreted as embryonic forms of socialist consciousness. Finally, football support is often part of a more general Orange popular culture which, as Bell argues

> ... functions to encourage localistic loyalties, provide public and recreational space for the marginalized young, and furnish the symbolic resources for the construction of a distinctively Protestant sense of community for an increasingly beleaguered people. (1990, p. 210)

Thus, football makes a positive contribution to Protestant working-class life in Northern Ireland and violent behaviour is seldom directly linked to football matches. It is doubtful, however, that the organisation and ethos of the game are of a wholly civilising character. Eric Dunning himself recognises that 'the theory of civilising processes is not a theory of necessary and irreversible progress' (1993, p. 55). Indeed, he points out that 'football hooliganism is indicative of the structurally generated unevenness with which the British civilising process has taken and is taking place' (1993, p. 64). In Northern Ireland, for example, far fewer women attend football matches than in other parts of the United Kingdom or farther afield. This may reflect a relatively low level of female involvement in the province's public life more generally, which in turn has important implications if one accepts the view that women contribute greatly to the direction and pace of the civilising process.

Although hooligan behaviour is not a regular feature of matches in Northern Ireland, the rough, working-class masculinity of those most often associated elsewhere with hooliganism certainly is. According to Dunning and his fellow researchers, 'the values which underlie hooligan behaviour at football matches and in match-related contexts are relatively persistent, deeply rooted and long-standing features of the communities of specific sections of the working class' (1986, p. 266). They argue that the identities of males from the 'rougher' sections of the working class thus tend to be based on what are, relative to the standards dominant in Britain today, openly aggressive forms of masculinity (Dunning et al., 1988). According to Dunning, such sections of the working class are characterised by 'segmental' bonding, more typical of traditional societies, rather than 'functional' bonding which is the norm in industrial societies. For a variety of reasons, segmental bonding is more conducive to affective masculinity than is functional bonding (Elias and Dunning, 1986, pp. 233–44). Above all, Elias and Dunning suggest, 'segmental groups in modern society are subjected to restraint from the outside but not, to anything like the same extent, from within' (1986, p. 243). Given the challenges currently faced by Protestant working-class youth in Northern Ireland and the fact that sections of the working class are characterised by the type of social bonds described by Dunning, it is not surprising that some young men resort to aggressive masculine behaviour.

David Morgan argues that 'the impact of prolonged unemployment and redundancy would seem to be a fruitful area for the exploration of masculinities' (1992, p. 118). Thus, as Bell suggests, the marching bands in Northern Ireland offer 'an alternative and increasingly aggressive assertion of masculinity for the marginalized young working-class male' (Bell, 1990, p. 104). They are 'markers of manhood ... now being constructed in the sphere of leisure at a time when traditional identities associated with the workplace and the wage packet are less available' (Bell, 1990, p. 104). Following a team or supporting the national side provides a similar outlet, not least because this too is related to the parental culture.

Football in Northern Ireland is infected by the same habits of male working-class life as elsewhere in the United Kingdom – heavy drinking, sexism, bad language and so on. But, more than that, for many supporters, regardless of which team they follow, watching football is intimately bound up with being an Ulster Protestant. For the most part, theirs is a secular or non-Christian Protestantism described by Norman Gillespie and his fellow researchers as 'a mixture of selective theological dogma, anti-Catholicism and pragmatic loyalism' (Gillespie et al., 1992, p. 135). Regardless of their lack of religiosity, however, the commitment of these secular Protestants to their native Ulster is undeniable. Referring to the importance of sport for the consolidation of national identity, Grant Jarvie comments that 'it is as if the imagined community or nation becomes more real on the terraces or the athletics track' (1993, p. 75). For many Northern Ireland Protestants, their imagined community is Ulster, the potent symbolism of which cannot be exaggerated. As Gillespie and his colleagues reveal 'One of the overriding patterns to emerge from our discussions with young Protestants is that when they speak of Ulster they are not merely referring to a place' (1992, p. 163).

This phenomenon is also explored by Bell for whom the mythic representation of the 'Protestant' people and their ideal-ised territory 'Ulster' is an attempt 'to resolve at the level of the imaginary, the real material contradictions confronting the Protestant working-class in contemporary Northern Ireland' (Bell, 1990, p. 23).

Sport and Allegiance

Although most of the intense rivalries in Irish League football are inspired by local identities (Linfield versus Glentoran, Glen-avon versus Portadown), it is not only when supporters of rival clubs join forces behind the Northern Ireland team that their shared loyalty becomes apparent. At club matches Loyalist songs are sung, often by supporters of both opposing teams, Northern Ireland flags are displayed at each end of the ground with slight modifications to indicate allegiance to a particular club and anti-Catholic comments are relatively common. Thus, regardless of which club they support, young working-class Protestant men are able to celebrate their allegiance to Ulster. The most potent symbols of Ulster which are present in Northern Irish football, however, are Linfield Football Club and the national team, together with Windsor Park, home ground of both. In the eyes of its devotees, each of these signifies the indomitable spirit of Ulster whatever the material and political threats to its continued existence as a distinct entity.

Linfield cannot be regarded as merely a local club since its support has come traditionally not only from the Donegall Road and Village areas of Belfast where Windsor Park is situated but from throughout Northern Ireland and from other Protestant areas of the city itself, notably the Shankill Road (Boal, 1970,

p. 389). This is not untypical of major clubs in other countries. As Bale notes, 'there has been an undoubted reduction in the degree of spatial circumstances of most football clubs' support' (1993, p. 61). Thus, 'if a "community" does still support a club it often embraces a wider geographical area than that in the immediate vicinity of the club's home stadium' (p. 61). In Northern Ireland, the "community" which supports Linfield is regarded by its members as the true Ulster Protestant working class even though actual members of that class support other teams and may even dislike Linfield with a remarkable degree of intensity. Furthermore, it is significant that for supporters of other clubs, Windsor Park, enemy territory during much of the domestic season, becomes a place of pilgrimage when the Northern Ireland team is playing.

An allegiance to Ulster is proclaimed by supporters at league and international football matches through various forms of uncivilised behaviour. Arguably the most serious of these are the anti-Catholic rhetoric and the vocal support for Loyalist paramilitary organisations, such as the UDA and the UVF, which have been directly responsible for the deaths of numerous Catholics over the past 25 years. These are persistent features of most football grounds even though Catholics play for all teams in the Irish League as well as for the national side and nearly every club receives some level of Catholic support. This can be explained in part by reference to the politics of division in Northern Ireland, and when the opposition on the field of play is supplied by Cliftonville, with a predominantly Catholic following (members of which are pleased to celebrate the activities of Nationalist paramilitaries or the Republic of Ireland) the message becomes more strident and is articulated by more supporters than normal. But how is this anti-social behaviour to be explained in less emotional circumstances?

Most of the abusive rhetoric emanates from members of the lower sections of the Protestant working class who are apparently unresponsive to the code of conduct demanded by the civilising process. They have also become increasingly disrespectful towards agencies of state control, notably the Royal Ulster Constabulary who are perceived as unfriendly towards Loyalist interests. In general, the attitudes of these football fans can be likened to those of young men who, in other circumstances, become football hooligans. According to Dunning and his fellow researchers, 'males from the "rougher" sections of the working class remain relatively unincorporated, and that means less subject to the sorts of "uncivilising" constraints and higher pressures which affect the members of higher classes' (Dunning *et al.*, 1988, p. 229). In Northern Ireland, however, such people rarely resort to hooliganism. Instead, they celebrate the achievements not only of their 'proxy warriors' on the field of play but also of those real warriors, belonging to the paramilitary organisations, who represent them in the wider community. For them, the football ground is their own public space in which they expect to be allowed to express their approval of anti-Catholic violence. Such behaviour is seldom condoned in other public places. Yet neither the police nor the football authorities, with a few honourable exceptions, have done much to eradicate it from Northern Irish football grounds.

Why is uncivilised, anti-Catholic rhetoric apparently condoned? First, it may be felt that the anti-social behaviour of certain groups of football supporters need not be a major cause for concern since it seldom leads directly to violence and, as a consequence, it pales into insignificance when compared with what has been happening in the wider community. Thus, the security forces have had neither the time, the resources nor any pressing need to stop young fans from expressing anti-Catholic sentiments. Second, there is a feeling that the songs and chants which are heard at football games are simply part of the social fabric of Northern Ireland. The supporters are carrying on a tradition. According to Bell, 'representations of heritage are no longer tied primarily to the workplace'. Instead, 'other more organic formations of heritage start to predominate within the lives of the young' (1990, p. 200). For Bell, the Loyalist marching bands perform such a role. Football support, however, can serve a similar function. In England, for example, where young working-class men have also been cut off from occupational and other traditions passed on through family and community, football, according to David Robins, 'is one of the most important elements of a continuing tradition' (1984, p. 53). So it is in Northern Ireland where it is no accident that a favourite song amongst supporters refers to inheritance: 'My old man said be a Linfield fan ... .' For Linfield, one can insert Glentoran, Portadown, Glenavon and so on. The message is essentially the same. Supporting a particular club or the Northern Ireland team is inherited and supporters expect (and are generally granted) the right to follow football in the traditional manner even if that means the construction of a fundamentally anti-Catholic ambience. Thus, the anti-social behaviour of fans is seen as both trivial and inevitable. This assessment, however, shows a marked lack of concern for the feelings of Catholic players and supporters.

A useful comparison can be made between this problem and the issue of racial abuse at football grounds in England and Scotland. Although less rooted in tradition than anti-Catholic rhetoric in Northern Ireland, racism was allowed to develop at British football grounds for many of the same reasons, as anti-Catholic sentiments have been accepted as part and parcel of football in the province. First, uncivilised chanting on the terraces was regarded as unrelated to and less problematic than hooligan violence. Second, racist abuse was interpreted within a purely footballing context and distinguished from racism in the outside world. Although fans taunted black players on opposing sides, they idolised their own clubs' blacks. This it was felt revealed that they were not really racists at all. The same theory could be applied to Protestant fans in Northern Ireland as regards Catholic players. Yet what is ignored in both cases are the feelings of those players who hear the followers of their club abusing people with their skin colour or religious beliefs. It is as if footballers are granted an honorary status – honorary whites, honorary Protestants – by some followers of the clubs for whom they play. Gradually the flawed logic of trying to make a special case for racism practised on football terraces has been recognised and, in both England and Scotland, the police, the football authorities and supporters themselves have taken steps to eradicate the problem.

Underlying the anti-racist campaign in British football are two important principles. First, there was a recognition that racist chants are offensive not only to black players from competing teams, but also to the entire black population, many of whom have been deterred from watching football because they judged that their presence would become unwelcome. Few black people in Britain are able to share the sanguine approach adopted by Liverpool's John Barnes in the face of racist jibes. According to Dave Hill, Barnes 'pre-empted his own initiation': 'He gave permission for his team-mates to, for better or worse, relate to him in the traditional Liverpool way. I'm black. It's a joke. Everyone relax' (1989, p. 130). Few black Britons could share the joke and similarly few Catholics in Northern Ireland can listen with equanimity to groups of young men singing about being 'up to their knees in Fenian blood'.

The second principle which prompted the anti-racist campaign in British football was a recognition of the possibility that the climate of hostility towards black people which surrounded football games could contribute indirectly to violent racist attacks. This is impossible to prove but, given that racially motivated violence is a serious problem, it was seen to be proper to target one of its potential sources. It is against the backdrop of anti-racism in British football that the relative silence surrounding anti-Catholic rhetoric at games in Northern Ireland can best be explored.

It is clear that football in Northern Ireland provides ample support for Stephen Jones' claims regarding the capacity of working-class people to secure some measure of control over important areas of their life. Whilst this has had some positive results, however, the overall consequences having been largely negative, not least because of the prevalence of certain forms of uncivilised behaviour making football grounds uncongenial places for most women, many members of the Protestant middle class and all but a handful of Catholics. There is, of course, a danger of becoming excessively squeamish about the behaviour of a single section of football supporters. As Guttmann points out, those who are not fully incorporated into society or subject to the civilising process are inevitably inclined towards behaviour 'which the upper and middle classes, differently socialised and with more to lose from a rocking boat, simply misinterpret' (1986, p. 169). The response which follows is described by Dunning as 'the reaction of the dominant "respectable" majority to the behaviour of people whose standards deviate for structurally identifiable reasons from their own' (1993, p. 64). Certainly there is little to be gained by moralising about the behaviour of some working-class Protestant football supporters.

Numerous political, social and economic factors have conspired to reduce the opportunities for these young men to express their masculinity and their sense of identity. Perhaps their uncivilised behaviour should be welcomed as preferable to engagement in Loyalist paramilitary violence as a response to their situation. For that to be the case, however, there would need to be convincing evidence that there has been no link between the behaviour of football fans and political violence.

According to Dunning, 'the level of violence in sport depends fundamentally on the level of violence in society at large' (1993, p. 67). An almost identical point is made by Guttmann who argues that 'when a society is torn apart by social conflict, conflict will occur in conjunction with sports as it does in conjunction with everything else' (1986, p. 164). There is an element of truth in these comments. Certainly the vivid imagery and the intense emotions on display at some football matches in Northern Ireland reflect the sectarian conflict. Rather than adding to the violence, however, the passion aroused may represent a valuable safety-valve. As Hobermann suggests 'The frequent association of sportive nationalism and domestic political tensions might even reflect a societal need for occasional cathartic outbursts to relieve feelings of anger and frustration' (1993, p. 20).

Conclusion

The absence of a serious hooligan problem adds further weight to this relatively positive assessment of uncivilised behaviour on the terraces. Ironically, perhaps some contribution is being made to the civilising process. Against this much too convenient conclusion, however, it must be restated that, leaving the Troubles temporarily to one side, Northern Ireland is not a particularly violent society. Thus, the relative insignificance of football hooliganism is scarcely surprising. Taking the Troubles into account, however, violence has been widespread throughout the Province for over 25 years and any possible connection between that violence and the anti-social behaviour of football fans becomes an important issue, arguably far more serious than football hooliganism.

It should be said at once that in any case football supporters (at least those who attend Irish League matches) represent a small percentage of the Northern Ireland population. Being predominantly working-class and male, they are also unrepresentative of the wider society as a whole. Furthermore, only a minority of these football fans are directly involved in anti-Catholic abuse and sometimes even their tone is moderated. Linfield supporters, for example, have been less overtly hostile to Catholics in recent years, during which time their team's improved performances have owed much to the arrival of Catholic players at Windsor Park. In general, however, at most Irish League clubs, an anti-Catholic atmosphere lingers. This does not mean that a majority of football fans or even most of those who indulge in abusive behaviour have been directly involved in violence against Catholics. They are not 'up to their knees in Fenian blood' whatever they may sing. Indeed, they might not have actually supported the Loyalist paramilitaries whose achievements their songs salute. Furthermore, it is impossible to establish a continuum linking anti-Catholic rhetoric at football games with sectarian violence. Neither, however, can it be safely argued that the two phenomena are totally unrelated. Whilst very few of the Protestants who attend football matches in Northern Ireland are or have been involved in violence, most of those who have acted violently towards Catholics have also taken part in the sort of celebration of working-class Protestant identity witnessed at football games. What influence has the general atmosphere at most grounds in Northern Ireland had on men who have, for a variety of reasons, a propensity for sectarian violence? What will be the impact on young boys who attend matches today and who are given the impression that anti-Catholic sentiments are condoned by their elders, by 'the People' who run football and even by the police? In the absence of answers to these questions, it behoves all the interested parties to consider very seriously how best to remove all forms of uncivilised behaviour from the terraces of Northern Ireland. Far from diminishing the importance of this issue, the cessation of paramilitary violence since 1994 makes it all the more necessary to confront sectarian attitudes, wherever they are manifested, and thereby weaken the potential support for any future resumption of violence.

More than that, it is important to address the social causes of violence in Northern Irish society from whatever source that violence comes and whatever its purpose might be. Necessarily this includes examining the cultural contexts in which men act aggressively. This is not to suggest that only men are criminally violent in Northern Ireland or to imply that women who engage in violence are freaks of nature (Smart, 1995). As Joyce Canaan suggests, however, male violence is 'central to masculinity in general and takes particular forms among distinct groups of working-class young men, which reveals much about their class and gender as well as their sexual orientation and age' (1991, p. 123). Male violence in Northern Ireland is by no means restricted to working-class men. It goes without saying that it is not exclusive to Protestant men either. This chapter, however, has been concerned with one of the important areas of social life in the province within which violence is provided with a structure of support; it so happens that this area is dominated by Protestant, working-class men.

6 The Culture of Contentment: The Political Beliefs and Practice of the Unionist Middle Classes

Colin Coulter

There exists within recent social scientific approaches to Ulster Unionism a disabling asymmetry. Social scientists have been perennially drawn to the intemperate and frequently impenetrable voices which emanate from the margins of the Unionist community. The recent fascination with the purportedly 'new Loyalism' articulated by those fringe Unionist parties which are organically associated with paramilitary bodies merely confirms the abiding fixation of academics with the exotica of contemporary Unionism (Todd, 1995). Preoccupation with the radical periphery of Unionist politics has ensured that social scientists have essentially left uncharted that rather more temperate ideological terrain occupied principally by the Unionist middle classes (Jackson, 1990). There is, therefore, a pressing need to map out the political beliefs and practice of middle-class Unionists. An adequate understanding of the ideological disposition of the Unionist middle classes demands an appreciation of their specific, essentially contradictory, experience of the period since the demise of Stormont. An account of the developments which have accompanied the era of Direct Rule is, therefore, required.

A Place Apart

One of the abiding concerns of the British political establishment since the creation of Northern Ireland has been to maintain a discreet political distance from the province (Aughey, 1990; Cunningham, 1991; O'Leary and McGarry, 1993;

Wichert 1991; Wright, 1987). This strategic imperative of the modern British State was inscribed in the actual terms of the partition settlement (O'Dowd, 1994). The establishment of a devolved assembly possessed of considerable legislative powers within the fledgling constitutional entity of Northern Ireland reflected primarily the ambition of the metropolis to remain aloof from the sectarian political affairs of the six counties. Given the historical anxiety of Westminster to keep the province 'at arm's length' the decision of the sovereign Parliament to dissolve the Stormont legislature and assume direct responsibility for the governance of Northern Ireland would appear to mark a radical departure. In reality, however, the introduction of Direct Rule signified a shift in the form but not the substance of British policy towards Northern Ireland (Wright, 1987). The strategies adopted by successive administrations of Direct Rulers have continued to be informed by the perennial conception of Northern Ireland as 'a place apart' (Rose, 1982). The official conviction that Northern Ireland represents a region irreconcilably 'different' from the rest of the state has pervaded the conduct of public policy in the six counties over the past quarter-century. The influence of this particular abiding ideology of the modern British State has been pronounced both in the realm of political affairs and in the sphere of social and economic concerns. The changes within each of these crucial areas of public policy wrought by the operation of Direct Rule will be considered in turn.

The Politics of Direct Rule

The dissolution of the Stormont regime furnished Westminster with the historic opportunity to govern Northern Ireland in a manner identical to the rest of the United Kingdom. Rather than treating Northern Ireland as an integral region of the State, however, the 'mother of parliaments' has preferred instead to deal with the six counties in a manner reminiscent of a distant colonial possession. The structures of authority through which Direct Rule has operated for more than two decades have been distinctly autocratic (Bloomfield, 1991; Livingstone and Morison, 1995; O'Leary and Arthur, 1990). Legislation pertaining to Northern Ireland is formulated and largely administered by individuals who remain unaccountable to the electorate of the province (Bradley,

1995; Hadfield, 1991; Weir, 1995). The substantial powers
afforded to the executive under the terms of Direct Rule
have frequently been employed to promote political enter-
prises seemingly inimical to the interests of the Unionist
community. Successive Direct Rule administrations have issued public guarantees of the safety of the Union. In spite of
these public declarations of constitutional fidelity, however,
the British political class has proved only too willing to
consider a future for the six counties beyond the environs of
the Union. At the heart of modern British policy is the
conviction that Westminster has no 'selfish, strategic or economic' interest in the Union with Northern Ireland and
would offer no resistance should the residents of the six
counties express a democratic preference to leave the United
Kingdom (Arthur, 1994; Ryan, 1994). The official indifference to the constitutional status of Northern Ireland codified
in the Anglo-Irish Agreement, the Downing Street Declaration and, most recently, the Framework Document adverts to
the subaltern status which Northern Ireland endures within
the United Kingdom. One has only to contrast the readiness
of the British political class to envisage a political destiny
for Northern Ireland without the Union with the virtual hys-
teria which has greeted attempts to reformulate the terms
under which Scotland should remain *within* the Union to
arrive at an understanding that the province represents a
rather less than cherished region of the modern British State
(Millar, 1995).

The political strategies instigated under the auspices of
Direct Rule have inevitably fostered the distrust of substantial
swathes of the Unionist community, its more affluent elements
included. The formal indifference towards the constitutional
status of the six counties articulated by the British political
establishment has been typically decoded by Northern Unionists as a veiled expression of the desire to be rid of the
troublesome territory of Northern Ireland. The abiding suspicion that the intentions of the metropolis towards the Union
are somewhat less than pure has exercised a pervasive, and
ultimately debilitating, influence upon the political imagination
of contemporary Unionism (Bew and Patterson, 1985). The disquiet of the Unionist population has been especially aroused by
the conduct of security policy over the period of Direct Rule.
The failure to effect a conclusive military defeat of Republican
insurgence has been broadly interpreted by Unionists as a

reflection of British indifference to the plight and welfare of the Northern Irish people. The suspicion grips the Unionist mind that had comparable levels of political violence occurred elsewhere within the United Kingdom the response of the repressive apparatuses of the British State would have been appreciably swifter and more vigorous.

The Political Economy of Direct Rule

The official construction of Northern Ireland as 'a place apart' has, therefore, exercised a tangible influence upon the political initiatives fostered under Direct Rule. The conception of the province as 'different' has proved politically iniquitous. The form and substance of Direct Rule have offered to 'the People' of Northern Ireland political and civil rights appreciably poorer than those enjoyed by their fellow British citizens. The notion that Northern Ireland is different has also guided the hand of Direct Rulers in the sphere of social and economic policy, but with starkly different consequences. The particular conditions which exist within the six counties have drawn British politicians to the belief that the social and economic policies introduced throughout the other regions of the state would be inappropriate – indeed calamitous – in the context of Northern Ireland. The British political establishment has held to the view that fiscal benevolence is required to promote those social conditions deemed conducive to the formation of a sustainable political settlement. Consequently, the period since the dissolution of the Stormont parliament has been characterised by distinctly generous levels of public provision (Wichert, 1991).

During the past two decades the funding of public services in Northern Ireland has doubled in real terms (Hewitt, 1990). The persistence of the war in the six counties has of course ensured that a substantial element of the enlarged public budget has been consumed by the grotesquely inflated expenditure of the military. The era of Direct Rule has also, however, witnessed significant improvement of state funding of vital areas of social provision including health, housing and education (Rowthorn, 1981). The funds which Direct Rule administrations have spent in Northern Ireland have drawn predominantly upon tax revenues generated within the province. An increasingly significant element of public expenditure in the region has, however, depended upon a direct subsidy from the British exchequer. The magnitude of the 'subvention' from Westminster provides arguably the starkest index of the instrumental dependence of Northern Ireland upon the British State under Direct Rule. The annual subsidy which the British treasury provides to the province rapidly approaches £4 billion (Hutton, 1994; Tomlinson, 1994). The existence of the subvention has become ever more indispensable to the economic health of Northern Ireland in recent times. Indeed, financial transfers from London currently constitute one-third of the region's gross domestic product (Anderson and Goodman, 1994; Hamilton, 1995).

The enormous increases in government spending occasioned by Direct Rule have facilitated a substantial expansion of employment opportunities in the public sector. At the outbreak of the present political conflict, the State offered employment to one-quarter of the Northern Irish workforce, a proportion which had remained unchanged over the preceding decade. The operation of Direct Rule has significantly swollen the ranks of public employees in the province (Borooah, 1993; McAuley, 1994). Of every ten individuals in work in Northern Ireland four are employed directly by the British State and another three employed indirectly. The era of Direct Rule, therefore, has established the British State as the absolute fulcrum of the Northern Irish economy (Pollak, 1993).

The Contented Classes

The conduct of social and economic policy since the demise of Stormont has transformed Northern Ireland virtually beyond recognition. The enormous expansion of public expenditure and employment which has attended Direct Rule has significantly augmented the general standard of living in the six counties. The material benefits of Direct Rule have, however, been neither universal nor evenly distributed. Contemporary Northern Ireland represents a social formation rather more polarised along class lines than a generation ago (Cebulla and Smyth, 1995; Milburn, 1994; Wichert, 1991). The virtually unpunctuated crises which have beset the local and global economies over the past quarter-century have condemned a substantial body of workers to the poverty of unemployment and many others to poorly paid service jobs on the margins of formal economic life. The advent of Direct Rule, in contrast, has heralded an era of unprecedented affluence for the Northern Irish middle classes. The focus of the discussion which follows falls primarily upon the Unionist elements among the province's 'contented classes' (Rolston, 1993).

The expansion of public employment which has accompanied Direct Rule has furnished occupational opportunities which have facilitated the emergence of a substantially enlarged middle class in Northern Ireland. Those individuals in the six counties who are employed by the British State typically enjoy rates of remuneration on a par with the rest of the United Kingdom. Public employees living in Northern Ireland, however, face lower living costs than their counterparts in the other regions of the State (MacKinnon, 1993). In particular, houses in the province are relatively inexpensive, presently running at only two-thirds of the United Kingdom average. The coincidence of salaries comparable to the remainder of the UK and relatively low house prices has afforded public employees in the six counties greater purchasing power than their counterparts 'across the water' (Cebulla and Smyth, 1995).

The appreciable affluence of the Northern Irish middle classes has been further underwritten by the industrial policies implemented by Direct Rule administrations. In the period since the demise of the Stormont parliament, the British political class has adopted a distinctly interventionist approach towards the Northern Irish economy (Cunningham, 1991; Tomlinson, 1994). The relatively generous practical and financial assistance tendered by the Northern Ireland Office has allowed indigenous enterprise to enjoy rates of profit which would not appear to be justified on grounds of performance (Teague, 1993b). Given that Protestants remain heavily over-represented among the remnants of the local bourgeoisie, the substantial benefits of the distinctly Keynesian industrial policies favoured under Direct Rule have inevitably accrued primarily to elements within the Unionist community.

The considerable affluence which the fiscal and industrial policies implemented by Direct Rulers have conferred upon the Northern Irish middle classes has in time found expression through increasingly conspicuous patterns of consumption (Breen, 1994; O'Faolain, 1993; Rolston, 1993). Over the last decade, the enhanced purchasing power of the professional and business classes has attracted to Northern Ireland those major retail chains which had previously shunned the province (Brennock, 1991). The recent establishment of Sainsbury outlets throughout Northern Ireland has merely confirmed that the bourgeois affluence generated under the auspices of Direct Rule has rendered the six counties an increasingly lucrative site for commercial enterprise.

Cultural Assimilation Under Direct Rule

The social and economic measures introduced since the abolition of the Stormont parliament have, therefore, established an instrumental bond between a substantial swathe of the Unionist community and the British State. The operation of Direct Rule has also radically altered the nature of the everyday life experiences of northern Unionists. Over the past two decades the Unionist middle classes in particular have been assimilated more fully into the mainstream of British social and political life. The restructuring of the Northern Irish economy effected by Direct Rule has bound the more affluent elements within the Unionist fold ever more closely to the rest of the United Kingdom. The pivotal role which the British State performs within the local economy has ensured that the organisation of work in the upper echelons of both the public and private sectors has, as Jennifer Todd (1987) acknowledges, come to be 'integrally tied to British policies and practices'. Consequently, numerous members of the province's professional and business classes have become drawn increasingly into channels of communication and career advancement which encompass the United Kingdom and centre upon the British State. These bonds are experienced in the guise of attending conferences and meetings in Great Britain, negotiation with state agencies and institutions, routine communications with fellow civil servants in other regions of the United Kingdom and so forth.

The growing association between the Northern Irish middle classes and the rest of the United Kingdom has found a pertinent expression in patterns of travel. The number of residents of the six counties who visit Great Britain has mushroomed over the period of Direct Rule. The growth of air travel in recent times has been particularly remarkable. In the early 1980s the major airlines established 'shuttle' services between the province and various locations in Britain, principally London. Although relatively expensive, these services have proved hugely popular, not least among the professional and business classes. As a result, in the decade after 1984 the number of flights to Britain from the province rose from 329,000 to approximately 500,000.

The bonds between the Unionist middle classes and the other regions of the state have been further enhanced by the growing propensity of their children to opt for British universities. In 1968, the year before the current political unrest erupted in earnest, only 326 students left Northern Ireland to attend university elsewhere within the United Kingdom. Over the period of the Troubles, however, it has become increasingly popular to study 'across the water' especially among the children of the Protestant professional and business classes (Gudgin and Elliott, 1994; McKittrick, 1991; Pollak, 1993). By the early 1990s the number of students from the province enrolling for their first year in British universities and polytechnics was approaching 3000. The increased popularity of Great Britain as a place to study means that there are presently over 8000 people from Northern Ireland attending institutions of higher education elsewhere throughout the United Kingdom. Moreover, given the political unrest and chronic unemployment which afflict the province, many of these migrants will choose not to return once their courses finish. The outcome of recent trends within higher education has, therefore, been the essentially permanent migration to Great Britain of many of the children of the Northern Irish salariat. In the process, an enduring emotional identification with the other regions of the United Kingdom has been established among elements of the Northern Irish middle classes.

The growing association of the more affluent elements among the Unionist community with British society has inevitably found reflection in terms of cultural consumption. In modern times the inhabitants of the six counties have come increasingly to look to Britain, and beyond of course, for their cultural resources. The advancing cultural dependence of the six counties finds a pertinent expression in patterns of newspaper readership. The highly regarded survey of social and political attitudes conducted by Richard Rose (1971) on the eve of the Troubles discovered that 32 per cent of people in the province read a British daily newspaper. The most recent edition of the *Northern Ireland Readership Survey* reveals that over the past quarter-century the consumption of British newspapers in the province has doubled. The penetration of the six counties by the British media which has developed apace over the period of Direct Rule has acted to incorporate elements within Northern Irish society into the cultural and political life of the British State. The omnipresence of British television, radio and newspapers in the province has ensured that the Unionist middle classes in particular have become readily familiar with the substance of contemporary political debate throughout the remainder of the United Kingdom. The pervasive influence of the British media has, moreover, furnished middle-class Protestants with the cultural resources to construct an imagined community which transcends the boundaries of the six counties and incorporates the entire United Kingdom. It has, in other words, fostered a profound cultural sense of Britishness.

Real and Imagined Communities

The process of cultural assimilation which has attended Direct Rule adverts to a pressing need to alter the manner in which we seek to understand the political imagination of contemporary Unionism. Social scientists have frequently suggested that Unionists define and construct the Union in distinctly metaphysical terms (Bruce 1986; O'Malley, 1990). The United Kingdom is assumed to represent for Unionists the abstract expression of an essentially spiritual, imagined community. While these readings have considerable validity, they tender none the less a strictly partial understanding of the Unionist mind. The Union exists not merely in the imaginations of Northern Unionists but also in their everyday lives. Middle-class Unionists in particular no longer inhabit the margins of British society. On the contrary, complex processes of change unleashed by Direct Rule have ensured that fragments of the Unionist middle classes have become direct participants in many spheres of the broader community of the United Kingdom. As a result, Northern Unionists' sense of Britishness has come to be produced and reproduced in not only the realm of philosophical abstraction, but also the prosaic realities of everyday life. In a sense, the existence of the Union is made real for middle-class Unionists every time they attend a conference or business meeting 'across the water', communicate with a fellow civil servant in London or Edinburgh, witness the departure of one of their children to a British university, listen to Radio Four or leaf through *The Times*. The processes of cultural assimilation occasioned by Direct Rule have served to ensure,

therefore, that for many Northern Unionists the Union represents not merely an ideological abstraction but also a lived
reality. The era of Direct Rule has, in other words, ensured
that the United Kingdom has come to constitute a community
that is not only imagined but real.

The Politics of Inertia

The conduct of public policy under Direct Rule has, therefore,
had a peculiarly contradictory effect upon the Unionist middle
classes. The conception of Northern Ireland as 'different' has
prompted the British political class to govern the six counties
in a distinctly colonial manner. The political form and substance of Direct Rule have inevitably sponsored among middle-
class Protestants that sullen disenchantment which pervades
the entire Unionist community. The construction of Northern
Ireland as 'a place apart' has produced a rather different, ultimately contradictory, expression in the realm of social and
economic policy. The assumption that the six counties offer an
inappropriate setting for the implementation of social measures
introduced elsewhere has ensured the survival in the province
of a welfarism abandoned a generation ago in the other regions
of the British State (Longley, 1994). The fiscal benevolence of
Direct Rule has afforded the Unionist middle classes both unprecedented wealth and enhanced literal and cultural experience of the social and political life of contemporary Britain.
Hence, the era of Direct Rule presents us with a particular
paradox. The execution of public policy over the past two
decades has simultaneously nurtured the alienation of middle-
class Unionists from the British state and ensured their
progressive assimilation into the mainstream of the broader
cultural community of the United Kingdom. It is this essentially contradictory experience of Direct Rule which has shaped
the political beliefs and practice of middle-class Protestants in
modern times.

The conduct of public policy since the dissolution of the
Stormont legislature has inevitably confirmed and nurtured the
seemingly innate conservatism of the Unionist middle classes.
Instrumental dependence upon the metropolis has prompted an
especially corrosive form of political impotence. Mindful of the
source of their appreciable wealth, middle-class Unionists have
typically proved unwilling to contemplate those radical

ideological and political projects which would threaten to alienate a distinctly materially benevolent British state. Accordingly,
the response of Protestant professionals to the recurring traumas
which have beset the Unionist community over the past couple of
decades has been characterised by a circumspection which has
given rise to an abiding inertia. The debilitating conservatism of
the Unionist middle classes found vivid illustration in the
emotional aftermath of the Anglo-Irish Agreement.

The advent of the Hillsborough Accord represented the most
profound crisis to have confronted Ulster Unionism for more
than a decade. Outraged that the Irish Government had been
afforded a consultative role in the governance of the province,
representatives of every shade of Unionist opinion gathered at
enormous public rallies to articulate vehement opposition. For
the first time in a generation substantial numbers of Unionist
professionals rubbed shoulders with even the more lumpen elements of their ethno-political kin. The trauma of the Anglo-Irish
Agreement appeared initially to have dispelled much of the quintessential conservatism of the Unionist middle classes. It became
quickly apparent, however, that the more affluent elements
within the Unionist fold possessed little appetite for the radical
demagoguery of street politics.

As the campaign of resistance against the Hillsborough
Accord grew ever more militant, the Unionist middle classes
became increasingly concerned at the prevalence of those extra-
parliamentary methods which promised to invoke the wrath of
the metropolis. The disquiet of middle-class Unionists was generated in particular by the organisation of a strike to vent
Unionist antagonism to the Agreement. An endeavour to recall
the glory of former days when the exercise of industrial might
and paramilitary muscle had secured political gain, the Loyalist
'day of action' called for 3 March 1986 inevitably produced
manifold incidents of violence and intimidation. Fearful that
the cause and reputation of Unionism would be irredeemably
tarnished, the voices of Unionist moderation were raised in
denunciation of the boorish excesses of the strikers. The Ulster
Unionist Party leader at that time, James Molyneaux, the ideological and physical embodiment of the circumspection of the
Unionist middle classes, pronounced that never again would he
lend support to those radical forms of political protest which
had produced the debacle of the 'day of action' (Aughey, 1989).
In future the Unionist case against the Anglo-Irish Agreement
would be pursued not on the streets of Ulster but rather in the

somewhat more dignified setting of the Palace of Westminster. The characteristically temperate strategy mapped out by Molyneaux astutely caught the mood of middle-class Unionists concerned at the potentially calamitous repercussions of Unionist militancy upon the demeanour of the British political class. The prudent parliamentarianism of the 'steady course' exercised a resonance among middle-class Unionists who, although anxious to articulate their antipathy to the Anglo-Irish Agreement, ultimately proved too fearful of alienating the metropolis to embrace those radical ideological and political departures which the gravity of the crisis occasioned by the Hillsborough Accord appeared to require.

The Politics of Ambivalence

The past couple of decades have fostered among the ranks of the Unionist middle classes the further ideological trait of a profound ambivalence towards the British State. The operation of Direct Rule has conferred considerable material and cultural benefit upon middle-class Unionists. The comparative profligacy of the British exchequer has underwritten the burgeoning affluence of the professional and business classes within the Unionist family. A substantial body of middle-class Unionists have come to be more fully assimilated than hitherto into the cultural and public life of the wider community of the United Kingdom. In recent times, moreover, elements of the Unionist middle classes have established enduring affective bonds with other regions of the state. The complex processes of social and cultural change unleashed by Direct Rule have persuaded many middle-class Protestants to regard themselves as integral members of an 'imagined community' which accommodates all of the diverse peoples of the United Kingdom. This process of ontological reflection has ensured that the Unionist middle classes in particular have come increasingly to define themselves as 'British'. The sense of Britishness possessed and articulated by middle-class Unionists remains, however, far from unequivocal. Whilst the Unionist middle classes readily identify with many of the rites and institutions of the British State, they also exhibit appreciable distrust of one of its principal components, namely the government of the day. The propensity of Westminster to govern Northern Ireland as 'a place apart' has served to alienate those elements of the Unionist community which have otherwise prospered enormously under the auspices of Direct Rule. The conviction that London does not genuinely have their interests at heart has prompted many middle-class Unionists to question their status as members of the complex ethnic kinship which constitutes the United Kingdom and to conceive of themselves not as British citizens but rather as British subjects. Their misgivings have thereby moved the Unionist middle classes to withhold their full consent from the metropolis and to append substantial qualifications to their vital sense of Britishness.

The essential ambivalence of middle-class Unionists has exercised a palpable influence upon their political outlook and practice in modern times. Since the mid-1970s a substantial swathe of the Unionist middle classes has offered consent to an ideological project which is typically denoted as 'integrationist' but which Bew and Patterson (1987a) have persuasively characterised as 'minimalist'. The strategy of minimalist integrationism embodies an aspiration that Northern Ireland be governed through a mode of Direct Rule which acknowledges the accepted standards of democratic practice. The integrationist philosophy clearly articulates the particular interests and experience of the Unionist middle classes over the preceding two decades. The realisation of the minimalist project would ensure that Direct Rule would become the permanent, democratised form of government for Northern Ireland. The strategy proposed by minimalist integrationists, therefore, dovetails conveniently with the specific class interests of those constituents of the Unionist community who have accumulated unprecedented wealth since the demise of the devolved assembly at Stormont. The minimalist project further accommodates the shifting everyday life experience of the Unionist middle classes under Direct Rule. The integrationist camp offer the view that executive authority over the affairs of Northern Ireland should be retained by the sovereign Parliament at Westminster. In this regard, the minimalist strategy encodes an aspiration that the residents of the six counties should be enabled to transcend the 'narrow ground' of provincial politics in order to participate in the wider, ultimately more cosmopolitan, public life of the state. It is entirely rational, therefore, that the philosophy of minimalist integrationism should have exercised an enduring appeal for that significant body of middle-class Unionists who have over the past twenty years become increasingly familiar with the substance and form of British political culture.

Hence, the minimalist integrationist project may be interpreted as an articulation of the growing cultural identification of
the Unionist middle classes with the wider environs of the
United Kingdom. The particular strategy advanced by minimalist integrationism also, however, intimates the limits of middle-
class Unionists' enhanced sense of Britishness. The philosophy of
integrationism embodies an ambition to participate in the political life of the state. The proponents of integration, however,
insist that the interests of the Unionist community cannot be
prosecuted within those political parties which can reasonably
expect to form a majority in the sovereign Parliament but which
have little sincere concern for the health of the Union. Rather,
the welfare of Northern Unionists can only be guaranteed by the
eternal vigilance of a Unionist voice which remains formally
independent from those parties which aspire to form Government and Opposition. At the heart of the integrationist project,
therefore, there exists a fundamental tension between an ambition to participate fully in the public life of the British State and
a concern to remain aloof from that system of party politics
which represents its principal medium. Minimalist integrationists exhibit a desire to take part in the political drama which
unfolds within the Palace of Westminster, yet prefer to remain in
the wings rather than occupy centre stage (Clifford, 1987). The
seeming anomalies of the integrationist project offer ideological
expression to the Unionist middle classes' profoundly contradictory experience of Direct Rule. The essential ambivalence which
pervades the philosophy of integrationism merely echoes that of
middle-class Unionists who identify readily with the rituals and
icons of the British State yet are simultaneously repelled by the
apparently perennial perfidy of its executive. It is precisely this
capacity to accommodate the equivocation of the Unionist professional and business classes which has underwritten the longevity
of the minimalist project.

In the atmosphere of flux engendered by the Anglo-Irish
Agreement, minimalist integrationism came under sustained
challenge from a nascent ideological sibling. The philosophical
construct of *electoral integrationism* rested upon the conviction that
Northern Ireland should be governed not as 'a place apart' but
rather as an equal and integral region of the British State. The
ideologues of electoral integration rehearsed those demands that
Direct Rule be rendered the permanent and accountable mode of
government for the province which had long since been the
standard fare of the integrationist wing of Ulster Unionism.

There was, however, one genuinely original component within
the formidable ideological armoury of electoral integrationism.
The advocates of electoral integration voiced the demand that the
British political parties establish constituency organisations
within Northern Ireland and admit to full membership the residents of the six counties. The decision of the parties of state to
organise throughout Northern Ireland would, the electoral integrationist movement counselled, usher in an era of genuinely
democratic government in the province. Admission to the party
political life of the State would afford 'the People' of the six
counties the opportunity to effect those relatively minor shifts in
the balance of political power which can transform Government
into Opposition (Clifford, 1986). Fearful of electoral retribution,
the parties at Westminster would be compelled to tailor their
policies to the interests and aspirations of the Northern electorate. The advent of electoral integration would, therefore, sound
the death knell of unaccountable government in Northern
Ireland (Davidson 1986).

The ideal of electoral integration appeared for a time to
have found a ready constituency among elements of the Unionist middle classes disgruntled at the political impotence and
philosophical dereliction of the Unionist mainstream. The
strategy of electoral integrationism exercised an appeal among
middle classes not least because it acknowledged the shifting
contours of their cultural identity and experience under Direct
Rule. The realisation of electoral integration would have afforded the more affluent strata within the Unionist fold the
opportunity to participate fully in the political life of that
cultural community of which they imagine themselves to be an
integral part. Admission to the party political life of the State
would, in other words, have enabled the Unionist middle
classes to offer ideological consummation to their burgeoning
sense of Britishness under Direct Rule. In spite of a brief
flirtation with the ideal of electoral integration, however, the
Unionist middle classes have ultimately proved unwilling to
embrace the radical prescriptions of the electoral integrationist
project. The insouciance of middle-class Unionists to the lucid
counsel of the ideologues of electoral integration has been
starkly evidenced in the fate of the Conservative Party since
the historic decision taken at its 1989 annual conference to
forward candidates for election in the province.

Although the Conservative Party is the 'natural' representative of their substantial economic-corporate interests, the

Unionist middle classes have steadfastly refused to cast their votes for the party. Consequently, the Conservatives suffered in Northern Ireland electoral performances which, even in the context of their current plight in many other regions of the State, have been thoroughly pitiful. The refusal of the Unionist professional and business classes to appropriate the ideal of electoral integration adverts to the essential ambivalence which informs their conception of the modern British State. The adoption of the electoral integrationist strategy would have allowed the Unionist middle classes to have affirmed their assimilation into the wider cultural environs of the United Kingdom. It would also, however, have required middle-class Unionists to have entrusted their political interests to those parties which aspire to govern the State. Inevitably they have proved unwilling to do so. The suspicion that the metropolis cares little for the health of the Union exercises sufficient hold over the imagination of contemporary Unionism to have ensured that even those fragments of the Unionist community which have garnered considerable benefit from the policies of successive Direct Rule administrations have proved unwilling to place their faith in those parties which seek to wield executive authority over the State. Rather the Unionist middle classes have preferred to hold true to the traditional minimalist axiom that the interests of Unionism are best served within the sovereign Parliament by a political voice which remains formally independent of the parties of state. The ideological preference of middle-class Unionists for minimalist rather than electoral integrationism suggests that they have ultimately proved content to inhabit the margins rather than the centre of that imagined community to which they express cultural and political devotion. In so doing the Unionist professional and business classes have acknowledged and announced the limits of their feelings of Britishness.

The Politics of Indifference

In the summer of 1993 the Opsahl Commission published reflections on the deliberations of one of the most extensive surveys of social and political life ever conducted in the north of Ireland. Among their diverse observations, the Opsahl Commissioners noted that the Northern Irish middle classes – and, in particular, the Unionist middle classes – have largely

abstained from involvement in the political affairs of the province over the period of the recent conflict (Pollak, 1993). The
absence of the 'contented classes' has, the Commissioners
insisted, exercised a distinctly debilitating influence upon the
political life of the six counties. The seeming indolence of the
professional and business classes has deprived the political
process of the energies and temperance of an element of Northern Irish society whose consent and participation are indispensable to the formulation of a viable settlement (Lister, 1995).
The refusal of the middle classes to engage in party politics
has, moreover, served to impoverish the wider realm of public
life. The apparent political apathy of the more affluent strata of
Northern Irish society proves emblematic of the inertia which
infects the public space of civil society (Lister 1995; Pollak
1993). The manifold iniquities authored by the indolence of
the Northern middle classes convinced the members of the
Opsahl Commission of the need to lure professionals back into
the party political affairs of the province. The return of the
middle classes represents, in the minds of the Opsahl Commissioners an essential precondition and harbinger of the regeneration of public life in the six counties (Pollak, 1993).

The characterisation tendered by the Opsahl Commission
bears considerable resemblance, of course, to the realities of
Northern Irish political culture. Over the past two decades the
Unionist middle classes in particular have remained aloof from
the typically prosaic concerns of party political life. The seeming political indifference of middle-class Unionists accords with
their particular experience of Direct Rule. The measures implemented by Direct Rule administrations of various hues have
invariably served the instrumental interests of the Unionist
professional and business classes. The relative benevolence of
the British exchequer has afforded to many residents of the six
counties a lifestyle that would induce envy among the middle
classes of every other region of the State. The conduct of
Direct Rulers has, therefore, largely eliminated the need for the
Unionist middle classes to intervene directly in political life in
order to alter the inflection of public policy. The absence of
Protestant professionals from local political parties owes its
origins not merely to the substance but also the form of Direct
Rule. Under bourgeois democracy the engagement of the
middle classes in political life articulates *inter alia* an ambition
to prosecute particular political interests and to acquire pres-
tige. The exhaustive powers appropriated by the executive

under the auspices of Direct Rule have ensured, however, that the province's political parties no longer constitute a source either of influence or status. Promotion through the ranks of the local parties has in recent times come to hold the prospect merely of attaining public positions which afford derisively menial powers. The essential autocracy of Direct Rule has, therefore, effectively eroded the principal reasons for the participation of the Unionist middle classes in party political life. It has thereby served to confirm the abiding impoverishment of the political culture which obtains within the six counties.

The observation offered by the Opsahl Commission that middle-class Unionists have opted out of the political affairs of Northern Ireland over the course of the modern Troubles is beyond dispute. Other aspects of the depiction of the relationship of the Unionist middle classes to the public life of the province embodied within the Opsahl Report are rather more contentious. The members of the Opsahl Commission appear to contest that the reluctance of Unionist professionals to enter party politics adverts to a corrosive political indifference which has precluded their participation in the broader realm of civil society. This particular characterisation fails, however, to stand up to close scrutiny. Although the Unionist middle classes have proved perennially reluctant to engage in party politics, their reticence should not be confused for political indifference or inertia. The more affluent elements within the Unionist fold have over the past couple of decades continued to pursue their particular interests. They have done so, however, not through the realm of party politics but rather within the broader sphere of civil society. Over the past generation the Unionist middle classes have come to channel their political energies not through the conventional medium of the local parties but rather through those professional bodies which give voice to their specific, sectional interests. Protestant professionals have, moreover, increasingly sought kudos not through election to public office but rather through ascent within those voluntary organisations whose upper echelons attract civic honours and invitations to those social occasions orchestrated by the Northern Ireland Office which offer a pastiche of that baroque Home Counties gentility so beloved of the Unionist middle classes.

The specific form which the political conduct of the Unionist middle classes has assumed over the period of Direct Rule has proved advantageous in numerous respects. The Unionist professional and business classes have proved able to prosecute their objectives with greater efficacy through the realm of civil society than the more conventional conduit of political parties. The various organisations which articulate the interests of middle-class Unionists within civil society are able to operate unfettered by the strictures and formalities of democratic practice. Those professional bodies which lend voice to the concerns of indigenous capital require no endorsement from the electorate of the province in order to negotiate with and exercise influence upon the Northern Ireland Office. Indeed, these pressure groups are often more likely to have the ear of government ministers than the representatives of political parties which enjoy substantial democratic mandates.

The pursuit of political objectives within civil society has further proved beneficial to the Unionist middle classes in the sense that it has allowed certain of their ideological formulations to assume a distinctly hegemonic character. Were the Unionist professional classes to have continued to have operated through local parties their conduct would have been readily exposed as an expression of certain sectional, exclusive interests. The particularism of the political projects to which middle-class Unionists offered their consent would have necessarily engaged the opposition of other elements of that complex configuration of sectarian class relations which obtains within the six counties. That area of public space which constitutes civil society, however, has proved a rather less contentious realm of political and ideological debate. Operating through those bodies which occupy civil society has enabled the Unionist middle classes to express their political interests in a manner which is ostensibly apolitical. The measures and values advanced by various professional organisations have been portrayed not as an articulation of the particular interests of the more elevated strata within Northern Irish society but rather as the tenets of universally beneficial common sense to which all can subscribe. The particularism of bourgeois ideology has been allowed to masquerade as the universalism of an enlightened civic conscience.

The particular manner in which the Unionist middle classes have sought to pursue their political interests under Direct Rule found pertinent illustration in the course of those tortuous events which culminated eventually in the paramilitary cease-fires of 1994. Pivotal moments in the evolution of the 'peace process' were marked by the issue of press releases by a body of individuals believed to have insights into the thinking of local capital (McKittrick, 1994). The clandestine group of one hundred senior professional and business figures, who, given the ethno-religious composition of the upper echelons of the occupational hierarchy in the province, may reasonably be assumed to hail from predominantly Unionist backgrounds, sought to offer their blessing and encouragement to the seemingly progressive trajectory of the political process. Influential players within the unfolding political drama within the six counties were exhorted to summon the energy and goodwill required to construct a durable settlement which would allow 'the People' of Northern Ireland to enjoy peace and prosperity. The specific form which the intervention of the Northern bourgeoisie in the 'peace process' assumed would appear instructive. Those Unionists who endorsed the various press releases which were issued could have, in principle at least, sought to stimulate and define political dialogue through participation as individuals within the local parties. They chose instead, however, to seek to exercise political influence through one of the essential components of civil society, namely the media. In so doing, a strategically important fragment of the Unionist middle classes exhibited an understanding that under the terms of Direct Rule particular interests may be most fruitfully prosecuted outside that realm of party politics wherein they are conventionally pursued. The endeavours of a hundred professional and business people to foster political dialogue illustrate the capacity of the Unionist middle classes to conceal the irretrievably sectional nature of their political interests and behaviour. The intervention of a predominantly Unionist element of the Northern middle classes represented an attempt to secure a specific class objective, namely to establish an enduring political stability which would furnish the conditions for renewed accumulation. Those bourgeois individuals who produced the relevant press statements proved able, however, to conceal the particularism of their concerns within a discourse which emphasised the benefits of political progress for everyone within the six counties. This discursive agility offers confirmation of the ability of the powerful within society to portray their political interests and ideological concerns as the common currency of all.

New Times

The particular ideological traits – inertia, ambivalence, indifference – which the era of Direct Rule has engendered among the ranks of the Unionist middle classes have served to undermine

political dialogue and progress in the province. The conduct of
the executive since the demise of Stormont has enabled and
encouraged the more affluent fragments of the Unionist community to remain aloof from the political process and to avoid
reflection upon the nature of their interests and identity. The
preference of middle-class Unionists to remain apart from party
political life has produced many deleterious consequences. The
inertia of the Unionist professional and business classes has
ensured the absence from the realm of political affairs of an
element of Northern Irish society whose magnitude and strategic importance render its participation indispensable to the
formulation of a conclusive constitutional settlement. The
seeming indifference of the Unionist middle classes has, moreover, acted to confirm and exacerbate the lethargy of the other
principal players within the political process. Finally, the
refusal of middle-class Unionists to engage with the realities of
political life has inevitably corrupted the imagination of modern Unionism. The absence of Protestant professionals from
public life has deprived Unionism of those temperate voices
which could perhaps have more ably charted a course through
the perilous processes of political dialogue and ideological renewal. The indolence of middle-class Unionists has thereby
served to confirm the political ineptitude and philosophical
poverty which blight contemporary Unionism.

The manifold crises which have befallen Unionism over the
past generation have failed to disturb the wealthier elements of
the Protestant community from their political and ideological
slumber. Even the profound crisis summoned by the Anglo-
Irish Agreement proved insufficient to convince middle-class
Unionists of the need for ideological rumination or sustained
political engagement. A couple of developments have occurred
in recent years, however, which possess some potential to dis-
pel the seemingly perennial torpor of the Unionist middle
classes. The decision of the Loyalist and Republican paramilitaries to halt their respective campaigns of sectarian violence
has radically altered the political climate within Northern
Ireland. Were the cease-fires to become permanent an environment would emerge which might encourage and enable the
Unionist middle classes to participate more fully in the political affairs of the six counties. As the pall of a quarter-century
of political violence gradually lifted, the Unionist professional
and business classes might summon the confidence and cour-
age to reflect upon and disseminate their political aspirations.

The activists who emerged from the ranks of the Unionist middle classes might bring to the political life of the province the more temperate and cosmopolitan outlook of a swathe of Northern Irish society which has, under Direct Rule, come to inhabit a cultural environment which transcends the narrow sectarian contours of the six counties. The intervention of middle-class Unionists in the political affairs of the province might, therefore, invest contemporary Unionism with a rather more liberal inflection. In prompting the ideological renewal of Unionism, the return of the Protestant professional and business classes would serve to establish one of the conditions vital to political progress within Northern Ireland.

The apparent philosophical and political indolence of the Unionist middle classes may be further undermined by the processes unleashed by the current reconfiguration of western European capitalism. The measures implemented by the metropolis since the dissolution of the Stormont legislature have conferred upon the Unionist professional and business classes unprecedented wealth. The operation of Direct Rule has ensured, therefore, that the constitutional status of Northern Ireland within the United Kingdom accords not merely with the Unionist middle classes' sense of ethnic being but also with their appreciable material interests. Current patterns of change afoot within western European capitalism, however, threaten to disturb the neat coincidence between the ethnic and class interests of the Unionist bourgeoisie. Recent endeavours to construct a Single European Market have inevitably inspired demands for greater economic co-operation across the Irish border (Anderson and Goodman, 1995). The strategy of integrating the two economies on the island has evidently exercised a resonance among the predominantly Unionist remnants of the Northern Irish bourgeoisie (Anderson and Shuttleworth, 1992, 1993; Hutton, 1994; Kearney and Wilson 1994; Munck and Hamilton, 1994; Purdy, 1994; Quigley, 1993; Smyth, 1994). The capital invested in the Irish Republic by Northern entrepreneurs has hitherto been decidedly negligible. The integration of the economic life of the island, therefore, offers enormous scope for the Unionist bourgeoisie to establish potentially lucrative undertakings south of the border (Hamilton, 1995). It does so, moreover, at a time when the prospect of a prolonged period of peace embodies the threat that the fiscal benevolence which has characterised the response of the British State to the war in the North of Ireland and which has underwritten the enviable lifestyle of the Unionist middle classes may begin to evaporate. The nuances of a shifting economic and political climate have conspired, therefore, to convince a significant element of the Unionist bourgeoisie of the benefits of business ventures across the border.

The construction of a unitary economy on the island clearly offers significant opportunities to fragments of the Unionist middle classes. The process also, however, threatens to present the Unionist bourgeoisie with certain profound political difficulties (Tomlinson, 1994). The harmonisation of the Irish economies would inevitably require the creation of appropriate supportive institutions (Anderson and Goodman, 1995). These bodies might over time come to appropriate and employ extensive powers which may not be accountable to the electorate of either State (Anderson and Shuttleworth, 1993). The endeavour to co-ordinate the economic life of the island would, therefore, establish the institutions of a fledgling unitary Irish State. Economic integration would, in other words, prepare the ground for political integration (Munck and Hamilton, 1994; O'Dowd, 1994; Sheehan, 1995). Hence, the process of integrating the economies separated hitherto by the Irish border threatens to confront the Unionist bourgeoisie with a profound dilemma (Anderson and Goodman, 1995). The strategy of economic integration evidently offers to establish the conditions of renewed accumulation. At the same time, however, it threatens to attenuate the constitutional status of Northern Ireland within the Union. While the Unionist business classes may prefer for a time to blithely overlook the potentially grave ramifications of the project which they appear to have endorsed, they may not prove able to do so indefinitely. Confronting the contradictions latent within the strategy of economic integration may perforce demand that the Unionist middle classes dispense with their erstwhile political and philosophical indifference. As the process of economic integration gathers pace the business classes within the Unionist fold may be compelled for the first time ever to evaluate the relative merits of the competing ambitions of accumulating wealth and retaining an undiluted sense of Britishness. In seeking to reconcile the conflicting class and ethnic interests which would emerge out of the construction of a unitary Irish economy, the Unionist bourgeoisie might eventually arrive at a clearer understanding of who they are and what they want. Alternatively, of course, these fragments of the Unionist middle classes might eschew such ontological reflection and resort to that profound ambivalence which has served them so admirably in the past.

The specific antinomies latent within the project of economic integration may also prompt the Unionist bourgeoisie to greater political activism. As the threat to the constitutional integrity of Northern Ireland embodied within endeavours to synergise the economic life of the island became apparent, elements of the Unionist community would inevitably become increasingly disgruntled. The need to preserve that environment of political harmony conducive to capitalist enterprise may compel the Protestant business classes to address the anxieties of the wider Unionist family. The Unionist bourgeoisie might be required to offer to their ethno-religious kin explanations and assurances concerning the pattern of economic development to which they had tendered their active support. While their counsel may not necessarily be articulated through the medium of the local parties, the Unionist business classes might be persuaded towards more explicit interventions in the perilous domain of Unionist politics.

The complex processes initiated by the reconstruction of western European capitalism may radically alter the ideological character and political conduct of contemporary Unionism. The development of cross-border economic co-operation would arguably afford the more elevated strata within the Unionist community greater experience and understanding of the Irish Republic. Those bourgeois Unionists who have through their professional lives become more culturally familiar with Southern Irish society might perhaps prove more tolerant of the formation of political institutions which acknowledged the relationships which conjoin 'the Peoples' of the island of Ireland. The creation of a unitary Irish economy may thereby serve to foster those liberal and inclusive voices which will be required to guide Northern Unionism through the difficult times which are undoubtedly to come. While the process of economic integration may inadvertently offer Ulster Unionists the ideological resources necessary to navigate the perilous terrain ahead, it may simultaneously accentuate the propensity of Unionism to schism.

The benefits which will accrue from a unitary Irish economy will of course prove far from universal. Fragments of the Unionist middle classes will derive considerable reward from enterprise which straddles the border. The bulk of the Unionist community, however, will experience the unification of Irish economic life as a project which offers few instrumental rewards but threatens to undermine the status of Northern Ireland within the Union (Anderson and Goodman, 1995). The process of economic integration promises, therefore, to open up lines of fissure within the Unionist community which broadly acknowledge the contours of social class. In doing so it would create the ideological space essential for the germination of class politics. We are faced with the apparent irony, therefore, that a process designed to foster the efficiency and authority of capital throughout western Europe may in the particular context of Northern Ireland serve to nurture a mode of political engagement which promises to erode the foundations of bourgeois hegemony.

Conclusion

Ulster Unionism currently faces the latest of a seemingly unpunctuated series of political crises. The paranoia which infests the political imagination of contemporary Unionism has ensured that many Protestants have chosen to interpret the IRA cease-fire as signifying that Republicans have secured substantial, albeit as yet unspecified, political gain. The tone and substance of the Framework Document have confirmed Unionists' gnawing conviction that the British political establishment possesses little sincere commitment to the Union. While the recent developments evidently represent a profound crisis for Northern Unionism, they also tender considerable opportunity. The prevailing climate of peaceful flux offers an environment conducive to political engagement and ideological renewal. The conditions which presently exist within the six counties possess some potential to persuade middle-class Unionists of the need to participate more fully in the political and intellectual life of the province.

Indeed, there are signs that the Unionist middle classes have begun to emerge from their political and ideological slumber. The successful candidature of Robert McCartney in the North Down by-election clearly articulated the concerns and galvanised the energies of, among others, a body of Unionist professionals dismayed at the substance and form of contemporary Unionism. The recent publication of a collection of impressively lucid defences of the Union edited by John Wilson Foster (1995) confirms the emergence of a substantial body of intellectuals willing to offer expression to a constitutional preference which had previously dared not speak its name. The formation in April 1995 of an organisation to articulate the case for the Union comprised specifically of professional and business people would suggest a realisation among the more affluent elements of the Unionist community of the urgent need to disseminate their beliefs and defend their interests. While there exists considerable evidence of growing energy among the ranks of the Unionist middle classes, it remains to be seen of course whether they possess the capacity for sustained political engagement. The Anglo-Irish Agreement produced a similar initial flurry of ideological activity among middle-class Unionists. The Unionist professional and business classes ultimately proved unable, however, to sustain their political interest, an inability illustrated by the rapid and ignominious demise of the Ulster Tories. Recent historical precedent would tend to cast doubt, therefore, upon the capacity of the Unionist middle classes to summon the energy and imagination required if contemporary Unionism is to navigate successfully the perilous waters which lie ahead.

7 Gender and Protestantism in Northern Ireland

Rosemary Sales

The dominance of the sectarian divide in Northern Ireland has marginalised concern with gender inequality. Politics, both formal and informal, have been centred around community loyalties, a situation which provides little space for alternative agendas. Women's rights have generally been seen as a lower priority than, or even in conflict with, the major political issues. While some women have gained prominence within the Nationalist and Republican movements in recent years, Protestant women have remained much less visible. The public face of the Protestant community is overwhelmingly male, represented by male political and Church leaders, many of whom have purveyed strongly anti-feminist views.

Despite an enormous literature on Northern Irish society and politics, the centrality of the Catholic/Protestant relationship has obscured the realities of other forms of inequality and division such as gender to varying degrees (Davies and McLaughlin, 1991). This situation is slowly changing, as a growing body of research and activity is directly addressing women's interests in a serious and structured manner. Despite the formation of the Women's Coalition, women are largely excluded from the political process. For example, no woman MP has been elected in Northern Ireland since Bernadette Devlin in the late 1960s, and representation at council level is noticeably low. In terms of other social and health issues, abortion is still illegal, and Northern Ireland has one of the most insufficient levels of childcare provision in western Europe. Furthermore, policies to support mothers who undertake paid work are generally underdeveloped and as a result females tend to be ghettoised into the part-time and lower-paid end of the labour market.

Research on gender inequality has generally avoided tackling the religious divide, either ignoring it altogether or giving it minimal attention. In general, studies which make connections between religion and gender tend to be given more prominence by women who can be described as either Nationalists or Republicans. Unfortunately, the specific experience of Protestant women has remained largely unexplored.

The conflation of national (or ethnic) identity with religious affiliation has strengthened the power of the Churches in the two communities as a focus for their 'common interests', with, for example, Church leaders usually called upon as spokesmen (*sic*) for their community. The dominatory role of the Churches has been combined with a constant promotion of conservative views on social issues, particularly in relation to the family and sexuality. Opposition to abortion and gay rights has been one of the few areas of agreement between politicians and clergy from both communities/traditions. The construction of political allegiances around religious identity, moreover, means that politicians are reluctant to challenge the Churches' teaching on these issues.

The establishment of Unionist hegemony, in Northern Ireland, prior to Direct Rule was accompanied by a tendency to exclude the majority of Catholics from state power. Such exclusionary tactics provided a wider role to the Catholic Church in social life. State schools, as a result, tend to be Protestant, while the overwhelming majority of Catholic children attend schools controlled by the Catholic Church (Murray, 1985). The Churches play a prominent part in other aspects of welfare provision (Morrow *et al.*, 1994). Furthermore, the prevalence of sectarianism and ethnic division has divided women and in turn made it difficult to pursue issues of common interest. Feminists have had to confront not only the ideological dominance of Church teaching, but the idea that to argue a position which challenges the prevailing politics of their community is disloyal (McLaughlin, 1986).

As noted, the rights of women have been seen as, at best, secondary to the national struggle (Ward, 1983). The Nationalist history of conflict against British state authority has nevertheless meant that Catholic women are more likely to have a tradition of rebellion and radicalism with which they can identify. The ties of Protestantism to Unionist hegemony have made it difficult for Protestant women to challenge the authority of 'their' state and political leaders. Those who fight for their own interests are seen as 'rocking the boat' (Gordon, 1990).

The past 20 years have seen major shifts within the Protestant community. Socio-economic restructuring, and the policy shifts brought about by 20 years of conflict have undermined the ascendancy and loosened the ties which have bound the Protestant community together. While the response has often been fear and defensiveness, it has also opened up new possibilities for women to become more active in economic and political life.

Ethnicity and Identity

Divisions between Protestant and Catholic in Northern Ireland reach into every area of life. Religion affects habitation, schooling and socialising. It also conditions employment outcomes, friendships, marriage, sports and consumption (Howe, 1990; Murray, 1985; Sugden and Bairner, 1993). Above all, for the overwhelming majority, it determines national identity and political allegiance. Religion is not an immediately visible identity. Protestants and Catholics look more or less the same, speak the same language, share much popular culture and watch the same television programmes. But segregation is more all-embracing than between apparently more dissimilar groups in Britain and Europe. The degree of separation is not constant throughout Northern Ireland. It is most intense within working-class areas, where residential segregation is highest (Dunn, 1995). In 35 of Belfast's 51 wards, the population was at least 90 per cent Catholic or Protestant in 1991. Residential segregation however remains high across Northern Ireland, with half the population living in areas containing over 90 per cent of one religion, while only 7 per cent live in areas with equal distributions (Murray, 1995, p. 218).

Residential segregation provides the basis for the promotion of distinct heritages and common sets of values and beliefs. This is compounded by the almost entirely segregated school system – many Protestants grow up with no social contact with Catholics and vice versa (Murray, 1985 and 1995). Contact between Protestant and Catholic is characterised by 'avoidance' (McAuley, 1994, p. 56). Social life depends on 'telling', the /syndrome of signs by which Catholics and Protestants arrive at religious ascription in their every day interaction' (Howe, 1990, p. 13).

While religious divisions are deeply embedded in the structures of economic, social and political life, they are also in another sense 'invisible'. Religion is rarely discussed in 'polite' society: 'There are two languages spoken. There is what you say in public and in "mixed" company and there is what you say in private, among your own people' (Bruce, 1994, p. vii).

Because religious identity has such wide-ranging meanings, this implies that whole areas of discussion are closed off. When discussing sectarianism in the workplace with trade union officers, the author was frequently told that 'religion doesn't matter here'. One official, to show how little religion mattered, assured me that 'we never discuss politics' in the union; thus inadvertently demonstrating the constraints which sectarianism places on debate. The need for 'telling' suggests that religion does indeed matter in social interaction (Howe, 1990; Bruce, 1994; McAuley, 1994).

While racist discourse has underpinned exclusionary practices, ethnicity, which does not depend on a supposed biological base, is a more useful concept in relation to Northern Ireland. Ethnic groups involve the social construction of an origin as a basis for community or collectivity. This origin, mythical or real, can be historically, territorially, culturally or physiognomically based. It can be internally constituted by the group or externally imposed, or both. Moreover, the idea of a common or shared fate can act in the same way (Anthias and Yuval Davis, 1992). Ethnic groupings are not fixed entities, but are constructed and reconstructed in relation to specific social process. They can, therefore, in other contexts lose their salience. For example, many Protestants experience a crisis in their 'British' identity on arriving in Britain where the distinction between Protestant and Catholic is barely appreciated, and they find themselves treated simply as Irish.

The concept of ethnicity provides a powerful framework for understanding the depth of social, economic and political separation of the two communities. Although they take a distinct form in Northern Ireland, they have similarities to other forms of ethnic division. The use of religion as a 'boundary marker' for ethnic divisions does not mean that the differences are about religion, a product of a peculiar Irish attachment to religious struggles. Sectarianism is to be understood not in terms of individual prejudice against people with different beliefs. As such, sectarian (or ethnic) divisions are embodied in concrete process of dominance and subordination (Shirlow and McGovern, 1996).

Discussions of ethnicity have given limited attention to gender (Davies and McLaughlin, 1991). Women are seen as guardians of the family, and transmitters of community values to the next generation. Rules governing sexuality may be tightly enforced, particularly when the community appears to be under threat. For some Northern Ireland Protestants, women who marry 'one of them' (a Catholic) are a symbolic affront to their own community (Bruce, 1992 and 1994).

Gendered ideologies have been prominent in the construction of the two communities. Nationalist mythology uses images of woman's eternal suffering ('Mother Ireland', 'dark Rosaleen') as a metaphor for Ireland's oppression. Derry City is known as the 'mother of us all' (McLaughlin, 1986). A prominent Nationalist image during the hunger strikes of the 1980s was the Virgin Mary watching over the dying prisoners. Republicans have also promoted more active images of Nationalist women as 'freedom fighters'.

There is no equivalent symbolic role for women in Protestantism, where worship of the Virgin Mary is strongly condemned (McWilliams, 1991 and 1994). The imagery of the Protestant community is masculine, whether it is bowler-hatted Orange men celebrating Protestantism's triumph at the Battle of the Boyne, the archetypal Protestant worker (the skilled male manual worker), the harsh fundamentalist rhetoric of Ian Paisley or the balaclava-hooded Loyalist paramilitaries.

Although the meanings attached to a person's identification with one community have little to do with religious belief, the Churches play a powerful role in cementing community identity. Church attendance is the highest in Europe outside the Irish Republic. Even among those who do not go to church, the rhetoric of religious identity is not distant. As argued by Morrow et al., 'Churches are integrated into the fabric of community lives and provide much of the framework within which apparently secular, social, personal and community life is lived' (1994, p. 19).

Their denominational nature means that an organisation 'makes real social differences between each group and confirms identities' (Morrow et al., 1994). The Churches promote and reinforce notions of deference and obedience, and conformity to a rigid code of sexual behaviour. The sexual division of labour in the Churches, with (predominantly) male clergy and a predominantly female membership whose role is largely confined to domestic tasks, symbolises gender relations in the wider sphere of social and political life.

Gender and Protestantism

The dominant ideologies of Protestantism make a sharp separation between male and female spheres. Protestant Churches according to O'Dowd have 'elevated conjugality over virginity [and] Protestant clergy were more likely to devolve the role of moral guide to husbands and fathers within the family' (1987, pp. 14–15).

Positions of power and influence are dominated by an almost exclusively male clergy. Women play a vital role within the congregation, but are 'marginalised or excluded from power' (Fraser, 1995, p. 23). The women's organisations of the Church reflect the 'picture of the woman as child-rearer and home-maker' (Morrow et al., 1994, p. 23). This domestic sphere is also under male authority. In the words of Ian Paisley, leader of the Free Presbyterian Church, 'I believe that the husband is the head of the wife and the home. I believe that the father should be prophet, priest and king in his home' (cited in Fairweather et al., 1984, p. 266).

Moreover, his wife Eileen Paisley has described herself as 'just a minister's wife. I think the husband is head of the home certainly ... marriage is a partnership with the man at the head' (ibid., p. 274).

This view of womanhood is deeply embedded in evangelical Christianity. In the literature of the temperance movement, women have been depicted as holding 'significant moral authority and moral power' (Brozyna, 1995, p. 160). This authority, however, was confined to the domestic sphere, and did not involve material power (Montgomery and Davies, 1991).

Paisley's Church represents a tiny minority of Protestant congregations. His influence is much broader through his political role as leader of the DUP. Paisley's religious and political movements represent major constituencies within the religious and political life of the province. Furthermore, by being available as a home for dissidents from the Irish Presbyterian Church and the UUP, the movements have acted to retard liberal tendencies in those organisations (Bruce, 1994, p. 21). The ideology promoted by these movements denies women legitimacy in the public sphere. Protestant political organisations perpetuate a strongly male culture, and the bonding rituals of Unionist hegemony, like the Orange Order or the Masons, have totally excluded or diminished the role of women (Gordon, 1990, p. 7).

Women have played a vital support role within the political parties. The Ulster Women's Unionist Council, formed in 1911, involved women in a variety of activities, including public campaigning. These activities allowed the predominantly upper- and middle-class membership to gain 'a sense of freedom and independence which was forbidden to them in other spheres' (Urquart, 1994, p. 116). However, women's role was tightly circumscribed: the Council refused to discuss women's suffrage, and 'no overt encouragement was ever given to women standing for parliamentary election in the period 1918–40' (Urquart, 1995, p. 111). No woman was elected to the Westminster Parliament, and only four to Stormont during its existence. Those women who have become active in politics and stood for elected office have rarely pursued an independent agenda. Councillor Iris Robinson, wife of the DUP deputy leader said that she did not pretend 'to be anything other than a simple housewife, one that loves her country deeply. I don't have any particular skills' (quoted in Hall, 1994, p. 27).

There have been some shifts in more recent years. The official language of equal opportunities has been incorporated into public policy statements. The appointment in 1987 of Rhonda Paisley, Ian Paisley's daughter, as DUP spokesperson for women's issues marked a recognition of the changing realities of women's position in the 1980s. Rhonda Paisley herself, in a piece entitled 'Feminism, Unionism and "the Brotherhood" ' (1992) criticised the male domination of Unionism and called for 'a radical re-think of our involvement in Unionist politics'. She has since resigned as party spokesperson, to be replaced by Iris Robinson.

The conservatism of mainstream politics has made it difficult for some Protestant women to find a positive identity as Protestants. The 'need for loyalty is operating as a regulator of women's lives, structuring their everyday lives, and maintaining their alienation from themselves and other women' (Moore, 1993, p. 78). The strong association of Protestantism with Unionism has meant that those women who have been active in progressive politics, for example in the women's movement or trade unions, have often found it difficult to identify themselves as part of the Protestant community. Protestants who reject Unionism are often assumed to be Catholics, an assumption it has sometimes been easier to leave unchallenged. More recently non-Unionist Protestant women have started to 'come out' as Protestants, and to reclaim a positive identity for themselves which is not based purely on negating their own back-ground and experience. According to Moore, 'Protestant women experience their lives as other, as other to Catholic women and Catholic domination in Ireland as a whole, and the British state and particularly to Protestant men in Northern Ireland' (1993, p. 2).

Conflict and the Protestant Community

National conflicts present contradictory possibilities for women. New opportunities are opened up as women take on roles which men are forced to abandon through imprisonment or military activity. On the other hand, men may step up efforts to control women and try to reinforce the boundary that separates their domain from the public sphere. In Northern Ireland the conflict has brought widening economic, social and political opportuni-ties, together with pressures to conform to traditional values. Inevitably, due to the contested nature of society, the impact and possibilities opened up have been very different for Irish Nation-alist and Unionist women. There has been more space for radical ideas within Irish Nationalism, and women have been more visible in politics, as spokespeople for their community and directly involved in the 'armed struggle' (Edgerton, 1986; Morgan and Fraser, 1995). For Unionists, feminism is associated with 'the other side [and] ... conflated with socialism and nation-alism, even Republicanism, and thus regarded as an object of suspicion' (Morgan and Fraser, 1994, p. 5).

This suspicion has been reinforced by responses to the con-flict from outside Northern Ireland. It has been claimed that:

> very few researchers have seemed to feel that looking in detail at the perceptions of Protestants themselves about the conflict will augment their understanding of the situation substantially ... research students appeared to find Catholics more sympathetic, more fashionable and more interesting subjects of study. (Moxon-Brown, 1983, p. 81)

Journalists are seen as only interested in Catholics, especially as international interest in and sympathy for the Republican hunger strikes developed. Protestants have tended to see intel-lectuals as hostile, which has 'cut them off from resources they could use for their own benefit', such as civil liberty groups (Nelson, 1984). Republican women have developed links with feminists in Britain and elsewhere, which have provided support in their struggle for a women's agenda. Protestants have been largely excluded from these sources of support and ideas. Evidently, such a feeling of betrayal and isolation does not provide a fertile ground for new ideas.

Twenty-five years of military conflict has inevitably had major implications for political priorities and the way politics is pursued. Militarism makes politics more secretive, placing a premium on community loyalty. This makes it difficult, and sometimes dangerous to raise agendas which conflict with the mainstream within the community.

The use of violence against the 'other side' has been sanctioned, or at least tolerated, by large sections of the population. While Republican violence has generally aimed at what they define as 'legitimate targets' (those with some connection with the security forces), Loyalists have more often engaged in purely sectarian killing. Some women have become involved themselves in military activity. There have been a significant number of Republican women prisoners for many years. Sinn Fein Women's Department's pamphlet *Women in Struggle* (1994) celebrates women's involvement in all aspects of the Republican movement, including as 'volunteers'. Some of those mentioned – Mairead Farrell shot dead in Gibraltar, the Price sisters who went on hunger strike in Brixton prison, and Sinn Fein vice-president Maire Drumm – are well-known names throughout Republican circles.

Much less is known about Loyalist women paramilitaries who appear to have had less independence within the movement (Morgan and Fraser, 1995). The Women's UDA was disbanded in 1974 following the murder by some of its members of fellow member Ann Ogilby, a married Protestant woman who took parcels to an unmarried prisoner. Her murder provoked revulsion throughout UDA circles (Fairweather *et al.*, 1984). While punishment of women who transgress has been tolerated among the Loyalist community, the fact that it was women, acting on their own initiative, who carried out this particularly brutal murder may have contributed to the condemnation of the Women's UDA. Due to this event and other circumstances, Loyalist women's activities have centred largely on support for male prisoners, and welfare work. Women whose husbands are imprisoned have had to renegotiate the domestic roles. This has not been easy, as one prisoner's wife explained:

I'm dreading him coming out! He always expected me to be perfect, I think all men do, but I've had to learn to be independent. If he's here he'll be saying I should be doing the dishes ... he's in for a shock, we've changed that much. (Fairweather *et al.*, 1984, p. 301)

As such the two communities have responded very differently to the presence of the security forces on the streets. For Nationalist women, this has been relatively straightforward. The army has been seen as an alien force, provoking hostility and/or indifference. The banging of dustbin lids to warn of the army's approach has been one of the most potent symbols of women's resistance. The experience of community resistance during the early 1970s helped politicise many Nationalist women, and has brought many into community activity. Republican women have also highlighted the specific ways in which women have been intimidated by the security forces, including strip searching and sexual assault (see, for example, Sinn Fein Women's Department, 1994).

The response of Protestant women has been more ambivalent. The army, and even more the police force, are seen as theirs. They did not develop the experience of resistance which has been such a powerful basis for community activism in the Nationalist community. Where conflicts have developed in recent years, the security forces are seen as betraying their own.

Gender Divisions of Labour

Women have experienced a major shift from the private into the public sphere in the past twenty years, as they have gained greater access to the labour market. This has given women greater autonomy and economic independence, making it more possible to challenge patriarchal authority in the home and in the public sphere. The restructuring of the labour market, which has brought more women into the new service-type employment and seen the decline of traditionally male manufacturing jobs, is part of a global process. Its impact has been particularly strong in Northern Ireland, with its peripheral location and its economic dependence on Britain. The economy is increasingly dependent on both public employment and on state support to maintain private employment (Rowthorn and Wayne, 1988; Teague, 1993a).

Women's employment also increased as a result of the expansion of welfare spending which occurred in the 1970s, partly as a response to the Troubles. Although political and economic crisis made it politically impossible to implement the full rigours of Margaret Thatcher's neo-liberal agenda in Northern Ireland, public spending cuts and deregulation have been introduced since the mid-1980s. Northern Ireland is the most economically deprived region in the United Kingdom and unemployment has consistently been above any other UK region (Policy and Planning Research Unit, 1994a).

According to the Equal Opportunities Commission (1993), women in full-time work have increased their share of earnings from just under 70 per cent of the male average in 1974 to just over 80 per cent in 1991. However, much of women's employment is part-time, poorly paid, insecure and largely unprotected by legislation. The official view is that religious inequality in employment is primarily a male problem. The persistence of the male unemployment differential (Catholics are approximately two times more likely to be unemployed than Protestants) has been the main target of policy. Women are assumed to face broadly the same experiences in the labour market. Research has been largely based on this assumption, focusing on either religion or gender. The employment profiles of Catholic women and Protestant women are more similar than those of Catholic and Protestant men. But while religious divisions are so embedded in the structures of economic and social life, they are bound to have implications for women's employment. These take a number of forms.

Women experience different relations in the labour market through their partners. The benefit system assumes women's dependence on the 'family wage' (sufficient to keep a man, dependent wife and children). Unemployed men lose benefit if their wives are employed. The disincentive is particularly strong for part-time work, where the income gained is unlikely to offset benefit losses. The expansion of women's employment has been highest among those married to men in full-time jobs. Women are most likely to be out of the labour force if their husbands are unemployed (McLaughlin, 1986). Because of the higher Catholic male unemployment, Catholic women's labour market activity rate reduced.

Social policy has been geared to the notion of a 'male breadwinner', but Policy Planning Research Unit figures suggest that less than three-quarters of Protestant men, and just over three-fifths of Catholics, are in the minimum position to fulfil this role. Those most able to earn a 'breadwinner wage' are most likely to have a wife in employment, compounding inequalities between households. As shown in Table 7.1 the participation rate among Catholic females is 10 per cent lower than for Protestant women.

Sectarianism also creates obstacles to workplace organisation, especially within mixed workplaces. The official trade union movement has found it extremely difficult to confront sectarianism. Until recently complaints of discrimination at work were liable to be dismissed as sectarian themselves (Rolston, 1981). In formal terms, the situation has changed substantially due to the implementation of fair employment legislation and the campaign against sectarianism launched by the Irish Congress of Trade Unions. However, at times the issue of fair employment has proved more intractable at branch level. One Catholic branch secretary, who felt she had been discriminated against, informed the author that raising the issue was 'too sensitive', as she felt that Protestant members would 'think I was raising it because I'm a Catholic and it would tear the branch apart'. Another union officer, when interviewed, was concerned that 'Protestants reject anti-government statements, because they think I'm getting at "their" government' (Interview: August, 1995).

This attitude promotes obstacles which impede discussions which might be considered part of normal trade union branch life. Most trade unionists still prefer to ignore religious divisions within their membership, and to act as if 'all that' was

Table 7.1 Activity, Unemployment and Employment by Religion and Gender, 1993 (% share)

	Protestant Male	Female	Catholic Male	Female
Activity Rate	83	64	80	55
Unemployment	11	7	23	11
In work	73	59.5	61.6	49

Source: Policy Planning Research Unit, 1994b

left outside the workplace (Campbell *et al.*, 1990). But this attitude, however well meaning, precludes confrontation of the issue, or of wider political debate. The workplace is potentially an important arena for organising in support of women's rights. Sectarianism has however made this a minefield, with many people preferring to avoid potentially dangerous or difficult issues.

Women and Political Organisation

Northern Ireland's current constitutional position has created a political vacuum, in which local people have little control over decision making. The formal political process has been dominated by the sectarian divide, with voters overwhelmingly giving allegiance to parties from their 'own side'. This construction of politics around community loyalties gives little space for raising issues of specific concern to women, particularly where they challenge the established view within the community (Birrell, 1983).

Although women have been, and continue to be, largely excluded from formal politics and the traditional parties, they have nevertheless become increasingly active in informal organisations. The range of organisations in which women participate is enormous, as is the degree to which these organisations have tended to reinforce women's traditional role or to challenge it. A common feature has been the reluctance to discuss 'sensitive issues', and an avoidance of potentially difficult areas. The organisations involving the largest numbers of women have been locally based groups which are not explicitly political, including charities, professional, social and leisure groups. These are often based around a local church (Morrow *et al.*, 1994). A study by Morgan and Fraser (1994) of women in informal organisations found that, even in mixed areas, these groups tend to have a membership almost exclusively of one community reflecting segregated social networks. Although religious differences were rarely absent, the Troubles were rarely discussed. Avoidance is constantly expressed in the phrase 'religion doesn't matter'. Fear of giving offence means that programmes tend to be resolutely uncontroversial, many emphasising the domestic role. These organisations therefore provided little space for overcoming barriers, even where membership is mixed.

The 1970s saw the development of feminist movements which challenged the conventional view of women's role, particularly on the control of sexuality. The Northern Ireland women's movement has faced enormous difficulties. As noted, the Churches have sustained a strongly conservative family ideology, which is underpinned by some of the most restrictive legislation in Europe. In addition, women face opposition from their own communities if they challenge community beliefs. Protestant women face a powerful fundamentalist opposition to demands for sexual freedom. Feminism is seen as alien to sections of the Protestant community and associated with Republicanism. One community worker, when interviewed, was threatened by people claiming to be speaking for Loyalist paramilitaries when she raised women's issues in 'their' area. She was told, 'watch your back, Fenian lover.'

The women's movement, like feminist campaigns everywhere, has split on grounds of ideology and tactics. But the sectarian divide has often been at the root of these divisions, and has proved the most intractable (Roulston, 1989). The Northern Ireland Women's Rights Movement, founded in 1975, has played a major role in feminist campaigning. The movement attempted to develop a strategy that would 'unite women from all political traditions or none' (Roulston, 1989, p. 225) and specifically engage working-class women. It avoided taking a position on the political situation, but this proved difficult to sustain since the priorities for its campaign by implication suggested that great progress could be made within the existing political framework. A split soon developed, with the formation of the Socialist Women's Group which believed that women should campaign against British rule, arguing that imperialism is crucial in sustaining women's oppression. Divisions became more intense during the hunger strike, when the issue of support for female Republican prisoners in Armagh jail 'became a metaphor for everything that has kept Irish women divided from each other' (Ward, 1991, p. 156).

By 1980 feminists were frustrated at their inability to develop a programme which could encompass all women's struggles without the danger of sectarian splits. The movement nevertheless achieved some notable successes. Divorce became easier in 1978, and the Equal Pay and Sex Discrimination Acts were transferred to Northern Ireland. The Equal Opportunities Commission for Northern Ireland (established under Sex Discrimination Act legislation) has been more proactive than the

equivalent organisation in Britain due to it being reprieved
from abolition after successful lobbying (McWilliams, 1991).
Legislation on domestic violence was amended in 1980, and
women's refuges started to gain funding and support. The
Northern Ireland Abortion Law Reform Association (NIALRA)
held a successful tribunal in 1987 to 'challenge the hypocrisy
of society' on the issue (NIALRA, 1989). Its campaign for the
introduction of the 1967 Abortion Act into Northern Ireland
has so far been unsuccessful.

The early 1980s saw women devoting their energies to more
practical issues as the possibility of building a united movement continued to elude them. Local women's centres have
been established across Northern Ireland, providing advice and
support for women, and a base for a range of activities, including research about women's needs, and education classes. While
explicitly feminist movements involved a relatively small
number of women, these centres have involved a much wider
spectrum. May Blood, Chair of the Shankill Women's Forum,
was part of a delegation of women's groups to an international
women's conference in Boston. Other delegates expressed
surprise that the women from Northern Ireland were mainly
working class, in contrast to the mainly middle-class delega-
tions from elsewhere.

Community organisations in which women have played an
active role have developed alongside the women's centres.
These developed as a response to the appalling problems of
social deprivation, particularly in the inner city. The Lower
Ormeau Road Drop-In Centre has its origins in campaigning
from the early 1970s against poverty, when women from the
area organised protests to City Hall. Work in the community
has traditionally been a 'safer' area for women's activity, not
quite part of the formal, public sphere. Community groups also
provide a space for more radical groups and individuals for
whom the concerns and practices of the formal political parties
hold no attractions (Nelson, 1984).

Protestant women were slower to become involved in community organisations. However, though Catholics still dominate
the 'community development' field, a substantial network of
both women's centres and community centres has developed in
Protestant areas. The Shankill Women's Forum was established
in 1994 to provide a focus for women in the area and a great
deal of work has been done investigating the needs of local
women.

The majority of these groups are in either Protestant or Catholic areas, and tend to serve one community or the other. The only women's centre in 'neutral territory' in Belfast is the Down Town Women's Centre in the city centre. This is also the most explicitly feminist. For other centres based within tight-knit communities, raising issues such as abortion, or lesbian rights would be problematic. They are dependent on their communities for support. The Lower Ormeau Road centre, for example, describe their position as 'family feminist'. As they have become more established with paid staff, they are increasingly dependent on funding, including funding from official sources. The Shankill Woman's Centre, for example, has recently moved into new and expanded premises within the Shankill Centre. Its Annual Report of 1995 nevertheless describes a range of activities outside the more traditional notions of appropriate activities for Protestant women, including classes in Women and Irish and trips to the Gaeltacht in the Irish Republic. Its programme of meetings has raised a number of extremely sensitive issues, including domestic violence and child abuse.

Women are working hard to overcome community divisions. The Women's Information Group organises monthly meetings in women's centres, alternating between Protestant and Catholic areas. A range of issues of concern to women are discussed in meetings which often involve between 150 and 200 women. Another notable example of co-operation was the joint approach by Falls and Shankill Women's Centres to Belfast City Council when funding for the Falls Centre was cut off; this led to the formation of the Women's Support Network.

A common theme expressed by staff at these centres was that they do not discuss the political situation. Even when the peace process was several months old, few discussed the issue openly, as it tended to be avoided in informal discussion in the centres. Great strides have been made in building co-operation, and in developing a range of services for women. But this approach does not allow a direct confrontation of sectarianism. While the issue is avoided, it does not necessarily become less virulent. Staff at the centres were able to point to the continuing hold of sectarian ideas among users of their centres. In 1994 one group of Protestant women retracted an invitation to a community activist, although this was not the ostensible reason, staff believed it was because she was a Protestant married to a Catholic.

Conclusion

Women have made substantial moves into the public sphere, both in employment and in the largely informal politics of community groups and women's centres. Men increasingly recognise women as 'the backbone of the community', although as one woman community worker asked, 'Are we going to be ousted when the men come out of jail?' Women remain nevertheless largely excluded from the formal political process, and this exclusion is evident in the lack of involvement, particularly of Protestant women, in the current negotiations around the peace process. As one group stated when interviewed:

> Women had no say in the peace negotiations ... they believe that women's concerns were important and need to be heard, and that women on both sides of the political and religious divide were more compassionate and tolerant than men and more ready to try to understand different points of view. (Interview: August, 1995)

But women cannot speak with one voice. The Peace People of the 1970s quickly built up enormous support on the basis that women could talk to each other where men had failed, and that if they stood together they could stop the violence. The energy and commitment soon dissipated as women were forced to take a position on security force violence, terrorism and traditional political divisions.

For many Protestant women there is a feeling of loss. The majority feel a strong British identity, but feel that Britain has let them down. There is an ambivalence about the future, with on the one hand a determination to hang on to their Britishness, but on the other a feeling of resignation to what they see as the inevitability of a united Ireland. Many Protestant women have and are losing trust in their traditional leaders, and many are consciously learning from the experience of Catholics in organising around new community politics. This new situation opens the space for more progressive politics, but, especially if little change is delivered, it could also produce a hardening of sectarian attitudes.

Women have started to talk to each other across the sectarian divide, but there is a need to go beyond avoidance of politics. Perhaps men have been supportive of women's community organisations precisely because they have not engaged in mainstream political debates, and can therefore be marginalised. The cessation of violence offers an opportunity to face divisions with 'dangerous honesty' (Inez McCormack in 1986, cited in Ward, 1991, p. 161) so that women's concerns can be placed at the heart of any new agenda for the future.

8 'Flying the One-Winged Bird': Ulster Unionism and the Peace Process

James McAuley

It is the latest stage of a malicious scheme by successive British Governments to push Northern Ireland out of the Union.

Revd William McCrea, DUP

It is a dishonourable blueprint for an all-Ireland.

Ken Maginnis, UUP

The Framework Document is not the basis for a settlement in Northern Ireland.

David Ervine, PUP

In order to create the conditions required for Unionist acquiescence, it was necessary to bring about a cease-fire. If this could be obtained, its benefits might be skilfully used to persuade a war weary populace to accept almost anything.

Robert McCartney, MP

Most people in Northern Ireland, and far beyond, have welcomed an end to 25 years of physical conflict. Yet, clearly, as the quotations above indicate, large sections of the Ulster Unionist community have approached what has become known as the 'peace process' with extreme reticence. Their response has, overtly at least, been one of unified resistance and mutual hostility. This was highlighted by the pictures, seen world-wide during the summer of 1996, of thousands of Orangemen in Drumcree bedecked in full marching regalia and claiming their 'right' to march anywhere in Northern Ireland. Those marchers, for around 72 hours, found themselves in a 'stand-off' with massed ranked forces of the Royal Ulster Constabulary barring their 'traditional' route in an effort to 'keep the peace'. This for many Unionists simply confirmed their worst fears. Indeed, according to several leading Unionists, the RUC were acting directly 'under Dublin orders'. Within the Unionist mind, their very identity was being threatened by a 'conspiracy' between the Irish and Westminster Governments. This was no simple difference over the route of a march, but rather a focal point in the 'final conflict' for Ulster.

There have, indeed, been many points of conformity in the Unionist rejoinder to the 'peace process'. Not least of these have been clear expressions of fear for the future of the Union. One notion that has continued to surface is that of a 'deal', which has been struck between the British and Irish governments and the Republican movement, in order to break the link between Northern Ireland and the rest of the United Kingdom. This has led many Unionists to conclude that the Framework Document was 'unacceptable', that one could not be a Unionist and negotiate within the terms of this Framework Document and that all efforts must be put into its opposition.

In reality, however, the pragmatic Unionist response has been more fragmented and varied, reflecting the nature of Unionism itself. This chapter will highlight the position of several major groupings: politicians, paramilitary groups, paramilitary prisoners and 'ordinary people', acting through community-based groups. The broad response of these groupings appears to be have converged around four major political locations: 'liberal' Unionism, 'traditional' Unionism, 'hard-line' Unionism and 'community' Unionism. These are not mutually exclusive positions, nor can they be directly equated with any particular party political grouping. None the less, they do mark the range of responses within Unionism. This chapter will briefly consider each in relation to an overview of the politics of contemporary Unionism.

Political Unionism

What then has been the main retort of the Unionist political leadership to the 'peace process'? Predictably, to the fore in the most candid opposition have been the DUP. Initially, they pledged to lead a sturdy campaign against 'the deal', claiming it as clear evidence of another 'sell-out', part of 'a dastardly scheme

to remove Northern Ireland from the Union' (Allister, 1988 and
1989). According to Peter Robinson, for example, the British
Government was engaged in 'an exercise of devilishly devised
constitutional engineering', designed so that 'the People' of
Northern Ireland were 'progressively conveyed towards all-
Ireland rule'. He believed this to be part of a long-term process,
further claiming that:

> The DUP warnings about the Government's intention and the trend
> underpinning the previous policy documents has been completely
> justified by the publication of the Framework Document. The DUP
> got it right each time and the Ulster people need to follow the advice
> of those whose judgement has been proved sound rather than those
> who got it wrong in 1980 and 1983. (1995, p. 15)

DUP thinking was clearly reflected in the publication, just ahead
of the Framework Document, of their own document, *Formula for
Political Progress* (DUP, 1996). This proposed the election of a
Northern Ireland Convention, which would discuss matters of
North–South concern with Dublin. The Government of the Irish
Republic, however, would be excluded from any involvement in
the internal matters of the United Kingdom. Anything else
would represent 'a total and absolute surrender to the Nationalist
agenda' (*Irish Times*, 21 February 1995).

Such notions have proved important in structuring the
DUP response. Almost every contested political event in recent
months has been reconstructed to provide 'evidence' for this
perceived sell-out. Hence, for example, the DUP bitterly
attacked the Northern Ireland Office over its handling of the
royal visit in March 1995. Paisley claimed that the policy of
not playing the National Anthem or permitting Union flags to
be waved was an 'insult' to 'the People' of Northern Ireland,
the throne, the monarchy and the Queen herself. Another DUP
source argued that the Northern Ireland Office had removed
the 'symbols of our nation'. Overall, the DUP have dismissed
the 'peace' process as a 'peace of surrender', and the decision of
the IRA to call a cease-fire as a mere 'tactical manoeuvre'. In a
statement issued by the party's executive the underlying
message was that the British Government could not be trusted:

> The British Government lied about its secret contacts with the IRA
> for two years, it lied about clarification of the Downing Street Decla-
> ration, and the Protestant community in particular simply cannot

believe that same Government has offered no concessions, no deals,
no bargain in return for the so-called cease-fire. (in possession of
author)

While the public face of the Ulster Unionist Party welcomed
the IRA cease-fire declaration, it was hardly with candour.
James Molyneaux, in the immediate post-cease-fire period,
spent much time issuing public assurances that 'no secret deals
had been done', and that the Ulster Unionists had not been
involved in any backstage negotiation. In broad terms, the
UUP continued to contend that the IRA cease-fire was of
extremely limited political value. Further, they continued to
insist that the guidelines for any further discussions should be
those parameters set out in the Downing Street Declaration.
Pragmatically, the issue of IRA weapons became central for the
Ulster Unionists, as they called for the immediate handover of
all paramilitary armaments and weapons.

Much of the Ulster Unionist response in the weeks after the
cease-fires surrounded debates concerning official legislation
and the fine detail of government publications. The parliamentary agreement and supposed 'special relationship' between the
Ulster Unionists and John Major's administration was also
clearly of some significance at this time. Overarching this,
however, was the belief that the issues on hand remained
'internal' to the United Kingdom, and a refusal to acknowledge
any wider 'international' dimensions to the peace process. The
focal point for Ulster Unionists remained firmly fixed on the
link with the UK and the make-up of any future devolved
administrative assembly in Northern Ireland. The present
leader of the UUP, David Trimble, set out the Ulster Unionist
agenda:

> We don't see any point in discussing what we would regard as a
> purely Nationalist agenda. If that is what the framework document
> is, then I'm afraid it, like so many other foolish documents of the
> past, will end up consigned to the dustbin ... It is our duty to renew
> the warnings in the hope the Government will reverse out of the
> cul-de-sac it has got itself into. (The *Independent*, 16 February 1995)

The mechanism for this resistance was thus seen as the UK
Parliament. Hence, until his resignation, James Molyneaux,
constantly called on the Commons to 'produce another consultative paper on which there could be widespread agreement'.

This was seen as their key response to the Framework Document. As such, it reflected a strongly traditionalist agenda set out by the Ulster Unionists. That is not to say that Unionism was completely ossified in its response. The election of Robert McCartney as an independent, United Kingdom Unionist, in a by-election for North Down, was hailed by some as a victory for 'liberal Unionism'. That said, he too articulated the clear view that the 'peace process' was part of a conspiracy against Unionists and the Union. Further, a central task of the British Government has been to promote 'propaganda to persuade the pro-Union majority that the benefits of the cease-fire are a fair price for the sacrifice of its British identity' (*News Letter*, 23 February 1995).

For McCartney, the proposed strategy for political settlement outlined in the Framework Document long pre-dated the cease-fire. The suspension of violence, however, was a necessary precondition for 'selling' it to Unionists. He therefore drew the following conclusions:

> The British Government has, at the least, offered a conditional surrender to the IRA. Peace on these terms could have been obtained at any time over the past twenty-five years. In the interim the dead have died in vain and the maimed remain mutilated for nothing. In an attempt to stand truth upon its head, the Unionist people who have suffered largely in silence will be castigated by the propaganda machines of both governments as negative obstacles to peace. Those who have bombed, murdered and maimed will be presented as peacemakers while the victims will be blackmailed with a resumption of violence if they do not acquiesce in the destruction of the Union. The good and the great, both lay and clerical, will be called in aid by the British political establishment to lend their voices to a constitutional conspiracy. (*Belfast Telegraph*, 6 June 1995)

McCartney, having taken this as his starting point has offered some important internal criticisms of Unionism. He claimed, for example, that since 1921, the Unionist Party has relied on two main factors: an in-built Unionist majority, and the manipulation of pro-Union paranoia about Northern Ireland's place within the United Kingdom. This constitutional anxiety was compensated for by an extreme sectarian loyalism. It is this McCartney challenges, arguing that if the benefits of the Union are to be made clear, and the Union is to be preserved, then there must be dramatic changes. In some senses what he seeks to project is Unionism with a human face; an articulation of the maintenance of the link with Britain, but with a high priority given to issues of social concern. Indeed, before his election, McCartney openly expressed support for 'New' Labour's social policies (The *Guardian*, 13 June 1995; *Belfast Telegraph*, 15 June 1995). There was much serious discussion in the days before his election as to whether McCartney would take the Labour whip at Westminster. Something that, in the end, he did not do.

Paramilitaries and the Peace Process

Central and fundamental to the dynamic of the Unionist response to the 'peace process' has been the position taken by Loyalist paramilitary organisations, especially the Ulster Defence Association (UDA) and the Ulster Volunteer Force (UVF). Their initial response was far from positive, maintaining as they did their military campaign, and murdering a Catholic man on the first day of the IRA truce. Within the next few weeks they were also responsible for bomb attacks on Sinn Fein's Falls Road office and at Connolly Station in Dublin. There were no automatic demands from within Loyalist paramilitaries for a cease-fire to follow their Republican counterparts.

This needs to be set in some context. Both the UVF and the UDA have expressed the belief in recent times, and certainly up to the point of the cease-fire, that their primary task was to engage in their own brand of 'counter-terrorism', and to 'terrorise the terrorists'. In reality, the focus of such campaigns has often been nakedly sectarian, targeting ordinary Catholics. Within the Loyalist paramilitary mind, however, such attacks were believed to be one way of isolating the IRA within its own community. As one UDA leader put it recently in seeking to explain the motivation behind such actions:

> The Catholic community as a whole had a major responsibility for the actions of the IRA. The IRA themselves said 'the day the wee woman on the Falls Road comes out and throws the rifle she has been minding onto the street, we will know we are in trouble'. (*Irish News*, 15 October 1995)

Led largely by an important internal grouping, most of whom were highly politicised by imprisonment in the 1970s and

1980s, the paramilitaries began to formulate a more coherent political response. In the weeks that followed, the contours of response of the Combined Loyalist Military Command (CLMC), representing the two major Loyalist paramilitary groupings, the UDA and the UVF, began to take shape. They sought answers to a number of key questions, including 'whether the IRA cease-fire was permanent; whether there were any 'secret deals' between IRA and the British Government, and whether Northern Ireland's position within the UK was assured' (*Belfast Telegraph*, 14 October 1994).

The Loyalist paramilitaries' response exemplified that of the wider Unionist community. It reflected, on the one hand, the suspicion of a 'dirty deal' between the British Government and the IRA. On the other, there was the understanding that the longer the IRA cease-fire continued, the more intense the pressure on Loyalist paramilitaries to respond positively would become. Finally, six weeks and one day after the IRA announced its cease-fire, the CLMC said that they would reciprocate, further declaring that the Loyalist cease-fire would be permanent unless Republican paramilitaries were to resume violence.

While the primary focus and actions of Loyalist paramilitaries have always been military there has also been a core political dimension, often crudely expressed, from within such organisations. That said, the contemporary political thinking of the Ulster Democratic Party (UDP) and the PUP can only be understood within the context of a distinct historical development.

'New Loyalism'?

So do the political parties that have emerged from the Loyalist paramilitaries mark a turning point? The UDA has since its formation been composed of a number of groupings, often stressing contradictory directions (McAuley, 1991a, 1991b and 1994). At various points throughout the organisation's history the UDA have sought to project a coherent political programme. Since the mid-1980s, however, their formal political project has been structured by the guidelines set out in a document entitled *Common Sense*, which amongst much else proposed the establishment of a devolved government in Northern Ireland on a power-sharing basis.

In the months following the IRA cease-fire there was clearly a further calibration in the organisation. Key individuals in the

UDA and UDP had attempted to move the UDA away from a purely military emphasis. This re-emphasis on the 'political' was seen by many as a necessary step to both counter what was seen as a Sinn Fein-set schedule and the continuing marginalisation of the paramilitaries from the political process. This basis for their political programme, however, remains somewhat dated, the *Common Sense* document now being over a decade old.

The other political grouping which has come to notoriety in Protestant working-class districts is the Progressive Unionist Party (PUP). It is this group which is most closely associated with the UVF, and which marks the latest in a series of attempts that this organisation has made to develop a political voice since 1974. Over the past two decades, the PUP has sought to create a political identity. At various times, it has described itself as a 'Socialist Unionist Party' and a 'fiercely British Party'. In recent years it has promoted a variety of policies including support for the organisation of 'British' political parties in Northern Ireland, the introduction of a Bill of Rights and the development of an integrated educational system. It has also promoted increased cross-border co-operation in non-executive matters such as agriculture, tourism, fishing and energy, and a series of detailed plans for the implementation of devolved government in Northern Ireland.

The contemporary PUP is highly captious in its relationship with the traditional Unionist political leadership. In particular, it is antagonistic towards the DUP and Ian Paisley as being isolated from the grassroots response to the 'peace process'. It has constantly claimed, for example, that Paisley and the DUP are unrealistic in the way they have sought to develop Unionist politics. It is, in particular, critical of the decision of the mainstream Unionists to 'exclude' themselves from the 'peace process', claiming that this has destroyed the possibility of any unified Unionist response.

While the PUP has, at times, remained rather indeterminate in its broad response to the 'peace process', it clearly is hostile to the leadership offered by 'traditional' and 'hard-line' political Unionism. It is also highly conscious of the fears expressed by the broader Loyalist working-class community that forms its main constituents. Indeed, it constantly project itself as the true representative of working-class Loyalist opinion (Bell, 1976 and 1984; Boulton, 1973).

Loyalist Prisoners

Vital to the dynamic of the paramilitary response to the 'peace process', and that of both the PUP and UDP, has been the position of Loyalist paramilitary prisoners. A continual proposition, manifest in the output of Loyalist paramilitary members for some time, has been their disillusionment at the lack of support given to them by Unionist politicians. This has especially been the case regarding those campaigns organised in recent years by prisoners' support groups over such issues as prison conditions and the physical segregation of Loyalist and Republican prisoners. There has also been constant criticism from within Loyalist paramilitary circles that it was their political leadership that manipulated or directed them into engaging in violent activities in the first place. Those politicians generated the situation, then washed their hands of them, condemning the paramilitaries for interpreting their calls too literally.

A conduit by which Loyalist prisoners would be able to express their views was, therefore, always likely to be of utmost importance, in any resolution. It was in this role that both the PUP and UDP came to prominence. UDA prisoners appeared, initially at least, to have been less willing to accept the notion of a cease-fire. This fell in line with the view of their Inner Council at the time, that the whole process marked a facilitation by the British Government to the Pan-Nationalist front. Within UVF ranks, the views of prisoners have always carried much weight, partly due to the UVF being a smaller organisation, and therefore the proportion of prisoners has always been higher. While the reaction of UVF prisoners could hardly be described as welcoming, they were keener to accept the notion of a cease-fire as part of an 'honourable' resolution to the conflict. They were 'guided' in this by an older, more politicised element within the PUP. According to several reports, however, the Loyalist cease-fire would never have occurred when it did, had it not found favour with Loyalist prisoners.

Underlying the willingness of both groups to support a cease-fire was the ability of key persons to convince them that in the background there was no mechanism for Irish Government 'interference'. As the cease-fires became established, the future of hundreds of 'political prisoners' moved to centre stage. Loyalist paramilitaries are currently calling for the implementation of an early release system, under the campaigning slogan of 'Free the prisoners – Free the process'. It is likely that this issue will reveal further fissures between the paramilitaries and traditional Unionist politicians.

Communitarian Unionism

Some of the most important consequences of the 'peace process' have been its effects at the community level. The consent of the Protestant working class, at least tacitly, was always crucial in ensuring any peaceful rejoinder to the issuing of the Framework Document. While there was obvious relief at the end to violence, in political terms, the broad response of working-class Protestants has been confused. At its most fundamental level their sense of Unionism has always rested on a sense of difference, of 'Britishness'. However, reaction to the 'peace process' has highlighted that there is no firm conception of what this means anymore within working-class Unionism. Certainly it does not mean accepting the legitimacy or political authority of the British state. This position has been manifest since the signing of the Anglo-Irish Agreement and reinforced throughout the contemporary peace process.

One consequence of recent events has been the opening up of disjunctions within Unionism. Evidence that this process is in operation, even if only to a limited extent, exists at several levels. It has been seen directly, for example, in the discussions and debates organised by community activists in Loyalist districts in the months following the cease-fires (Hall, 1995).

One optimistic reading of the 'peace process' is that the cease-fires have opened up some room for debate within Loyalist communities. This may be the experience of those groupings who have been particularly marginalised, such as Protestant women. Whilst recognising that this is a highly diverse grouping, a common experience is that they have been excluded from any visible participation in the public arena (McAuley, 1994). Certainly, there appears to be some recent evidence, albeit largely anecdotal, that Loyalist women may be creating the opportunity to discuss their own identity and social relations in a more meaningful way, in the absence of overt paramilitary violence.

A fuller flavour of the contemporary debates at the community level can be gleaned from the publication, *Beyond the Fife and Drum*, following a conference organised by Ian Paisley, Jnr, in 1994. The headings under which the event was reported are themselves illuminating: 'What is a Protestant'; 'Protestant Culture – What Culture?'; 'Next Century Unionism? – the potential for 2020 and beyond'. Such topics have hardly been central to Unionist discourse throughout the past quarter of a century.

While much of the above can be regarded as positive, within Loyalist heartlands, negative feelings have also been openly expressed. At one level these involve a clear perception of political alienation and marginalisation, both politically and socially, of the Protestant working class, from contemporary events. As one report compiled by leading community activists put it:

> The Protestant working class feels increasingly isolated by its enemies and betrayed by its friends. All shades of Nationalist opinion have now openly joined forces to either coerce or gradually prise the Protestant community away from its 'Britishness'. And the British on the mainland never really cared that much anyway. (Hall et al., 1994, p. 23)

At another level, there has been the openly articulated view that too many concessions have been made to Sinn Fein and the 'Pan-Nationalist Front'. That this feeling exists in the wider Protestant community was highlighted recently, when leading members of the Presbyterian Church, led by Moderator Dr John Ross, met with the Prime Minister, to voice their concerns about the direction that the 'peace process' was taking. Just before the formal meeting, the Revd Samuel Hutchinson, General Secretary of the Presbyterian Church in Ireland, said they would be reporting a change of mood among many Protestants. He claimed that many believed that 'the ship of state has [been] tilted towards the South not London' and that there was a broad perception that 'ever since the Anglo-Irish Agreement most of the concessions have been one sided, and a bird with one wing can't fly' (cited in Graham, 1995, p. 32).

There have then been a variety of signals from community groups and community organisations over the past few years. One important set of messages surrounds the discontent of many 'ordinary' Protestants with the political representatives of Unionism. Many have been increasingly rearticulating the view that the fears of many grassroots Protestants have been fuelled by Unionist politicians who have cared little for the real needs of the working class. There is then some evidence of a shift back towards the community as the basis for political expression for the Protestant working class. Does this mark a sea change? Some recognition by the Protestant working class that 'traditional' Unionist parties cannot represent their interests? To fully explain this, it is necessary to consider the place of contemporary events within the Loyalist 'worldview'.

Paramilitaries and the Protestant Working Class

The two groupings – the paramilitaries and the DUP – that have always claimed to speak for working-class loyalism, have historically occupied different if sometimes overlapping positions in the politics of the Protestant working class. In broad terms, the attitude of such communities to Loyalist paramilitaries, and their violence, has always been ambivalent. However, the paramilitaries have always been at their strongest when they have been able to claim some legitimate role as 'defenders of Ulster' (witness the Ulster Workers' Council strike of 1974), and as part of the community they have claimed to defend (Fisk, 1975). Overarching all the different roles fulfilled by the Loyalist paramilitaries has always been the need for such organisations to justify their very existence. The transition from 'soldiers' to political representatives has been open to widespread suspicion. This is particularly the case within the very Protestant working-class communities they claim to represent. Since the cease-fires, however, both the PUP and UDP do appear to have offered some alternative to working-class Unionists.

Clearly this has not been well received by all Unionists. Tensions still remain. For example, although the Ulster Freedom Force (UFF) has expressed its support for the progress made by its political wing, the UDP, it has continued to voice concern regarding the wider direction taken by Unionism (*Irish News*, 13 October 1995). The UFF still claims to feel deluded by politicians and their lack of concern for Loyalist prisoners in particular. In the same interview, it offered sharp criticism of the DUP leader Ian Paisley, whom it claims was 'stuck in the same old ranting mode. It is getting monotonous for Loyalists. He used us in the past but he will not be using us in the future' (*Irish News*, 13 October 1995).

Indeed, both the UDP and PUP remain unconvinced of the leadership qualities of the traditional Unionist politicians. Here the UDP summarises its views on the last quarter-century:

> The larger political parties have tried to bring peace to our troubled land and failed. For 25 years these groupings have retreated in the face of British Government pressure without fighting back using realistic political principals. For 25 years they have allowed the Pan Nationalist Front to set the agenda. (*New Ulster Defender*, Vol. 1, No. 13)

The views currently being expressed by the PUP, UDP and those who have acted as spokespersons for Loyalist paramilitaries must be set against the expanse of opinions and options currently on offer to Protestant workers. This has been recognised from a variety of sources. Hence, exactly one year after the Loyalist paramilitaries called a cease-fire the *Irish News* wrote the following:

> The political representatives of loyalism have distinguished themselves by making a positive contribution to the debate. Unlike representatives of the two main Unionist parties, they have been prepared to take their arguments to 'the People' who matter both in the United States and in Ireland.
>
> It could be said that one of the most important contributions the Ulster Democratic and Progressive Unionist parties have made this past year is forcing the other Unionist groups to look again at their tactics. That is welcome. Unionism has been badly served by politicians who have refused to engage with others. Both the UDP and the PUP deserve considerable credit for breaking that mould. (*Irish News*, 13 October 1995)

Crucial in this process is the willingness, or not, by at least some sections of the Protestant working class, to reassess their own position, and to challenge the authority of the established Unionist political leadership. Certainly, there are those who still wish to reinforce the traditional Unionist agenda. It is here that the DUP has remained to the fore. The reaction of this section of Loyalism was predictable. Criticism of the Unionist position, either external or internal, no matter how constructive, has been condemned as heresy and weakness.

The Reconstruction of Contemporary Loyalism

Who speaks for the Protestant working class in the contemporary period? The DUP has consistently talked in terms of 'Unionist alienation', arguing that the British Government has 'psychologically abandoned Northern Ireland' and that they 'plan to physically disengage as soon as circumstances permit a total withdrawal' (*New Protestant Telegraph*, 12 June 1995).

This can be seen as a consistent line from the DUP, since at least the signing of the Anglo-Irish Agreement in 1985. It is a common view amongst DUP members that it has largely been their actions, and particularly the leadership of Ian Paisley, which have stopped Westminster 'selling out' Ulster into an All-Ireland. The DUP has for some years regarded the British Government as being in 'default'. A decade ago, it was expressed in the *Protestant Blue Print*:

> [The DUP] reaffirms the party's total and undivided commitment to stepping up the campaign of opposition to the [Anglo-Irish] Agreement which has effectively established joint authority over this province. Democracy has been rejected ...
>
> If the government persists in forcing this undemocratic and unworkable agreement down the throats of the Ulster people against their wills then the consequences will be upon their own heads. The Ulster Unionist people are not turning for the price of acquiescence is the destruction of Northern Ireland as part of the United Kingdom. (1986, p. 2)

Central to the self-image of the DUP is the claim that it is they who will take action to 'defend Ulster against its enemies'. Another factor in this self-projection is of the DUP as unified in opposition. The Framework Document as drawn up by the British and Irish Governments cannot even be on the agenda. Those who dissent from this, including the UDP and PUP, are branded as guilty of 'treachery', involved in a 'pan-Nationalist inspired peace process', or 'dupes of the Northern Ireland Office'. Rather there must be no sign of compromise. Indeed, for the DUP the present policy

> has elevated Nationalism and ... Republicanism and has alienated Unionism. The British Government are running to embrace the apologists for murder and are dismissing the representatives of 'the

People'. Only those Unionists in the fringe parties who parrot the
Government's lies and fall for the Sinn Fein strategy by complying
with the peace process only they will be accorded a place because
they pose no threat to the political machinations of this Government.
(*New Protestant Telegraph*, June 1995, p. 2)

In trying to dismiss these groups it is Paisley who still seeks
to project himself as true defender of the Unionist cause. Any
form of negotiation with the Republican movement or the Irish
Government represents 'surrender' and may lead to the possibility of ultimate defeat. Further, the British Government cannot be trusted to secure Northern Ireland's future in the UK.
This was made clear by Paisley himself when he stated, 'Far
from being a bulwark of the Union, its aim is the breaking of
the Union. It triggered off a whole series of capitulations by
the Government' (*Belfast Telegraph*, 19 December 1994).

The implications from this are clear. Anyone beyond the
DUP cannot be trusted to defend Northern Ireland's constitutional position. This view has been increasingly and strongly
repeated in the contemporary period.

The Political Future – 'New' and 'Old' Unionism?

Despite its attempt to project a unified response, therefore,
Unionism is clearly in some state of flux. Immediately following the cease-fires the DUP appeared to have failed in its
attempt to assume its usual central role in the Loyalist
response. It was marginalised, both ideologically and pragmatically, in terms of its actions at a local level. Unlike in
the past, Paisley was unable to reconstruct hegemonic Unionism under his direct control. Indeed, those closest to the
paramilitaries came, at times, to the fore in representing
working-class Loyalism.

In response, the DUP has continued to project the 'crisis'
surrounding the 'peace process' as 'the final conflict' in the
battle for Ulster. There remain several items on the political
agenda that are not open to any future negotiations. These
surround several core issues: a reconfirmation of Northern Ireland's constitutional position within the UK, all legislation for
Northern Ireland should be included in UK Bills, a return of
local control to politicians in Northern Ireland, and no 'special
place' for Dublin (*Belfast Telegraph*, 28 August 1994).

What is the appeal of this perspective? Protestant working-class consciousness and ideology is, of course, not stable or homogeneous. Such ideology is fragmentary, internally contradictory and built on the incomplete forms of thought which people use to make sense of their everyday lives. It is within these frames of thought that everyday political calculations and decisions are made. It is at this level that the Protestant working class make sense of their social worlds by use of 'common-sense' ideas and explanations.

The reproduction of such 'common-sense' ideas has always helped explain the success of the DUP. This has become clearer as fuller negotiations around the 'peace process' have developed. One of the major appeals of the DUP to the Protestant masses has always been its promise to defend 'Ulster', in whatever is its current hour of need. The evidence for this 'defence' is based on reference to strong links with the past, particularly those elements of Irish history that have been selected to form the coherent self-conception of Protestant Unionist identity. It is this direct link into this strong collective identity and the broad sets of ideas within the community which explains the DUP success. Within the context of everyday values and beliefs it is the DUP who is still best able to articulate such issues.

It also partly explains the political failure of those political organisations most closely associated with Loyalist paramilitaries. Any support for Loyalist paramilitaries in working-class areas has always been conditional, best seen in terms of 'crisis management' and in practical terms, the perceived need for 'defence'. Loyalism still, of course, rests on a series of common understandings and symbols that gives the ideology its coherence. Protestant workers generate their own consciousness and their own culture, by which they make sense of their world. This 'common-sense' understanding determines what is, and what is not, acceptable, what can and cannot be done in given conditions. It is this 'common-sense' understanding that will determine the response to the 'peace process'. As disillusionment with the 'peace process' continues, and as the feeling of stagnation amplifies, mainstream Unionism is likely to further reconstruct around the DUP position.

A further consideration here must be the election of David Trimble as Ulster Unionist leader. His presence offers a further dynamic within Unionism. For the first time in many years there exists the distinct possibility of a coming together of

many of the strands within Unionism to form a united entity.
Both Trimble and Paisley have now openly articulated the
belief that it is Dublin and 'pan-Nationalism' that continues to
dictate both the policy and tempo of the 'peace process', and
that this must be resisted by the construction of a united
Unionist front.

This largely involves an ideological conjunction, a restating
of political Unionist hegemony around the DUP. Paisley has,
for example, claimed, with some justification, that Trimble's
victory was based on his articulation of DUP policies. One
pragmatic manifestation of this has been Trimble's active promotion by both Unionist leaders of a new elected Assembly or
Convention for Northern Ireland. There are several possible
readings of this. Clearly, one reason is the attempt to impose
an 'internal' solution, and thus by-pass any agreed development
by the Irish and British Governments. A less obvious reason,
however, is that the electoral profile of such an assembly
would, probably, largely exclude both the PUP and UDP. As
such these groupings would be politically and ideologically isolated within the Unionist bloc. There is a clear internal
agenda, to delegitimise the PUP and the UDP as the voice of
working-class unionism.

Conclusion

The various Unionist grouping have reacted strongly to challenges to their core identity, both internal and external, perceived or otherwise. There has been an attempt to reconstruct
the core hegemony of Unionism around the leadership of Ian
Paisley, and now David Trimble. This has been at the heart of
the response to recent 'set pieces', such as the re-routing of
Orange parades, or the 'failure' to play the National Anthem at
the Queen's visit. Further, this strong response is still in a
situation where any 'real' negotiations over mutually antagonistic agendas are not taking place. If and when the Peace Process
moves towards structured talks, this position is likely to
harden. British Government hopes seem to rest with the view
that, the longer widespread violence remains absent, the less
likely is it that any paramilitary group will have the momen-
tum, or support, to resume armed conflict on the scale previously witnessed. That said, time in itself will not bring
together the differing political dimensions, or restructure

Northern Ireland into a society based on a commonly agreed and accepted politic. The best hope for that surely remains through agreed negotiation, where the different factions of Unionism, and all other political voices, are represented.

9 Counter-Insurgency, Deindustrialisation and the Political Economy of Ulster Loyalism

Mark McGovern and Peter Shirlow

This chapter examines the ideology of Ulster Loyalism and how this political framework has been central within the construction of previous and contemporary modes of social regulation in Northern Ireland. In agreeing with Lipietz that a central aim of regulation theory must be to comprehend 'how every country functions, what it produces, for whom, how, what the forms of wage relations are, what successive regimes of accumulation developed and why' (1986, p. 25), we also stress the need to consider the process of socio-cultural antagonism in the formation and direction of socio-political regulation.

A central argument, presented within this paper, is that at no time in Northern Ireland's history has the State, in whatever form, been capable of producing a long-term non-conflictory socio-political project capable of resolving the conflict between the pro-British and pro-Irish sections of the population (Stewart, 1991). Moreover, the analysis presented stresses that the contemporary mode of social regulation (MSR) has not been based upon the removal of conflict but instead has been centred upon policies of conflict management and attempted socio-political 'normalisation', policies which, we argue, have merely ensured 'some regularity within social regulation' (Lipietz, 1986, p. 19).

In examining the transition to post-industrialism we acknowledge that although this shift has produced similar socio-economic profiles in various localities throughout the European Union, this does not necessarily mean that such evident similarities have the same socio-political consequences, nor will they be understood, or explained, in the same manner (Baker, 1983; Shirlow and Shuttleworth, 1994). It is in this sense that we focus upon the relative autonomy of ideology and collective consciousness as a determining factor on social action; the way, in other words, material change is perceived within the context of a pre-existing, if discursive, ideological framework. In examining the socio-political nature of State-directed policy making within Northern Irish society we analyse the impact of distinct socio-regulatory forms upon the cultural and political profile of Ulster Loyalism, and more specifically the factors which produce Protestant working-class alienation and support for Loyalist paramilitarism.

Theoretical Perspectives: Loyalism and Sectarianism

Since the late 1960s and early 1970s the demise of Unionist hegemony, the imposition of Direct Rule and the direction of IRA violence stimulated the political activities of Ulster Loyalists. The threat to the Northern Ireland State that each of these developments conjured up in the minds of Ulster Loyalists led directly to the mobilisation of paramilitary groups, in the 1960s, and brought to the fore the politics of contestation between the Protestant and Catholic working classes (McAll, 1990; Todd, 1987).

The central political goal of Loyalism is to maintain the existence of the Northern Irish State, either through the current constitutional link between or by establishing Northern Ireland as an independent entity. By and large the term 'Loyalist' is usually engaged to refer to the more intemperate and/or populist supporters of the Unionist cause; those who are willing to countenance draconian state action or the use of paramilitary violence in order to sustain the Northern Irish State (Bairner, 1986).

Loyalist paramilitaries are groups which adopt such features and which infer or expound support for the goals of Loyalist ideology (McAuley, 1994). There are two main Loyalist paramilitary groups, who prior to the recent cease-fire, were actively and openly engaged in political violence: the UVF and the UFF, the latter – the Ulster Freedom Force – being the military wing of the Ulster Defence Association. Between 1966 and the end of 1993 Loyalist groups are known to have killed 911 people, over 25 per cent of the total number of those murdered. The overwhelming majority of Loyalist murders have been essentially random sectarian assassinations of Catholics. However, violence alone does not clarify how sectarianism functions as a social and ideological occurrence – it is only one mode of sectarianism and is in fact rooted in the social processes which make sectarian division an everyday reality (Brewer, 1992).

Sectarianism is an often misunderstood term, not least because it is to a great extent under-theorised (Bell, 1990; Brewer, 1992). If we examine sectarianism as a specific form of ethnic difference this allows theoretical perspectives developed in relation to the study of ethnic relations, divisions and conflicts to be employed in the analysis of sectarian social relations. Such a conception of sectarianism ensures that, whilst religious affiliation is established as a primary discourse of ethnic separation, religion is not recognised as the 'subject' of conflicting interest but as a symbol of conflict, representing a means to identify, express, historically root, 'legitimate' and 'give meaning' to resource competition.

Defining the sectarian 'Other' results in 'the imposition, by one set of actors upon another, of a putative name and characterisation which affects in significant ways the social experience of the categorised' (Jenkins 1994, p. 199). The construction of the Catholic community as the 'Other' of Loyalist ideology must be seen in this vein. Ethnicity, in terms of an Ulster Protestant identity, within the framework of Loyalist ideology, is inevitably predicated upon the negative categorisation of Catholics. This in turn acts as a means to sanction the procedure of sectarianised power relations at the level not only of 'ideas' and 'individual action' but also in terms of 'social structure'. Sectarianism therefore emanates as a pivotal mode of domination and boundary demarcation.

The sectarian nature of Loyalist ideology is also combined with the Loyalist sense of 'Siege' (McGovern, 1994). The Siege culture focuses upon formations which distinguish the 'we' from the 'they', thereby fortifying group unity and providing a rationale for group action (Aughey, 1989; Baker, 1983; Graham, 1994b). As such the consequential issue of concern is based upon constituting how the ideology of Siege within Ulster Loyalism can be conceived, and why the discursive dynamic of the Siege mentality correlates with the changing socio-economic conditions facing sections of the Protestant working class (Bell, 1990; Cohen, 1985).

That world-view is firmly established upon the overruling binary opposition, of the Collective Self and the Collective Other, and upon the construction of a necessary relationship between the two. As far as Loyalism is concerned each of these (the Collective Self, the Collective Other, and their interaction) may be defined in terms of a key ethno-political thesis or action. The Collective Self, the Ulster Protestant/Loyalist community, the 'elect', is defined in terms of 'Loyalty'. The Collective Other is the 'Threat', which can come from a host of social groups or agencies but which is principally assembled in terms of the Catholic/Nationalist community. The mediating manner which delimits the inevitable relationship between the two is the notion of 'Defence'.

The 'Loyalty' which is so substantial in the construction of the Collective Self can be given to institutions or groups such as the UUP, the British State or paramilitary organisations, ideals or principles or to a range of communal and inter-personal relationships (neighbours, family, fellow-workers). What is important too is that through the enunciation of allegiance these miscellaneous loci of self-identity can be fused: loyalty to the state, to the Union, to the local community and the family blend to mean one and the same thing, the 'British/ Protestant way of life'. The Collective Self is, in other words, built upon the sum of the social relationships experienced by someone growing up within a Loyalist community, framed within a particular value system which is in turn related to an ethno-political identity.

The 'Threat' of the Collective Other represents the antith-esis of the Collective Self. This involves the attribution of disapproving values, actions and beliefs to the Other. At the same time, through the discourse of 'threat' any provocation to, or change in, the status of the 'Loyal People' is encoun-tered within the context of conventional lines of division and conflict. More important is the recognition that a loss of socio-economic status, which is the outcome of deindustriali-sation and the onset of post-industrialism, is 'recognised' as another example of Catholic besiegement, aided and abetted by the folly of a British state which fails to come the 'assuagement' of the assaulted people and discharge the obli-gations owed to the Loyal. As a result, the 'Loyal People' must defend themselves. 'Defence' thus emerges as the primary discourse defining the mediating practice between the Self and the Other; the conceptual ordering of inter-communal relations. Through this sectarianised consciousness a transformation in the regime of accumulation which gives rise to the post-industrial mode of social regulation, becomes merely the latest onslaught to hit the besieged garrison. Far from being understood as a reflection of global economic change, or of antagonisms rooted in the social relations of production, it is sectarian competition, the threat of the Other, which provides the basis of explanation.

It is within this context of sectarian domination that any analysis of the relationship between economic structures and social relations in Northern Ireland, and of social and political regulation by the State, must be examined alongside a comprehensive understanding of the historic place of sectarianism. Similarly, the changing nature of the economic order and the consequent implications this has for the regulatory practices of the State, must be seen to have powerful ramifications for the reproduction of sectarian relations.

Regulation Theory and the State in Northern Ireland

In adopting a regulationist approach we identify the link between regulatory practice and the production and reproduction of sectarianised social relations. This is achieved through an examination of how epochal shifts in the character of capitalism in Northern Ireland during the industrial and post-industrial phases of capitalist development have produced important alterations in the mode of social regulation and the production and reproduction of sectarian ideologies. Before examining the modes of social regulation which have operated within Northern Ireland, and the interactive relationship each mode of social regulation has had upon Loyalism, it is necessary to sketch out briefly the theoretical perspective being employed in the analysis of state and economy.

Perhaps the most prevalent contribution of the regulation school lies in its theorisation of the impact that political and social relations play within the conception of capitalist reproduction and crisis – the so-called mode of social regulation (MSR). According to Aglietta (1979) modes of social regulation play a consequential part in fixing the integrity and unity of the capitalist accumulation process in the medium term. The stabilisation of a MSR with a certain model of consumption and production transpires under what is termed a 'regime of accumulation'. Regimes of accumulation summarise stages of capitalist development in which the reproduction of capital can take place in a comparably crisis-free environment. Within this conception the MSR serves to facilitate, negotiate and normalise crisis tendencies through internalising and containing the contradictions which emerge within capitalism.

However, the deployment of social regulatory forms will eventually be overcome by inherent crisis tendencies within the accumulation process which will exceed the moderating and equilibrating effects of the MSR and in due course the regime of accumulation will be dismantled and/or broken down. In order to surmount this predicament through the restoration of capitalist growth, a new constructional coupling between the MSR and regime of accumulation must be secured.

As such the regulationist approach permits a full consideration of how the formation of regimes of accumulation are interlinked to complex socio-political processes (Harvey, 1989). However, it is true to state that regulation theorists have tended to concentrate upon the relationship between economic structure, the social relations of production and consumption, and have fairly narrowly defined the socialisation processes which reproduce those relationships. A particularly startling gap, within regulation theory, is the absence of any coherent analysis of the role of gender and ethnic relations in much of this work. However, the core concepts of the regulation approach, and in particular the concept of MSRs, if allied to more culturally and politically-oriented approaches can allow for a complex and integrated analysis of political economy that marries a materialist critique of contemporary capitalism with insights provided by aspects of cultural theory.

Within the context of Northern Ireland, we argue that three regulatory modes have been evident since the partition of Ireland in 1921: a pre-Fordist MSR, in operation from 1921 to the 1950s; a limited-Fordist MSR (1950s–1970s) and a post-industrial MSR (1970s–1990s). Each successive MSR has been clearly influenced by the politics of cultural opposition between the pro-Irish and pro-British sections of Northern Ireland's population.

As with all western economies, state regulation and intervention in Northern Ireland has been disciplined by the need to compensate for market failures and the need to promote economic growth structures (Callinicos, 1989; Harvey, 1989; Lipietz, 1986; Murtagh, 1993). It has similarly inured wage earners to the perpetuation of capitalist production through a mix of workplace and social regulation (Teague, 1993b). The socialisation of labour in relation to the conditions of capitalist production, in Northern Ireland as elsewhere, has centred upon various mechanisms of social control, persuasion, education, training and the mobilisation of social forces.

However, Northern Ireland is reasonably peculiar in that the mobilisation of social forces has been continually bound to the unleashing of distinct and sectarian socio-political sentiments. In other words, the conditions of capitalist production are continually understood in relation to competing sectarian and social identities. The creation of distinct modes of social regulation have therefore not been concerned solely with the resolution of accumulatory crises and antagonisms between capital and labour, but also with the management and/or sustainment of sectarian competition.

The Pre-Fordist MSR (1921–1950s)

Any analysis of the socio-political construction of sectarianism and social regulation must begin with the legacy of Unionist domination. The partition of Ireland in 1921 effectively created a Protestant pro-British majority in both political and economic terms. However, the fact that there was a Protestant and pro-British majority did not automatically mean that the Protestant working class would serve the interests of Unionist-controlled industry and the State.

The newly formed state's power holders were fearful of three possible political outcomes. First and foremost was the fear that the Protestant working class would engage in socialist/ labourist politics; secondly the anti-sectarian position of several prominent trade unionists engendered the belief that the emergence of pan-community politics would similarly undermine the dominance of the Protestant bourgeoisie. The final threat was the Catholic minority whose support for unification with the Southern regime threatened the very survival of the State (Bew et al., 1979).

In order to convert these pressures it was essential for the Protestant bourgeoisie to bond together a political and cultural alliance which removed the threat of the Protestant working class engaging in political activities beyond Unionist Party control. This cross-class alliance was consummated through a range of alternatives open to the State in Northern Ireland. Firstly, the fact that the Southern regime was predominantly Catholic played upon Protestant working class fears that unification would undermine their religious and civil liberties.

Secondly, the dominance of agriculture in the South and the threat of losing Empire-based markets through the onset of Irish unification aroused Protestant working class suspicions that merging with the Southern regime would not serve their immediate material interests (Pringle, 1984). In socio-political terms the Protestant working class united with the bourgeoisie, not out of simple bigotry, but to preserve a unique way of life, on the island of Ireland, which they perceived as being under threat (Stewart, 1991).

As such, disunity between Protestants and Catholics became Unionism's *sine qua non*. In terms of the socio-regulatory form adopted, Unionism chose the option of promoting and reproducing an economy and civil structure which visibly excluded the Catholic masses; the MSR which operated during this period was a mode of sectarian regulation.

The State's corroboration of sectarian activities remained an important element in the reproduction of the class bloc. The essential basis for the reproduction of the class bloc was the State's sensitivity to the political impact on the Protestant masses of changes in their material conditions. In terms of creating a socio-regulatory format capable of removing Protestant working-class hostility toward the State, Unionists constructed a state which served, whenever possible, the relative material interests of the Protestant working class through promoting discriminatory employment, voting and housing allocation structures. This in turn promoted the loyalty of Protestant workers toward the State and employers, and in so doing exacerbated sectarian divisions through material and political influence (Farrell, 1980).

The domination of certain key industries (shipbuilding, linen and heavy engineering) which were dependent upon Empire-based markets produced a fragile and narrowly-based economy whose viability was being called into question almost from the moment the State was born. The pre-Fordist regime of accumulation was highly dependent upon the production of capital goods and very low levels of consumer production compared to the UK. Industrial wages during the 1920s and 1930s were on average 40–45 per cent lower than in the UK, a situation which reflected stagnant markets, low productivity growth rates and declining output. Population decline and the detachment from the Southern Irish market combined with the over-reliance upon Empire-based markets to thwart the necessary dynamic for self-sustaining domestic-led economic growth (McGovern and Shirlow, 1997).

Accumulation patterns were incapable of halting the continual growth in unemployment between the 1920s and the Second World War due to the failure of industrialists and the government to promote diversification, productive reorganisation and scale production. The failure of the bourgeoisie to diversify into new markets or to adopt new technologies in order to stimulate productivity growth rates led not only to the onset of deindustrialisation but also to significant growths in unemployment and underemployment. Indeed, during the period 1925–35 unemployment grew by 342 per cent and staple industries such as shipbuilding and linen shed 57 per cent and 41 per cent of their respective workforces.

The dominance of free-market policies supported by the Unionist bourgeoisie permitted only token government support for industry which did little to broaden Northern Ireland's industrial base or alleviate unemployment growth rates. The failure to provide significant job opportunities meant that politicians and employers had to vigorously practice discrimination, in employment, in order to ensure that the material position of the Protestant working class was maintained. The adoption of Keynesian-type intervention within the economy was frowned upon by the majority of Unionist politicians who viewed income support, education reform and state planning as a version of 'creeping socialism'. The ruling class was totally subordinate to the ideology of Empire and was therefore unable to implement the sort of radical measures needed to shift the economy away from deindustrialisation and the maintenance of inefficient units of production.

In any case the loyalty of Protestant workers to theSstate and owners of capital meant that there were few Protestant workers clamouring for social reform due to their allegiance towards sectarian labour practices and the exclusion of Catholics from the workplace (O'Dowd, 1980). In essence this was because the Unionist–Protestant working-class alliance was the perfect embodiment of the pre-Fordist MSR and ensured a paternalistic populism which suited some Protestant workers and their religious and social identity.

In the post-war period, global restructuring saw the re-emergence of deindustrialisation in certain economic sectors, and most notably those which had previously been central to the Northern Irish economy. More importantly the sectarian practices which had been promoted up to and during the Second World War were now beginning to influence the politics of the Catholic minority who in the 1950s began to challenge their socio-economic and political exclusion within Northern Irish society. The mode of sectarian regulation which was adopted during this period was creating tensions which would eventually lead to the dissolution of Unionist hegemony and the onset of nearly thirty years of paramilitary violence.

The Limited Fordist Regime (1950s–1970s)

After the Second World War the demand for social democracy and the idea of social citizenship, so central to the Fordist compromise, were placing Unionist rule and the prevailing MSR under increasing strain. It was within this context that the 1950s and 1960s saw the emergence of what may be termed a 'Limited Fordist' MSR and a variety of new political forces.

The accumulation process adopted in the post-war period was 'limited' in that although the State became more interventionist through the funding of social programmes in order to maintain the level of total consumption, it and the owners of business failed to promote Fordist production methods, a mode of monopoly regulation, and a distinct link between productivity and wage growth rates capable of forming mass markets for consumer goods. Instead the accumulation strategy was shifted onto the attraction of mobile capital investment as the Northern Irish economy increasingly became a site of neo-Fordist production (Munck, 1993).

The continual loss of jobs in traditional industries deeply affected a Protestant working class for whom such industries formed the core of employment opportunities, and thus of access to goods and resources. It similarly challenged a local bourgeoisie whose claim to political leadership was founded on a paternalistic relationship with the Protestant working class. In the space that opened up as a result, the first shards of serious disaffection within the Unionist political bloc appeared and took shape not only in the Protestant working class's growing interest in Labour politics during the 1960s but also in the politics of hard-line Loyalism.

It was at this stage that Northern Irish society entered into a highly complex and contradictory period in which the Unionist bourgeoisie struggled to maintain its socio-regulatory influence. The first task facing the Unionist establishment was the need to redefine its relationship with a Protestant working class which had begun to clamour for social reform due to the influence of Labourist politics. However, this relationship could not simply be restored or renewed through placating some Protestant workers unless the rewards of social reform perpetuated sectarian labour practices.

As such the creation of a new MSR had two premises. First and foremost was the need to advance a brand of welfarism and social regulation which represented adopting welfarist policies in order to woo back disenchanted Protestants. Secondly, there was the need to assure sections of the Protestant working class that such reforms would not involve a strategy for reform in the areas of civil rights and discrimination.

However, not only did Unionism have to redefine its relationship with the Protestant working class but it had to respond to the minority Catholic population whose material and political needs had been either neglected, rejected or suppressed during the pre-Fordist regime. The endurance of political and economic alienation was no longer acceptable to sections of a Catholic minority which began to promote collective action as an expression against the perpetuation of sectarianised modes of social regulation.

The Unionist establishment was caught in a quandary. If they responded to Catholic grievances, through promoting a non-sectarian MSR, they would fractionalise the cross-class Unionist bloc. However, if they did nothing then they opened themselves up to the possibility of British State intervention and/or open civil war. Unable to provide a non-sectarian MSR the Unionist establishment attempted to convince Catholics and the British and Irish Governments that reform was inevitable, while, convincing the Protestant working class that the opposite was the case (McGovern and Shirlow, 1997).

Inevitably, the direction of social welfare and industrial location became crucial points of contention as Catholics and Protestants looked for signs, in each area, of transformation and continuity respectively. Unable to break away directly from sectarianised practices, the Unionist regime supported mobile capital investment in predominantly Protestant areas at the expense of the predominantly Catholic and depressed western region of Northern Ireland (Purdie, 1991).

Given that the State was now even more clearly involved in social and economic planning than ever before, the role of the State as an agency directing resources to either deconstruct or maintain sectarianised social relations was brought to the fore by such activities as the location of mobile capital investment. For Catholics there appeared to be a yawning chasm between the State's rhetoric of citizenship and what was construed as the State's practice of maintaining Protestant privilege. For many Protestants the very opposite was the case. As such the perpetuation of a sectarian MSR during the period of limited Fordism dashed Catholic expectations at the same time as it fanned the fears of a Protestant working class; enured to a sense of its right to privilege on the basis of its manifest loyalty.

Although the State had been determined to maintain the material position of the Protestant working class, the ambiguity of Unionism's rhetoric fuelled suspicions that the rationale of the Protestant State was now under constant attack. The eventual dissolution of Unionist hegemony was not merely centred upon Unionism's failure to satiate the socio-political aspirations of the minority population. It was similarly influenced by the advent of Unionist tokenism towards Catholics and the suspicions this aroused among the Protestant working class. Moreover, the failure of the Unionist regime to provide a set of regulatory practices capable of removing Catholic hostility towards the State increased tensions between working-class Protestants and Catholics. For many Protestant workers the failure of the State to police and ultimately suppress Catholic-led hostility and socio-political aspirations fuelled the re-emergence of Protestant paramilitaries.

As the cross-class alliance between the Protestant bourgeoisie and the working class began to dissolve, some Protestant workers increasingly looked to politicians and community leaders who spoke the language of suppression and draconian State action against the Catholic minority. In the vacuum which now existed between the State and the Protestant working class the UVF was relaunched and began to engage in a sectarian campaign of murder and intimidation of Catholics.

The violent murder of Catholics by the UVF, the impartiality of State policing and the onset of rioting between Catholic and Protestants led to the re-formation of the IRA. The activities of Loyalist paramilitaries and the failure of the State to respond adequately to the socio-economic demands of Catholics encouraged support for the politics of Republicanism and the use of violence in order to remove what was perceived as a state beyond reform. In the late 1960s and early 1970s Northern Irish society was plunged into open violent conflict as

Republicans fought for the dissolution of Unionist and then British hegemony and Loyalists fought to maintain sectarian modes of domination and the constitutional link with the UK.

During this period the Unionist regime failed to create a socio-regulatory format capable of transforming the very society which it had created and as a result the Protestant working class began to operate as defenders of the sectarianised practices which operated during the pre-Fordist MSR even though such defence strategies only drew the two communities into intense political and violent opposition. In the violent crisis which was stimulated by the collapse in the regulatory capability of the Unionist establishment the British State imposed Direct Rule, in 1972, and began the slow process of rebuilding a new form of social regulation.

'Post-Industrialism' in Northern Ireland: 1970s–1995

The evolution of a post-industrial economy in Northern Ireland has been characterised by continued deindustrialisation and by the state's adoption of economic strategies designed to 'manage' armed socio-political conflict (Cebulla and Smith, 1995). To no small degree these two elements of profound and devastating economic change and a long-term political crisis that has centred on the very existence of the State have been very much interwoven and have made the period since the early 1970s both economically and politically distinctive.

The manufacturing sector that exists today is a mere shadow of its former self (Munck, 1993; Teague, 1993b). Between 1950 and 1994 there was a 58.4 per cent decline in manufacturing employment. Moreover, during the period 1971–1991 there was an employment shortfall of 28.9 per cent, a rise in registered unemployment of 14.6 per cent and a 12.2 per cent growth in out-migration (Borooah, 1993). There has, however, been a significant 22.8 per cent increase in service and public sector employment between 1950 and 1993. Between 1974 and 1992 employment grew significantly within the health and social services (+27.8 per cent), education (+26.3 per cent) and security services (+54.3 per cent) sectors. The aggregate growth within the security services sector has undoubtedly been the most obvious economic impact of state strategies of conflict management. However, it must be stressed that public sector employment has been artificially inflated by the state in order to offset the destabilising effect of job loss within the manufacturing sector (Rowthorn and Wayne, 1988).

The other major factor which keeps the Northern Ireland economy from terminal collapse is the large injection of public money or 'subvention' from the British exchequer. In 1993 the subvention was estimated to be worth approximately £3.5 billion or 35.8 per cent of Northern Ireland's GDP. The level of state subvention and the regulation of public sector-driven growth clearly indicates the pressure on the British Government (given the continuation throughout the 1980s of socio-political conflict) to maintain a modicum of social stability (Cebulla and Smith, 1995).

As with other parts of the post-industrial world the private services sector is increasingly promoted as the way out of this economic morass. Retail-based economic growth has, however, already led to the emergence of a low-income economy. The redevelopment of Belfast's city centre as a shopping emporium, targeted at the upper- and middle-class shopper, has seen an expansion in low-income, part-time and largely female labour 'opportunities'. In 1992 the average wage among retail workers in Belfast was 42 per cent below the UK average, and over 62 per cent of the jobs created in the city centre between 1984 and 1991 went to part-time female workers (Shirlow, 1995).

These standard features of the post-industrial economy – flexible labour markets, deindustrialisation and the creation of low-income service employment – have had a myriad of effects upon the class structure and, as a consequence, on the political fabric of Northern Ireland. In terms of Northern Ireland's social structure, two broad trends have been most evident: the first is the growth of well-paid white-collar employment among upper- and middle-income groups; the second is a rise in unemployment, low-paid employment and underemployment among an increasingly marginalised working class (Shirlow, 1995).

The implications of this process in Northern Ireland are manifold but two features are of particular importance. The growth and maintenance of public service employment has created a distinct and large middle class, the majority of whom receive incomes much higher than the Northern Ireland average and who also enjoy the highest disposable income rates in the UK. Yet perhaps the single most politically significant aspect of this process is that the public sector includes a more or less equitable proportion of Catholics in relation to the total adult population (Cormack et al., 1993).

The result of both these processes is a tendency to consoli-
date non-sectarian middle-class solidarity while at the same
time alienating sections of both the Catholic and Protestant
working-class (O'Connor, 1994). For many working-class
Catholics, the benefits accruing from 25 years of struggle, in
which, they could legitimately argue, they have borne the
brunt of suffering, are passing them by (Rowthorn and Wayne,
1988). On the other hand, for many working-class Protestants
their denial of entry into new labour markets which require
educational qualifications or skills they do not possess is not
acknowledged as the consequence of economic restructuring,
but of a Protestant middle class that has deserted them and a
Catholic population who are, in socio-economic terms, in the
ascendant. It is in the often ugly and dismal space created by
these twin processes of alienation and social marginalisation
that the emergent mode of social regulation is being forged.

For the British State the Northern Ireland 'problem' has
never been one which threatened any fundamental economic or
strategic interest. It has, however, represented a fundamental
political threat through challenging the State's legitimacy. In
order to undermine this challenge the British State has constructed a comprehensive apparatus (and a coherent discourse) of
coercion and consensus building in an attempt to resolve and
remove socio-political hostility in Northern Ireland (Anderson
and Goodman, 1995; Rolston, 1995).

The onus has therefore been upon the British State to
develop a series of regulatory practices which will limit the
apparent challenge to its legitimacy. (Tomlinson, 1993). This
in turn has been pursued through a policy of socio-political
'normalisation', and the adoption of socio-regulatory practices
whose primary goal is to construct a set of socio-political relationships which, it is hoped, will transcend sectarian hostilities
and provide socio-economic stability. As such the primary goal
of State intervention has been to police and/or contain the
conflict on the one hand and provide new socio-regulatory
mechanisms and class structures on the other.

Containing the conflict, in order to provide a semblance of
political normality, is clearly linked to the defeat of the Republican and Loyalist paramilitaries through a range of options
open to the British State. The most obvious form of containment has been based upon military control and the use of
military intelligence. The British State's long-term strategy has
been to isolate the conflict in both spatial and ideological

terms. Spatially, the conflict was to be 'contained' to the territory of Northern Ireland itself and, even more specifically, to
certain working-class areas. Ideologically, the State has represented itself as both a positive agent of conflict control, and as
one which is extraneous to the reproduction of the conditions
which produce violence. The 'problem' was thereby 'contained'
to the context of inter-communal strife.

Other forms of containment have been undertaken through
the suspension of habeus corpus and the instigation of Emer-
gency Powers Acts. However, such draconian State actions have
also been paralleled by the slow de-escalation and demilitarisa-
tion of the political environment. The British State, aware of
the impossibility of complete military control, has policed the
paramilitaries to a standstill situation in which the Republican
movement, in particular, is forced to acknowledge that its military tactics can never fully succeed with their stated aims and
objectives. The low-intensity counter-insurgency strategy of
'containment' was therefore born out of the overarching ethos
of 'normalisation'. It has not, however, been the only strategy
of conflict management.

The economy of Northern Ireland, more than that of any
other state in western Europe, is characterised by an abnormal
public-sector dominance. The economics of post-industrialism
in Northern Ireland, with the virtual collapse of a sustainable
private sector and the evolution of a heavily subsidised
economy, places the State at the centre of economic management, which, in turn ensures that the regulation of the
economy is a principal component of 'normalisation'.

The direction of economic policy as an overall strategy of
conflict management is clearly linked to the politics of regulatory practice in Northern Ireland. As noted previously, the
Northern Irish economy is kept afloat through the Westminster
subvention and the support given for unprofitable investment
by the British State in both the public and private sectors. The
use of the subvention is clearly linked to the over-arching
desire to keep the economy afloat and ensure that the activities
of paramilitaries do not undermine the functioning of the
economy.

As such the Government has increasingly used financial
resources in order to govern and direct the conflict in recent
years. The use of resources has been based upon two distinct
policies. First, around 10 per cent of the total government
subvention between 1982 and 1994 was pumped into deprived

communities in an attempt to convince these communities that
the State is responding to high levels of social marginalisation
(data supplied by the Northern Ireland Office). Unlike in other
regions of the UK, the State has continued to sponsor public-
sector housing and increasingly higher levels of investment in
community groups and their related activities (McGarry and
O'Leary, 1995). Moreover, the direction of State funds within
deprived communities, especially in Republican communities,
has been motivated by the State's desire to present itself as
politically neutral, interventionist and concerned. However, the
primary use of funds (nearly 90 per cent) has been to support
public- and private-sector investment, as it is within this form
of expenditure that the State has recognised the possibility of
achieving greater political consensus through subsidising the
middle and upper-income groups.

The direction of investment and resources, the creation of
new strategies regulating labour markets, indeed, the whole
pattern of regulation governing production and consumption,
while obviously responding to more widespread influences has
also been governed by the need to reimpose the authority of
the state. Other strategies include the reorganisation of economic activity and of labour markets to facilitate cross-border
co-operation, the attempted depoliticising of marginalised working-class communities and the absorption of the Catholic
middle class into a new political consensus.

This form of counter-insurgency has been tied to an attempt
to reconstitute the structure of cross-class, communal political
alliances and to reinvent the spatial loci of competing political
identities. Socio-economic policy making and anti-sectarian legislation have been implemented in order to try and create a third
tradition which is capable of living with the evident ambiguities
within Northern Irish society (O'Connor, 1994). This third tradition can be denoted as those who are in favour of integrated
education and who are keen to share a more liberal political
agenda which may include joint-authority or Irish federalism. In
effect the British State has tried to create a middle ground in
Northern Irish society for those who are opposed to the sectarian
politics of Unionism and Irish Nationalism/Republicanism.

What draws together and defines the various elements
which constitute the politics of 'normalisation' is the State's
primary desire to present itself as the sole site of legitimate
authority. It does this by representing Northern Ireland as a
'normal' liberal democratic regime beset by the abnormality of

an atavistic sectarian war and anachronistic political concerns. It should also be remembered, however, that the aim is also to provide an environment conducive to the operation of a capitalist economy. While the politics of 'normalisation' can, and sometimes (as in the case of anti-discrimination legislation) do involve the State in the promotion of policies and strategies which may be regarded as 'positive', it is necessary to develop an analysis which understands these policies within a critical perspective on the role of the State in modern capitalist societies. That is to say, while aspects of State regulation are 'progressive' in their incremental outcomes, the context of their implementation and the overarching rationale of their operation is the extent to which they can 'ensure the crisis-free production of social relations over a certain period of time' (Lipietz, 1986, pp. 20–1).

Although it has produced a process of only slow and unclear change, post-industrialism has created the circumstances for a relatively recent (yet potentially profound) shift in the operation of state policy of 'normalisation' in two particular ways. First, it has become increasingly apparent that sectarianised politics no longer ensure the crisis-free reproduction of social relations. Second, the particularity of the Northern economy upon which Unionism was constructed has disappeared (Munck, 1993).

In particular, a great regulatory emphasis has now been placed upon the absorption of middle-class Catholics into the realms of political and social power. That is the logic of recognising the 'cultural identity' and 'aspirations' of Catholics, and of promoting power-sharing as the basis for a future internal settlement. It is similarly the logic of arriving at some sort of cross-border accommodation which will both deliver this political goal and relocate economic activity with an aim to expanding the productive capacities and market opportunities of the island as a whole (Anderson and Goodman, 1995).

Within Northern Ireland, the drift of economic strategy is similarly designed to reconstruct labour markets to allow equal access for Catholics and Protestants who are trained and educated for white-collar middle-class employment, and to deny such access more equitably amongst the marginalised working class. That is the political logic behind the liberal conception of equal opportunities promoted by the Fair Employment Commission (formerly known as the Fair Employment Agency). It is also the political logic of flexible labour markets and the expansion of poorly paid, less secure and increasingly feminised employment patterns for whole sections of Northern Ireland's population (Cebulla and Smith, 1995). This marginalisation of working-class employment is, of course, a well-known aspect of post-industrial 'normality'; it is also, in Northern Ireland, a strategy of counter-insurgency, aimed at developing middle-class as opposed to working-class consensus.

Post-Industrialism and the Protestant Working Class in Belfast: The Dimensions of Deindustrialisation

Post-industrialism has had a very particular impact upon the Protestant working class. To understand the direction the politics of certain sections of the Protestant working class is currently taking, it is necessary to understand how these processes have been experienced. It is first necessary, however, to understand what these processes have been.

The clearest indicator of deindustrialisation is the changing nature of the labour market. The two broad trends which have characterised the Northern Ireland economy – the growth of public- and private-sector white-collar employment and the decline of blue-collar manufacturing jobs – has been nowhere more starkly apparent than in Belfast. While aggregate employment in Belfast fell by a mere 0.78 per cent between 1961 and 1991, this masks profound shifts in the sectoral balance of the labour market. In the same period, manufacturing employment fell by just over 70 per cent, while jobs in private services increased by 54 per cent and employment in the public sector increased by a staggering 158 per cent (Shirlow, 1995).

In reality the share of employment held by those who reside within the Belfast Urban Area has fallen by over 38 per cent since 1970; a situation which clearly indicates that de-industrialisation has been accompanied by a rapid process of suburbanisation which has 'emptied out' many traditional working-class areas of the city and severely altered the age and income balances within the local urban populations (McGovern and Shirlow, 1997).

A variety of factors, including low levels of educational attainment and the collapse in manufacturing employment, have ensured that many people from these deprived urban communities have found access to the post-industrial labour markets increasingly difficult, a situation which is clearly indicated by the growth in welfare dependency within the Belfast urban area; between 1971 and 1991 the share of those whose livelihoods were dependent upon state-sponsored welfare rose from 31.1 per cent to 58.1 per cent (McGovern and Shirlow, 1997).

These processes of social restructuring are not unique to Belfast, and it is certainly not one unique to the Protestant working class in the city. It is important to stress that Catholic working-class areas still have unemployment rates double those of the city's average. The average unemployment rate in the six most deprived Catholic wards – Falls, Whiterock, New Lodge, Ardoyne, Upper Springfield and Clonard – grew by 36.1 per cent between 1971 and 1991, and now stands at 45.5 per cent. In the six most deprived Protestant wards – Crumlin, Shankill, Woodstock, Woodvale, Island and Duncairn – the unemployment rate is 28.3 per cent, and has grown by some 28 per cent in the same period. The idea, often portrayed by Loyalists – that Protestants have lost out because great gains have been made by the Catholic working class – is, quite simply, not true.

However, there is some evidence that indicates (at least to some degree) that a greater 'equity of emmiseration' is taking place. For example, the growth in Protestant male unemployment between 1971 and 1991 was 28 per cent higher than that in Catholic areas. Moreover, higher employment rates in Protestant working-class areas do not necessarily mean a substantial difference in standards of living. In terms of average household incomes, the percentage share of those households in Belfast whose average incomes are 25–80 per cent less than the Northern Ireland average are relatively similar for Protestants (68.7 per cent) and Catholics (73.9 per cent). In 1971 the six most deprived Protestant wards had household incomes which were 18 per cent higher than in the six most deprived Catholic wards. In 1991 the gap had narrowed to 7.2 per cent (McGovern and Shirlow, 1997).

For many working-class Protestants, the very industries (in particular shipbuilding and engineering) which formed the basis not only of their relative economic well-being, but also of their political allegiance and their construction of community identity have gone. Three-quarters of jobs lost within Belfast's manufacturing sector were previously held by those from Protestant working-class communities (Shirlow, 1995). What this indicates is that the MSR which ensured a unity of identity and purpose between Protestant labour and capital is no more.

It is this decline in the economic position of sections of the Protestant working class which defines the politics of contemporary Loyalism.

The limited convergence in the marginal status of Catholic and Protestant workers has fuelled a growing animosity amongst many Protestants (the oft-talked about Protestant working-class 'alienation'. While occasionally being directed toward the State and the Protestant middle class, this animosity is more usually funnelled into sectarian competition and antagonism. Crucially, for the politics of Loyalism, it is not a transformation in the regime of accumulation and congruent mode of social regulation which is to blame for the loss of Protestant working-class status, for many Ulster Protestants it is the rise of the Catholic community on the back of IRA violence. It is this logic which underwrites the view of a senior UDA figure in a recent interview: 'The IRA want us and our industry on its knees. They think they will take away our livelihood and then we will submit' (Interview: September, 1994).

The erroneous perception held by sections of the Protestant working class that their economic plight is due to a growth in employment for working-class Catholics has led directly to the targeting of Catholic workers in predominantly Protestant workplaces as part of the recent Loyalist paramilitary campaign. Between 1992 and 1994, 18 Catholic workers, who had no paramilitary connections, were killed by Loyalist paramilitaries, the majority of these attacks taking place in staunchly Loyalist areas of East Belfast. That these workers were killed was not simply due to the fact that such Catholics were easy targets for Loyalists intent on sectarian assassination, it also represented the most obvious and extreme response to the notion of a Catholic-inspired loss of Protestant status. When questioned about these attacks one prominent UVF spokesperson commented:

> You have to blame the IRA. If they didn't fight a war and intimidate our people we wouldn't mind them working here. But if they don't stop then targeting Catholics is part of our war.
>
> Anyhow, they get jobs and are helped and we are simply left behind by a Government that doesn't care. (Interview: October, 1994)

The notion that the collapse of the economy and the decline in the position of Protestants is the result of IRA violence and a policy of state appeasement in response is similarly evidenced in attitudes toward the Fair Employment Commission and anti-discrimination legislation. Many Loyalists deny that anti-Catholic discrimination exists, and tend rather to 'explain' any relative disadvantage with reference to supposed defects in the character of the Catholic community itself. Similarly, the imagined relationship between the Protestant working class and the State is constructed around the concept of Loyalty, and that the faithfulness of Protestants to the State should be rewarded by the State. It was precisely this relationship which underwrote the previous mode of social regulation. It is the perception that, through such strategies as Fair Employment legislation, the State is abdicating its responsibilities to the 'loyal people', that leads to a growing unease with the role of Britain. An interviewee closely linked to the Ulster Defence Association emphasised this perspective:

> Fair employment is against the Protestant people. Such policies are an attack against Protestant livelihoods. It's simple. The Fenians [an abusive name for Catholics] and their IRA have bombed the Brits into submission. It is the start of the process in which they will secure a united Ireland. (Interview: December, 1994)

Conclusion

The need to provide socio-regulatory processes during the period of conflict has in turn meant that the British State has deployed planning and industrial support structures which are unprofitable in economic but not necessarily political terms. The overall result is that conflict management in Northern Ireland has produced a unique socio-regulatory form compared to the UK and other European Union states. This uniqueness is tied to the role that sectarianism plays within the construction and reproduction of politicised identities. Tentative success, in political terms, has been forthcoming due to the emergence of a Catholic middle class which is less nationalistic in its political aspirations. However, both working-class communities have remained committed to the binary opposition between Loyalism and Republicanism.

The role of Loyalism clearly indicates how class relationships in Northern Ireland, as elsewhere, clearly cross-cut politics, economics, ideology and culture. It also illustrates the

manner in which class relationships are experienced and perceived as sectarian relationships. It is in this sense, too, that
the discourses which constitute sectarianism are reproduced
through the 'lived experience' of the spatial, social and institutional segregation that characterises parts of Northern Ireland,
and which is most acute in certain working-class areas.

Sectarianised social relations, and a sectarianised world-
view, are therefore embedded in the regularised social experience of people in those areas. The boundaries between the
communities are produced not only in terms of consciousness
and ideology, but in physical-spatial terms and through social
practice. In effect it is the permanence and sustainability of
sectarianism which has not been effectively challenged during
the post-industrial era.

The adoption of a regulationist perspective in order to analyse
the politics of state regulation in Northern Ireland provides the
opportunity to explore how the construction of politicised identities influences and is influenced by the nature of socio-political
change. However, it also indicates the weaknesses in the means
being deployed at present in order to provide sustainable and real
'normality' within Northern Irish society. If anything, the contemporary regulatory practices of the British State have failed to
acknowledge or address the politics of sectarian opposition. The
result has been the reproduction of a new socio-political environment which seems increasingly 'normal', especially since the
emergence of the 'peace process' and the cessation of paramilitary
violence. Moreover, in terms of socio-political regulation it is
clear that an overall regulation of sectarian competition and
animosity is beyond the capacity of the British State.

Bibliography

Adamson, I. (1978) *The Cruthin* (Belfast: Donard).

Adamson, I. (1982) *The Identity of Ulster: The Land, the Language and the People* (Belfast: Nosmada).

Adamson, I. (1991a) *The Ulster People* (Bangor: Pretani Press).

Adamson, I. (1991b) *The Identity of Ulster* (Bangor: Pretani Press).

Aglietta, M. (1976) A Theory of Capitalist Regulation (London: NLB).

Agnew, J. A. (1987) *Place and Politics: The Geographical Mediation of State and Society* (Boston: Allen and Unwin).

Allister, J. (1987) *Alienated but Unbowed: a Unionist Perspective on the Origin, Meaning and Future of the Anglo-Irish Agreement* (Antrim: East Antrim DUP).

Allister, J. (1988) *Irish Unification – Anathema. The Reasons Why Northern Ireland Rejects Unification with the Republic of Ireland* (Belfast: Crown).

Allister, J. (1989) *The Unionist Case: The Forum Report Answered* (Belfast: DUP).

Althusser, L. (1971) *Lenin and Philosophy and other essays* (London: New Left Books).

Anderson, B. (1983) *Imagined Communities* (London: Verso).

Anderson, J. and Goodman, J. (1994) 'Northern Ireland: Dependency, Class and Cross-Border Integration in the European Union', *Capital and Class*, vol. 54.

Anderson, J. and Goodman, J. (1995) 'Euro-Regionalism: National Conflict and Development' in Shirlow, P. (ed.) *Development Ireland: Contemporary Issues* (London: Pluto).

Anderson, J. and Shuttleworth, I. (1992) 'Currency of Co-operation', *Fortnight*, no. 312.

Anderson, J. and Shuttleworth, I. (1993) 'Bordering on the Difficult', *Fortnight*, no. 313.

Anthias, F. and Yuval-Davis, N. (1983) 'Contextualizing feminism – gender, ethnic and class divisions', *Feminist Review*, vol. 15.

Anthias, F. and Yuval-Davis, N. (1992) *Racialised Boundaries* (Routledge: London).

Arthur, P. (1994) 'The Anglo-Irish Joint Declaration: Towards a Lasting Peace?', *Government and Opposition*, vol. 29, no. 2.

Ascherson, N. (1991) 'Europe of the Regions' in Crozier, M. (ed.) *Cultural Traditions in Northern Ireland* (Queen's University, Belfast: Institute of Irish Studies).

Aughey, A. (1989) *Under Siege: Ulster Unionism and the Anglo-Irish Agreement* (Belfast: Blackstaff).

Aughey, A. (1990) 'The "Troubles" in Northern Ireland – Twenty Years On', *Talking Politics*, vol. 3, no. 1.

Aughey, A. (1991) 'Unionism and Self-Determination', in Barton, B. and Roche, P. (eds) *Northern Ireland: Myth and Reality* (Aldershot: Avebury Press).

Bairner, A. (1986) 'The Battlefield of Ideas: The Legitimation of Political Violence in Northern Ireland', *European Journal of Political Research*, vol. 14.

Baker, A. R. H. (1992) 'Introduction: On Ideology and Landscape' in Baker, A. R. H and Biger, G. (eds) *Ideology and Landscape in Historical Perspective: Essays on the Meanings of Some Places in the Past* (Cambridge: Cambridge University Press).

Baker, D. G. (1983) *Race, Ethnicity and Power: A Comparative Study* (London: Routledge).

Bale, J. (1993) *Sport, Space and the City* (London: Routledge).

Barrett, M. and McIntosh, M. (1980) 'The Family Wage', *Feminist Review*, vol. 16.

Barry, J. (1991) *Women in Local Politics* (Aldershot: Avebury).

Bell, D. (1990) *Acts of Union: Youth Culture and Sectarianism in Northern Ireland* (London: Macmillan).

Bell, G. (1976) *The Protestants of Ulster* (London: Pluto).

Bell, G. (1984) *The British in Ireland: A Suitable Case for Withdrawal* (London: Pluto).

Bennett, R. (1994) 'Deconstructing Deconstruction', The *Guardian*, 16 July.

Berresford, Ellis P. (1993) *James Connolly: Selected Writings* (Harmondsworth: Penguin).

Bew, P. (1994) *Ideology and the Irish Question* (Oxford: Oxford University Press).

Bew, P. and Patterson, H. (1985) *The British State and the Ulster Crisis: From Wilson to Thatcher* (London: Verso).

Bew, P. and Patterson, H. (1987a) 'Unionism: Jim Leads On', *Fortnight*, no. 256.

Bew, P. and Patterson, H. (1987) 'The New Statement: Unionism and the Anglo-Irish Agreement' in Teague, P. (ed.) *Beyond the Rhetoric: Politics, the Economy and Social Policy in Northern Ireland* (London: Lawrence and Wishart).

Bew, P., Gibbon, P. and Patterson, H. (1979) *The State in Northern Ireland* (Manchester: Manchester University Press).

Bew, P., Gibbon, P. and Patterson, H. (1995) *Northern Ireland: Political Forces and Social Classes 1921–1994* (London: Wheatsheaf).

Birrell, D. (1983) 'Local Government Councillors in N.I.' in Gallagher, T. and O'Connell (eds) *Contemporary Irish Studies* (Belfast: Institute of Irish Studies).

Bloomfield, K. (1991) 'Who Runs Northern Ireland?', *Fortnight*, no. 300.

Boal, F. W. (1970) 'Social Space in the Belfast Urban Area' in Stephens, N. and Glasscock, R. E. (eds) *Irish Geographical Studies* (Belfast: Queen's University of Belfast).

Borooah, V. K. (1993) 'Northern Ireland – Typology of a Regional Economy' in Teague, P. (ed.) *The Economy of Northern Ireland: Perspectives for Structural Change* (London: Lawrence and Wishart).

Boulton, D. (1973) *The U.V.F.: 1966–73* (Dublin: Torc Books).

Bowman, J. (1982) *De Valera and the Ulster Question, 1917–1973* (Oxford: Clarendon Press).

Boyce, D. G. (1991, 2nd ed.) *Nationalism in Ireland* (London: Routledge).

Bradley, C. (1995) 'Keeping a Secret', *Fortnight*, no. 335.

Brady, C. (ed.) (1994) *Interpreting Irish History: The Debate on Historical Revisionism* (Dublin: Irish Academic Press).

Breen, S. (1994) 'Middle Classes Find a Silver Lining', *Red Pepper*, no. 5.

Brennock, M. (1991) 'Guess Who's Coming to Belfast?', The *Irish Times*, 23 March.

Brewer, J. D. (1992) 'Sectarianism and Racism, and their Parallels and Differences', *Ethnic and Racial Studies*, vol. 15.

Brodie, M. (1980) *One Hundred Years of Irish Football* (Belfast: Blackstaff).

Brozyna, A. (1994) '"The cursed cup hath cast her down": Constructions of Female Piety in Ulster Evangelical Temperance Literature, 1863–1914' in Holmes, J. and Urquart, D. (eds) *Coming into the Light* (Queen's University of Belfast: Institute of Irish Studies).

Brown, T. (1985) *The Whole Protestant Community* (Derry: Field Day).

Brown, T. (1991) 'British Ireland' in Longley, E. (ed.) *Culture in Ireland: Division or Diversity* (Queen's University of Belfast: Institute of Irish Studies).

Brown, T. (1992) 'Identities in Ireland: The Historical Perspective' in Lundy, J. and Mac Poilin, A. (eds) *Styles of Belonging: The Cultural Identities of Ulster* (Belfast: Lagan).

Bruce, S. (1986) *God Save Ulster: The Religion and Politics of Paisleyism* (Oxford: Oxford University Press).

Bruce, S. (1992) *The Red Hand: Protestant Paramilitaries in Northern Ireland* (Oxford: Oxford University Press).

Bruce, S. (1994) *The Edge of the Union: The Ulster Loyalist Political Vision* (Oxford: Oxford University Press).

Callinicos, A. (1989) *Against Postmodernism: A Marxist Critique* (Cambridge: Polity).

Campbell, R., McWilliams, M. and Morrissey, M. (1990) *Women, Household and Employment in Northern Ireland* (Unpublished Report for EOCNI).

Canaan, J. E. (1991) 'Is "Doing Nothing" just boys' play? Integrating feminist and cultural studies perspectives on working class young men's masculinity', in Franklin, S., Lury, C. and Stacey, J. (eds) *Off Centre. Feminism and Cultural Studies* (London: HarperCollins Academic).

Cebulla, A. and Smyth, J. (1995) 'Industrial Collapse and Post-Fordist Overdetermination in Belfast' in Shirlow, P. (ed.) *Development Ireland* (London: Pluto).

Clarke, J. (1978) 'Football and Working Class Fans: Tradition and Change', in Ingham, R. (ed.) *Football Hooliganism. The Wider Context* (London: Inter-Action Imprint).

Clayton, P. (1996) *Enemies and Passing Friends* (London: Pluto Press).

Clifford, B. (1986) *Government Without Opposition* (Belfast: Athol).

Clifford, B. (1987) *The Road to Nowhere* (Belfast: Athol).

Clyde, T. (ed.) (1987) *The Selected Prose of John Hewitt* (Belfast: Blackstaff).

Cohen, A. P. (1985) *The Symbolic Construction of Community* (London: Tavistock).

Colley, L. (1992) *Britons: Forging the Nation* (London: Yale University Press).

Conservative Central Office (1992) Press Release, 22 February.

Cormack, R. J., Gallagher A. M. and Osborne, R. D. (1993)

Fair Enough? Religion and the 1991 Census. (Belfast: Fair Employment Commission).

Cosgrove, D. E. (1993) *The Palladian Landscape: Geographical Change and its Cultural Representations in Sixteenth-Century Italy* (Leicester: Leicester University Press).

Cunningham, M. (1991) *British Government Policy in Northern Ireland, 1969–89: Its Nature and Execution* (Manchester: Manchester University Press).

Davidson, J. (1986) *Electoral Integrationism* (Belfast: Athol).

Davies, C. and McLaughlin, E. (1991) *Women, Employment and Social Policy in Northern Ireland: A Problem Postponed?* (Belfast: Policy Research Institute).

Deane, S. (1988) 'Reconciliation of Cultures: Apocalypse Now', in Falconer, A. (ed.) *Reconciling Memories* (Dublin: Columba).

Dewar, M. E. (1958) *Why Orangism?* (Belfast: Historical Committee of the Grand Orange Lodge).

Dunlop, J. (1995) *A Precarious Belonging: Presbyterians and the Conflict in Ireland* (Belfast: Blackstaff).

Dunn, S. (1995) 'The Conflict as a Set of Problems' in Dunn, S. (ed.) *Facets of the Conflict in Northern Ireland* (Dublin: St Martin's Press).

Dunn, S. and Morgan, V. (1994) *Protestant Alienation in Northern Ireland: A Preliminary Survey* (University of Ulster: Centre for the Study of Conflict).

Dunning, E. (1993) 'Sport in the Civilising Process: Aspects of the Development of Modern Sport', in Dunning, E. G., Maguire, J. A. and Pearton, R. E. (eds) *The Sports Process. A Comparative and Developmental Approach* (Champaign, Illinois: Human Kinetics Publishers).

Dunning, E., Murphy, P. and Williams, J. (1988) *The Roots of Football Hooliganism. An Historical and Sociological Study* (London: Routledge and Kegan Paul).

DUP (1986) *Protestant Blue Print* (Belfast: DUP).

DUP (1992a) paper presented to Strand 1, May.

DUP (1992b) 'Impediments to Progress', 27 May.

DUP (1993) *Breaking the Logjam* (Belfast: DUP).

DUP (1995) *The Framework of Shame and Sham* (Belfast: DUP).

DUP (1996) *Formula for Political Progress* (Belfast: DUP).

Eastern Health and Social Services Board (1991) *Equal Opportunities Monitoring Report* (Belfast: Equal Opportunities Unit).

Edgerton, L. (1986) 'Public Protest, Domestic Acquiescence: Women in Northern Ireland', in Ridd, R. and Callanan, H.

(eds) *Caught up in Conflict: Women's Responses* (London: Routledge).

Elias, N. and Dunning, E. (1986) *Quest for Excitement, Sport and Leisure in the Civilising Process* (Oxford: Basil Blackwell).

Elliot, M. (1985) *Watchmen of Sion: the Protestant idea of liberty* (Derry: Field Day).

English, R. and Walker, G. (1996) (eds) *Unionism in Modern Ireland* (Gill and MacMillan).

Equal Opportunities Commission for Northern Ireland (1993) *Where do Women Figure?* (Belfast: EOCNI).

Evans, E. E. (1981) *The Personality of Ireland: Habitat, Heritage and History* (Belfast: Blackstaff).

Fairweather, E., McDonagh, R. and McFadyean, M. (1984) *Only Our Rivers Run Free* (London: Pluto).

Farrell, M. (1980) *Northern Ireland: The Orange State* (London: Pluto).

Fisk, R. (1975) *The Point of No Return: The Strike which Broke the British in Ulster* (Deutsch: London).

Foster, J. W. (1991) *Colonial Consequences: Essays in Irish Literature and Culture* (Dublin: Lilliput).

Foster, J. W. (1995) (ed.) *The Idea of the Union: Statements and Critiques in Support of the Union of Great Britain and Northern Ireland* (Vancouver: Belcouver).

Foster, R. F. (1989) 'Varieties of Irishness', in Crozier, M. (ed.) *Cultural Traditions in Northern Ireland* (Queen's University of Belfast: Institute of Irish Studies).

Foucault, M. (1973) *The Birth of the Clinic* (London: Tavistock).

Fraser, G. (1995) 'The Backbone of the Church: Women and the Protestant Churches in Northern Ireland' (Queen's University Belfast: Paper presented to conference on 'Protestantism and Identity', February 1995).

Gellner, E. (1983) *Nations and Nationalism* (Oxford: Basil Blackwell).

Gillespie, N., Lovett, T. and Garner, W. (1992) *Youth Work and Working Class Youth Culture. Rules and Resistance in West Belfast* (Buckingham: Open University Press).

Girard, R. (1987) *Things Hidden Since the Foundation of the World* (London: Athlone).

Goodall, D. (1995) 'A Country is part of who you are', *Parliamentary Brief*, vol. 2, no. 2, Spring.

Gordon, H. (1990) *Women, Protestantism and Unionism: Women in Ireland in the 1990s* (Report of conference organised by WEA Women Studies Branch, October 1991).

Graham, B. J. (1994a) 'No Place of the Mind: Contested Protestant Representations of Ulster', *Ecumene*, vol. 1.

Graham, B. J. (1994b) 'The Search for the Common Ground:
Estyn Evans's Ireland', *Transactions of the Institute of British
Geographers*, N.S. vol. 19.

Graham, B. J. (1994c) 'Heritage Conservation and Revisionist
Nationalism in Ireland', in Ashworth, G. J. and Larkham,
P. (eds) *Building a New Heritage: Tourism, Culture and Iden-
tity in the New Europe* (London: Routledge).

Graham, B. J. (1995) 'Unionist Ulster: A Rhetoric Lacking
Place' (Queen's University of Belfast: Paper presented to
conference on 'Protestantism and Identity' February).

Graham, B. J. and Proudfoot, L. J. (1993) (eds) *An Historical
Geography of Ireland* (London: Academic Press).

Graham, I. (1995) 'Protestant Leaders in Plea to Major', PA
News Release, 17 July.

Gudgin, G. and Elliot, S. (1994) 'Democracy Postponed', *Fortnight*, no. 327.

Hadfield, B. (1991) 'Northern Ireland Affairs and Westminster',
in Roche, P. and Barton, B. (eds) *The Northern Ireland Question: Myth and Reality* (Aldershot: Avebury).

Hall, M. (1985) *Ulster – The Hidden History* (Belfast: Pretani).

Hall, M. (1988) *Twenty Years: A Concise Chronology of Events in
Northern Ireland, 1968–1988* (Belfast: Island).

Hall, M. (1995) *Beyond the Fife and Drum* (Belfast: Island).

Hall, M. *et al.* (1994) *Ulster's Protestant Working Class: A Community Exploration* (Belfast: Island).

Hamilton, D. (1995) 'Peripherality and the Political Economy of
Northern Ireland', in Shirlow, P. (ed.) *Development Ireland*
(London: Pluto Press).

Hargreaves, J. (1994) *Sporting Females. Critical Issues in the History and Sociology of Women's Sports* (London and New York:
Routledge).

Harvey, D. (1989) *The Condition of Postmodernity: An Enquiry
into the Origins of Cultural Change* (Cambridge, MA: Basil
Blackwell).

Harvie, S. and Sugden, J. (1994) *Sport and Community Relations
in Northern Ireland* (University of Ulster: Centre for the
Study of Conflict).

Hennessey, T. (1993) 'Ulster Unionist Territorial and National
Identities 1886–1893: Province, Island, Kingdom and
Empire', *Irish Political Studies*, vol. 8.

Heslinga, M. W. (1971) *The Irish Border as a Cultural Divide: A*

Contribution to the Study of Regionalism in the British Isles (Assen: Van Gorcum).

Hewitt, V. (1990) 'The Public Sector', in Harris, R. *et al.* (eds) *The Northern Ireland Economy* (Harrow: Longman).

Hill, D. (1989) *'Out of His Skin'. The John Barnes Phenomenon* (London: Faber and Faber).

Hoberman, J. (1984) *Sport and Political Ideology* (London: Heinemann).

Howe L. (1990) *Being Unemployed in Northern Ireland* (London: Routledge).

Hutton, W. (1994) 'The State We're In', *Fortnight*, no. 333.

Hutton, W. (1995) *The State We're In* (London: Jonathan Cape).

Jackson, A. (1989) 'Unionist History', *Irish Review*, Autumn.

Jackson, A. (1990) 'Unionist History (ii)' *Irish Review*, vol. 8.

Jackson, A. (1996) 'Irish Unionism', in Boyce, D.G. and O'Day, A. (eds) *Modern Irish Hisotry: Revisionism and the Revisionist Controversy* (London: Routledge).

Jarvie, G. (1993) 'Sport, Nationalism and Cultural Identity' in Allison, L. (ed.) *The Changing Politics of Sport* (Manchester: Manchester University Press).

Jenkins, R. (1982) *Hightown Rules. Growing Up in a Belfast Housing Estate* (Leicester: National Youth Bureau).

Jenkins, R. (1983) *Lads, Citizens and Ordinary Kids. Working-class Youth Life-styles in Belfast* (London: Routledge and Kegan Paul).

Jenkins, R. (1994) 'Rethinking Ethnicity: Identity, Categorisation and Power', *Ethnic and Racial Studies*, vol. 17.

Johnson, N. C. (1993) 'Building a Nation: An Examination of the Irish Gaeltacht Commission Report of 1926', *Journal of Historical Geography*, vol. 19.

Jones, G. S. (1983) *Languages of Class – Studies in English Working Class History 1832–1982* (Cambridge: Cambridge University Press).

Jones, S. G. (1988) *Sport, Politics and the Working Class. Organised Labour and Sport in Inter-War Britain* (Manchester: Manchester University Press).

Kearney, R. and Wilson, R. (1994) 'Northern Ireland's Future as a European Region', *The Irish Review*, vol. 15.

Kennedy, J. (1989) *Belfast Celtic* (Belfast: Pretani).

Laclau, E. (1979) *Politics and Ideology in Marxist Theory* (London: Verso).

Lee, J. J. (1989) *Ireland Politics and Society, 1912–85* (Cambridge: Cambridge University Press).

Lipietz, A. (1986) *Mirages and Miracles* (London: New Left Books).

Lister, R. (1995) 'Social Policy in a Divided Community: Reflections on the Opsahl Report on the Future of Northern Ireland', *Irish Journal of Sociology*, vol. 4.

Livingstone, S. and Morison. J. (1995) 'An Audit of Democracy in Northern Ireland', *Fortnight*, no. 337, Special Supplement.

Long, S. E. (1978) *The Orange Institution* (Belfast: Orange Order).

Longley, E. (1994) 'A Northern "Turn"', *Irish Review*, vol. 15.

Loughlin, J. (1990) 'Some Comparative Aspects of Irish and English Nationalism in the late Nineteenth Century', in Hill, M. and Barber, S. (eds) *Aspects of Irish Studies* (Belfast: Institute of Irish Studies).

McAll, C. (1990) *Class, Ethnicity and Social Inequality* (Quebec: McGill-Queen's University Press).

McAuley, J. (1984) 'Will Ulster Fight?', *New Society*, 11 July.

McAuley, J. (1991a) 'Cuchulainn and an RPG-7: The Ideology and Politics of the UDA', in Hughes, E. (ed.) *Culture and Politics in Northern Ireland* (Milton Keynes: Open University Press).

McAuley, J. (1991b) 'The Protestant Working Class and the State in Northern Ireland since 1930: a Problematic Relationship', in Hutton, S. and Stewart, P. (eds) *Ireland's Histories* (London: Routledge).

McAuley, J. (1994) *The Politics of Identity: A Loyalist Community In Belfast* (Aldershot: Avebury).

MacDonagh, O. (1983) *States of Mind: A Study of Anglo-Irish Conflict 1780–1980* (London: George Allen and Unwin).

Macdonald, M. (1986) *Children of Wrath* (Oxford: Clarendon).

McGarry, J. and O'Leary, B. (1995) *Explaining Northern Ireland.* (Oxford: Blackwell).

McGovern, M. (1994) 'The Siege Myth: The Siege of Derry in Ulster Protestant Political Culture 1689–1939', unpublished PhD thesis (University of Liverpool).

McGovern, M. and Shirlow, P. (1997) 'Sectarianism, Regulation and the Northern Ireland Conflict', *Reclus: Journal de L'Espace Geographique*, vol. 37.

McIntyre, A. (1995) 'The Republican's peaceful gamble', *Parliamentary Brief*, vol. 3, no. 2, Spring.

MacKinnon, I. (1993) 'Ulster Few Enjoy a Golden Age', The *Independent on Sunday*, 8 August.

McKittrick, D. (1994) *Endgame: The Search for Peace in Northern Ireland*, (Belfast: Blackstaff).

McLaughlin, E. (1986) 'Maiden City Blues' unpublished PhD thesis (Queen's University of Belfast).

McNamee, P. and Lovett, T. (1992) *Working Class Community in Northern Ireland* (Belfast: Ulster People's College).

McWilliams, M. (1991) 'Women in Northern Ireland: An Overview' in Hughes, E. (ed.) *Culture and Politics in Northern Ireland* (Buckingham: Open University Press).

McWilliams, M. (1994) 'The woman "other"', *Fortnight*, no. 328.

Mallory, J. P. and McNeill, T. E. (1991) *The Archaeology of Ulster: From Colonization to Plantation* (Queen's University of Belfast: Institute of Irish Studies).

Mann, M. (1986) *The Sources of Social Power, Vol. 1: A History of Power From the Beginning to AD 1760* (Cambridge: Cambridge University Press).

Mansfield Jr, H. C. (1983) 'The Forms and Formalities of Liberty', *The Public Interest*, no. 70.

Mansfield Jr, H. C. (1987) 'Constitutional Government: The Soul of Modern Democracy', *The Public Interest*, no. 86.

Marr, A. (1992) *The Battle for Scotland* (Harmondsworth: Penguin).

Milburn, A. (1994) 'Class Act', *Fortnight*, no. 328.

Millar, F. (1995) 'Battle for the Union to be Held on English Soil', *The Irish Times*, 16 January.

Miller, D. (1978) *Queen's Rebels: Ulster Loyalism in Historical Perspective* (Dublin: Gill and MacMillan).

Molyneaux, J. (1992) Press release for Ulster Unionist Party, 13 July.

Montgomery, P. and Davies, C. (1991) 'A woman's place in Northern Ireland', in Stringer P. and Robinson, G. (eds) *Social Attitudes in Northern Ireland* (Belfast: Blackstaff).

Moore, R. (1993) *Proper Wives: Orange Maidens or Disloyal Subjects: Situating the Equality Concerns of Protestant Women in Northern Ireland* (Dublin: National University of Ireland).

Morgan, D. H. J. (1992) *Discovering Men* (London and New York: Routledge).

Morgan, V. and Fraser, G. (1994) *The Company We Keep* (University of Ulster: Centre for the Study of Conflict).

Morgan, V. and Fraser, G. (1995) 'Women and the Northern Ireland Conflict: Experiences and Responses', in Dunn, S. (ed.) *Facets of the Conflict in Northern Ireland* (Dublin: St Martin's Press).

Morrow, D. (1991) *The Churches and Inter-Community Relation-*

ships (University of Ulster: Centre for the Study of Conflict).

Morrow, D. *et al.* (1994) *The Church and Inter Community Relations* (University of Ulster: Centre for Study of Conflict).

Moxon-Browne, E. (1983) *Nation, Class and Creed in Northern Ireland* (Aldershot: Avebury).

Munck, R. (1997) *The Irish Economy: Results and Prospects* (London: Pluto).

Munck, R. and Hamilton, D. (1994) 'A Disintegrated Economy', *Fortnight*, no. 324.

Murray, D. (1985) *Worlds Apart: Segregated Schools in Northern Ireland* (Belfast: Appletree).

Murray, D. (1995) 'Culture, Religion and Violence in Northern Ireland' in Dunn, S. (ed.) *Facets of the Conflict in Northern Ireland* (Dublin: St Martin's Press).

Murtagh, B. (1993) *Planning and Ethnic Space in Belfast* (Coleraine: University of Ulster Press).

Nairn, T. (1977) *The Break-Up of Britain* (London: Verso).

Nelson, Sarah (1984) *Ulster's Uncertain Defenders: Protestant Political, Paramilitary and Community Groups and the Northern Ireland Conflict* (Belfast: Appletree).

NIARLA (1989) *Challenge the Hypocrisy of Society* (Belfast: NIARLA).

Ormsby, F. (1991) 'Introduction', in Ormsby, F. (ed.) *The Collected Poems of John Hewitt* (Belfast: Blackstaff).

O'Brien, C. Cruise (1994) *Ancestral Voices* (Dublin: Poolbeg).

O'Connor, F. (1994) *In Search of a State* (Belfast: Blackstaff).

O'Dowd, L. (1980) 'Shaping and Reshaping the Orange State: An Introductory Analysis', in O'Dowd *et al.*, *Northern Ireland: Between Civil Rights and Civil War* (London: CSE Books).

O'Dowd, L. (1987) 'Church, State and Women: The Aftermath of Partition' in Curtin, C., Jackson, P., and O'Connor, B. (eds) *Gender in Irish Society* (Galway: Galway University Press).

O'Dowd, L. (1994) *Whither the Irish Border: Sovereignty, Democracy and Economic Integration in Ireland* (Belfast: Centre for Research and Documentation).

O'Faolain, N. (1993) 'The Discreet Charm of the Northern Bourgeoisie', The *Irish Times*, 23 March.

O'Leary, B. and Arthur, P. (1990) 'Northern Ireland as a Site of State and Nation-Building Failures', in McGarry, J. and O'Leary, B. (eds) *The Future of Northern Ireland* (Oxford: Oxford University Press).

O'Leary, J. and McGarry, J. (1993) *The Politics of Antagonism: Understanding Northern Ireland* (London: Athlone).

O'Malley, P. (1990) *Northern Ireland: Questions of Nuance* (Belfast: Blackstaff).

Ó Tuathaigh, G. (1991) 'The Irish-Ireland Idea: Rationale and Relevance', in Longley, E. (ed.) *Culture in Ireland: Division or Diversity* (Queen's University of Belfast: Institute of Irish Studies).

Paisley, I. (1973) *My Father and Mother* (Belfast: Martyrs Memorial).

Paisley, I. (1991) Statement by Dr Paisley MP, MEP at the Plenary Session of Strand 1 Talks, Stormont, 14 June.

Paisley, R. (1992) 'Feminism, Unionism and "the brotherhood"', *Irish Reporter*, no. 8.

Policy Planning Research Unit (1994a) *Continuous Household Survey* (Belfast Policy Planning Research Unit).

Policy Planning Research Unit (1994b) *Continuous Household Survey* (Belfast Policy Planning Research Unit).

Pollak, A. (ed.) (1993) *A Citizens' Enquiry: The Opsahl Report on Northern Ireland* (Dublin: Lilliput).

Pred, A. (1984) 'Place as Historically Contingent Process: Structuration and the Time-Geography of Becoming Places', *Annals of the Association of American Geographers*, vol. 74.

Presbyterian Church of Ireland (1986) *Report of the Government Committee* (Dublin: Presbyterian Church of Ireland).

Pringle, D. (1984) 'Marxism, the National Question and the Conflict in Northern Ireland: A Response to Blaut', *Antipode*, vol. 11.

Progressive Unionist Party (1996) 'War or Peace: Conflict or Conference', Policy Document of the Progressive Unionist Party.

Purdie, B. (1991) 'The Demolition Squad', in Hutton, S. and Stewart, P. (eds) *Ireland's Histories* (London: Routledge).

Purdy, M. (1994) 'Hands Across the Border', *Belfast Telegraph*, 25 October.

Quigley, G. (1993) 'Missing the Message', *Fortnight*, no. 319.

Ricoeur, P. (1982) 'Science and Ideology', in Thompson, J. B. (ed.) *Hermeneutics and the Human Sciences* (Cambridge: Cambridge University Press).

Robins, D. (1984) *We Hate Humans* (Harmondsworth: Penguin).

Robinson, P. (1985) *Ulster in Peril: An Exposure of the Dublin Summit* (Belfast: DUP).

Rolston, B. (1981) 'The Limits of Trade Unionism', in O'Dowd *et al.* (eds) *Northern Ireland: Between Civil Rights and Civil War* (London: CSE Books).

Rolston, B. (1993) 'The Contented Classes', *Irish Reporter*, vol. 9.

Rolston, B. (1995) 'Selling Tourism in a Country at War', *Race and Class*, vol. 37.

Rose, R. (1971) *Governing Without Consensus* (London: Faber).

Rose, R. (1982) 'Is the UK a State? Northern Ireland as a Test Case' in Madgwick, P. and Rose, R. (eds) *The Territorial Dimension in UK Politics* (London: MacMillan).

Ross, W. (1992) Press release from Ulster Unionist Party, 13 July.

Roulston, C. (1989) 'Women on the Margin: the Women's Movement in Northern Ireland, 1973–1988', *Science and Society*, vol. 53.

Rowthorn, B. (1981) 'Northern Ireland: An Economy in Crisis', *Cambridge Journal of Economics*, vol. 5.

Rowthorn, B. and Wayne, N. (1988) *Northern Ireland: The Political Economy of Conflict* (Oxford: Polity).

Ryan, M. (1994) *War and Peace in Ireland: Britain and the IRA in the New World Order* (London: Pluto).

SDLP (1992a), Agreeing New Political Structures, May (Belfast: SDLP).

SDLP (1992b), Response Paper, Strand 1, 24 July (Belfast: SDLP).

SDLP (1992c), point made at Structures Sub-Committee Meeting, 12 May (Belfast: SDLP).

SDLP (1992d), Requirements for New Structures, June (Belfast: SDLP).

Sheehan, M. (1995) 'Stark Choices for the North: The Economy and the Peace Process', *Irish Reporter*, no. 17.

Shirlow, P. (1995) 'Contemporary Development Issues in Ireland', in Shirlow, P. (ed.) *Development Ireland: Contemporary Issues* (London: Pluto).

Shirlow, P. and McGovern, M. (1996) 'Sectarianism, Socio-Economic Competition and the Political Economy of Ulster Loyalism', *Antipode*, vol. 4.

Shirlow, P. and Shuttleworth, I. (1994) 'The Fear of Employment', *Parliamentary Brief*, vol. 3, no. 3.

Sinn Fein Women's Department (1994) *Women in Struggle* (Belfast: Sinn Fein Women's Department).

Smart, C. (1995) *Law, Crime and Sexuality: Essays in Feminism* (Sage: London).

Smith, A. (1986) *The Ethnic Origins of Nations* (London: Basil Blackwell).

Smith, P. (1986) *Why Unionists Say No* (Belfast: Joint Unionist Working Party).

Smyth, M. (1994) 'Powerful Corridor', *Fortnight*, no. 333.

Smyth, W. J. (1993) 'The Making of Ireland: Perspectives and Agendas in Cultural Geography', in Graham, B. J. and Proudfoot, L. J. (eds) *An Historical Geography of Ireland* (London: Academic Press).

Sparke, A. W. (1994) *Talking Politics: a Wordbook* (London: Routledge).

Stewart, A. T. Q. (1967) *The Ulster Crisis* (London: Faber and Faber).

Stewart, A. T. Q. (1977) *The Narrow Ground, Aspects of Ulster, 1609–1969* (London: Faber and Faber).

Stewart, P. (1991) 'The Jerrybuilders: Bew, Gibbon and Patterson – the Protestant Working Class and the Northern Ireland State', in Hutton, S. and Stewart, P. (eds) *Ireland's Histories* (London: Routledge).

St John Ervine (1949) Craigavon: Honest Ulsterman (London: Allen and Unwin).

Sugden, J. and Bairner, A. (1993) *Sport, Sectarianism and Society in a Divided Ireland* (Leicester: Leicester University Press).

Teague, P. (1993a) 'Not a Firm Basis', *Fortnight*, no. 317.

Teague, P. (1993b) 'Discrimination and Fair Employment in Northern Ireland', in Teague, P. (ed.) *The Economy of Northern Ireland: Perspectives for Structural Change* (London: Lawrence and Wishart).

Todd, J. (1987) 'Two Traditions in Unionist Political Culture', *Irish Political Studies*, vol. 2.

Todd, J. (1995) 'History and Structure in Loyalist Ideology: The Possibilities of Ideological Change', *Irish Journal of Sociology*, vol. 4.

Tomlinson, M. (1993) 'Policing the New Europe: The Northern Ireland Factor', in Bunyan, T. (ed.) *Statewatching in the New Europe: A Handbook on the European State* (Nottingham: Statewatch).

Tomlinson, M. (1994) *Twenty Five Years On: The Costs of War and the Dividends of Peace* (Belfast: West Belfast Economic Forum).

Tonkin, E. (1992) *Narrating Our Pasts: Social Construction of Oral History* (Cambridge: Cambridge University Press).

Trimble, D. (1986) Press release for Ulster Unionist Party, 2 October.

Trimble, D. (1988) 'Initiatives for Consensus: A Unionist Perspective' in Townshend, C. (ed.) *Consensus in Ireland: Approaches and Recessions* (Oxford: Oxford University Press).

Tuan, Yi-Fu (1991) 'Language and the making of place: a narrative-descriptive approach', *Annals of the Association of American Geographers*, vol. 81.

Ulster Unionist Party (1984) *The Way Forward* (Belfast: UUP).

Ulster Unionist Party (1986) *Ulster Must Say No* (Belfast: UUP).

UUP (1992a) *Nature of the Northern Ireland Community*, (Belfast: UUP).

UUP (1992b) paper submitted to Strand 2, 7 July.

UUP (1992c) letter to Sir Ninian Stevens, 26 October.

UUP (1992d) paper submitted to Strand 3, 30 June.

Ward, M. (1983) *Unmanageable Revolutionaries* (London: Pluto Press).

Ward, M. (1991) 'The Women's Movement in the North of Ireland: Twenty Years On', in Hutton, S. and Stewart, P. (eds) *Ireland's Histories* (London: Routledge).

Watson, G. (1991) 'Landscape in Ulster Poetry', in Dawe, G. and Foster, J. W. (eds) *The Poet's Place: Ulster Literature and Society* (Queen's University of Belfast: Institute of Irish Studies).

Weir, S. (1995) 'Aloof in Quangoland', *Fortnight*, no. 335.

Whannel, G. (1983) *Blowing the Whistle: The Politics of Sport* (London: Pluto).

Wheeler, R. F. (1978) 'Organized Sport and Organized Labour: The Workers' Sports Movement', *Journal of Contemporary History*, vol. 13, no. 2.

Whitson, D. (1990) 'Sport in the Social Construction of Masculinity', in Messner, M. A. and Sabo, D. F. (eds) *Sport, Men, and the Gender Order* (Champaign, Illinois: Human Kinetics Books).

Wichert, S. (1991) *Northern Ireland since 1945* (London: Longman).

Williams, A. M. (1994, 2nd ed.) *The European Community: The Contradictions of Integration* (Oxford: Blackwell).

Wright, F. (1987) *Northern Ireland: A Comparative Analysis* (Dublin: Gill and Macmillan).

Index

Index compiled by Peter Shirlow